CONTENTS

SECTION TWO: Male Power and the Sexual Abuse of Girls
Conference. Manchester, January 1982.

SECTION THREE: Women Against Violence Against Women
Conference. London, November 1981.

PREFACE

This is a selection of papers taken from the following National Women's Liberation Conferences:

Sexual Violence Against Women, Leeds 1980.
Women Against Violence Against Women, London 1981.
Male Power and the Sexual Abuse of Girls, Manchester 1982.

Women, in Britain, have been organising against male violence for years, in Women's Aid, Rape Crisis Centres and more recently in Women Against Violence Against Women groups all over the country.

These papers are part of the ideas and debates going on in the Women's Liberation Movement in the early 1980s. The ideas in them come from our lives and our experiences. Some papers were written by groups, others are signed by individuals; none were written in total isolation, and most were written in haste — just before the conferences.

They were written to be shared with other women and to spark off discussions at conference workshops. Not all the workshops had papers. Not all workshops talked specifically about the papers — with hundreds of women there why should we?

What do we expect our conferences to achieve? At least an end to isolation — 'Am I the only woman who has this problem/thought this/been worried about that?' Many of us come wanting answers and solutions *now*. Most of us go away with new questions. At best they give us encouragement, hope, a new awareness.

These papers contribute to a new way of seeing the world as it is, and hopefully to changing it for the better.

Sandra McNeill & dusty rhodes

INTRODUCTION

Discussion before and during these conferences helped us to understand how crucial men's sexual violence is to the maintenance of men's domination over women. It became clear how the experience or threat of men's aggression kept women afraid and 'in their place', despite all the talk of 'equal rights' and 'equal opportunities'. Nearly all aspects of the everyday lives of women and girls are affected by the fear, the reality of men's sexual violence. Women experience a well-justified anxiety when they are followed by men on the street. Even when we pass groups of children or youths in broad daylight we are subjected to harassment, insults, gratuitous comments — and required to respond more or less politely to escape further aggression.

Experience of being assaulted or reading about women being assaulted can keep women locked in their homes in the evening, which effectively imposes a curfew on women. But home is no safe place for women either. Women may have to deal with voyeurs and obscene telephone callers at the least, brutal violence or rape by the men they live with at the worst (and everything in between). Fathers, husbands, brothers, uncles, sons — none are exempt — not to mention live-in-lovers, lodgers, etc. Experience of such violence makes women insecure even in the place supposed to be women's haven, the home. At work women are subjected to harassment which takes a variety of forms ranging from comments on their appearance, remarks, innuendos and suggestions designed to establish men's sexual power, "touching up", through to rape and even murder. In childhood girl children are trained not to be adventurous either by experience of assault or indecent exposure or quite justified warnings by adult women of what might befall them if they exercise their citizen's rights of walking in a park or playground.

The minimum effect of all this experience — from some of which no woman is immune — is to undermine our confidence and restrict our movements. It is a substantial reason why women are apparently cautious about strange territory and new experience. Women cannot be called timid who have continually defied the attempts of young, mature and old males to terrify us — from showing us 'nasty' things in matchboxes when we are children to films and porn about the brutalisation of women, to actual sexual harassment and brutalisation. We defy the attempts, but they understandably leave their mark.

A number of papers focus particularly on pornography, women-hating films, and sex advice literature because they are propaganda which justifies and publicises new techniques, or new versions of old techniques, for the humiliation of women. We believe they do encourage men to assault women, and that they serve to further undermine women — both by alienating us from our bodies, and by constantly showing us images of ourselves as humiliated victims.

The conference papers explore in detail women's experience of all these forms of men's violence and more, and when put together as a whole they provide a devastating indictment of the system of sex slavery under which women live. They show how the whole range of men's violence to women — from the insistence on crippling 'fashions' through to incidents of rape and murder — operate as threats to our lives and well-being, and blocks to our freedom, our creativity, and our self-respect.

Some of the critics who have been most hostile to our campaign against men's violence have claimed that the women involved believe that men's aggression is somehow natural and biological and cannot change. At these conferences women have sought to understand where men's violence came from. We have concluded that men's sexual behaviour has been socially constructed to be aggressive, exploitative, objectifying. It is not nature that has constructed this effective system for the subordination of women. The system is constructed by men, in men's interests, for the benefit of all men.

As we learn more about male violence we can become more clear; feminists are beginning to seek out and make specific connections between race, class, lesbianism and gender in relation to male violence. Violence against Black women, for example, may be both racist in its intention and aimed specifically at Black women as women — for example, when National Front men rape Black women.

**Why did it take so long
to begin to look at male violence to women?**
Because, at these conferences, we have looked both at everyday experiences of harassment and at some of the extreme forms of male violence to women, we have had to face many accusations: we were being sensationalists, or we were confirming women's role as victim. In fact, we see connections between all forms of male violence and are convinced that we must look at and understand and publicise such issues as the murder of women by men, before we can begin to bring such violence to an end. Problems do not go away if we avoid looking at them.

Nonetheless, we realise that there are forceful reasons why feminists have taken so long to directly confront the many forms of male violence to women. One reason is that women have been socialised to see anyone's pain, to exert ourselves on anyone's behalf, to join anyone's struggle but our own.

Women are murdered daily simply for being women and their deaths go largely unnoticed and ungrieved by even the women's movement. We see women as being involved in a liberation struggle comparable in its intensity and in the casualties incurred with other liberation struggles around the globe, in which the casualties of war are remembered and mourned. Women's deaths at the hands of men are not unimportant. We have to start our fight from where we are rather than seeing other people's struggles as more important. We can no longer overlook the suffering and death of women.

Another reason why it has been difficult to confront the issue of male violence to women is the need to survive from day to day without too much fear. Recognition of the danger can cause us to hide our heads in the sand. But we believe that we can fight back more powerfully if we can really know and understand what is happening to us. We can gain strength from our anger and our grief.

Sheila Jeffreys, Sandra McNeill & dusty rhodes

Dedicated to all our Revolutionary Feminist Sisters

There are some glaring omissions in this collection of papers. On the whole, however, they reflect the discussions at the times of the conferences. We regret the absence of papers dealing with violence against particular groups of women.

WOMEN'S LIBERATION NATIONAL CONFERENCE

SEXUAL VIOLENCE AGAINST WOMEN

ROYAL PARK SCHOOL,
QUEENS ROAD,
LEEDS, 6.

NOV. 22/3 1980
WOMEN ONLY 10 a.m.

THIS IS YOUR
CONFERENCE
PASS

Please
do not
lose it.

Social: (not included in
registration fee)

Theatre, Disco
Film.

OUR STRATEGIES AND TACTICS

PORNOGRAPHY

RAPE

PROSTITUTION

MARRIAGE

SEXUAL HARASSMENT AT WORK

INCEST

WHY THIS CONFERENCE?

It is two years since the Bristol Anti Rape Conference. FAST* meetings have become a space where women involved in different Rape Crisis Centres (RCC) discuss the problems they are having. More women should be involved in discussions about rape.

We want the theme to be broader than rape, and to include sexual harrassment, incest, sexual abuse of children, prostitution. We want to talk about the politics of anti rape action. This should not be left to women in RCCs. Women in RCCs did not want to be split off from the WLM.

They needed to feel their politics supported. They wanted cross fertilization of their ideas with other feminists.

We also want to ask, is a feminist response to rape automatically just counselling and running phone lines. What else do we think there should be? We want to focus on what we as feminists can do about sexual violence — as well as saying what we think it is, why it happens, and how it affects women. One suggestion is that for part of the conference we have block workshops on strategy and tactics.

We have not yet finalised details of conference structure. This planning meeting was attended by women from Leeds, London, Nottingham and Birmingham Rape Crisis Groups as well as women from Leeds and Nottingham. Planning meetings are open to any women and we can organise a fares pool.

*Feminists Against Sexual Terrorism.

Notice in WIRES, (Women's Information and Referral Service) July, 1980.

WOMEN, ANGRY AT MALE VIOLENCE, SAY:
'RESIST THE CURFEW!'

Hundreds of angry women staged a militant protest in Leeds last Saturday. Angry at advice to stay indoors since the last 'Ripper' killing, five hundred women marched with torches through town, stormed into the Odeon Cinema (which was showing the film *Dressed to Kill*), and challenged men in the street, asking them where they were at the time the 'Ripper' killed Jacqueline Hill.

The march was organised by Women Against Violence Against Women. We reprint their statement in full below:

'We mourn Jacqueline Hill, and all the other women who have died at the hands of·the 'Yorkshire Ripper. And we are angry.

We are angry at being told to stay at home after dark. Why must we women restrict our lives when it's men who are to blame? Many women work at night: they can't stay at home. Anyway, home may not be safe for many of us. A quarter of all the crimes of violence reported is wife battering. And we're expected to take this without defending ourselves.

On Monday this week, Charlene and Annette Maw were sentenced to 3 years for killing their drunken violent father in self-defence. We demand their immediate release, and the right of every woman to defend herself against male violence.

We totally reject the way the press label women 'respectable' or not. We will not be judged and divided into the 'pure' and the 'fallen'.

We know that when this 'Ripper' is caught, women will not be safe. Everywhere women are murdered, raped and battered by men daily. We will carry on fighting until every woman can live without fear of being attacked by men.

We demand:
- Police — release your information on the 'Ripper'!
- Every woman's right to self-defence!
- Curfew on men, not women!

Leeds Other Paper, 28 November 1980.

12

PORNOGRAPHY

Why should we as feminists campaign against pornography?
Pornography includes all forms of visual and verbal humiliation of women for the sexual titillation of *men* from Page 3 in the Sun to striptease and flagellation movies, plus the exploitation and humiliation of women for economic gain, e.g. advertising, entertainment, etc.

Social control of women
It is effective in the social control of women as the strength, dignity and confidence of every women is undermined by those images and their messages are internalised.

Backlash against the Women's Liberation Movement
At the same time the massive boom in pornography of the last ten years can be seen as a backlash to the gains that women have made in this time. It compensates men for the threat to their status by providing them with images of women as victims and slaves in every newspaper and on every street corner. It seeks to invalidate all the claims to equality, and ensures that all males will see their women teachers, doctors, secretaries, etc. as a 'piece of ass'. As pornography shores up the confidence of men and undermines that of women, it also clearly reveals that reality of power. You may think you've come a long way baby, but it is clear that men rule when the culture is flooded with images of women as no more than tools for men's delight. Another reaction to the threat of Women's Liberation is that men incorporate and parody it in porn, in order to remain in control e.g. portrayal of lesbians in films and the way the 'liberated female' has replaced the 'German governess' in certain kinds of sado-masochistic material. Meanwhile the promotion of 'sexual confession' novels by 'liberated' women keeps our sexuality within the mainstream of porn, and so makes it acceptable.

Towards a self-defined sexuality
Pornography is male-defined sexuality. Women cannot reach a self-defined sexuality while surrounded by the male view of what sex is and of what women are. The prevailing view of sex in porn is that not only can sex be separated from love,

13

but from humanity. Rife at the moment are photos of female genitalia with no face or even body attached. At the same time sex is presented as a package, separable from the rest of our life and human experience. The view of women in pornography is that they are passive, depersonalised objects of male aggression, contempt and experimentation. An attack on porn, as a symbol and support of patriarchy, is therefore vital in our struggle towards a self-defined sexuality.

The real effects of porn.

Porn has real terrifying effects. It validates men in not seeing, whilst it facilitates and justifies rape, violence, verbal and physical abuse. Pornography could never on its own be responsible for the way men treat women, as it does in itself symbolise the fear, contempt and aggression which all men feel for all women and which permeate our culture. However its universal availability does legitimise each man's feelings. When porn was 'under the counter', men might have reason to feel guilty over their rape fantasies which were apparently socially disapproved of, and guilt can be inhibiting. Now a generation of male British youth has been reared and weaned in full page spreads of female genitals ('split beaver' as it is known in the trade) and of vile sadistic practices which are apparently approved of since they are in W.H. Smith.

The revolutionary potential of an attack on porn

A Feminist attack on porn would not just be reformist. As the frightening realities of sex-war and sex-oppression which are exemplified in porn come into focus, the class-consciousness of women will be built. A main object of action around porn would be to mobilise that anger and hate of all women in the fight against male supremacy. Until now the natural horror and disgust of most women at porn has been labelled puritanical and prudish and derided by the ruling male ideology of the sexual revolution. Now we must validate the disgust, identify its real cause (the obvious humiliation and degradation of women in porn, which each woman knows applies to her) and enlist the 'prudishness' of all our sisters in the struggle. If all women decided that porn should not exist and smashed and destroyed it on newstands, bill-boards, in the windows of sex-shops, on the streets of

14

Soho, and demanded their right never to be insulted in public again, then at least it would be driven underground. This could only be a beginning since the end of the struggle could only be the destruction of male supremacy itself.

And Mary Whitehouse

It can be difficult for those of us who were reared in the 'sexual revolution' of the 60's to work out a clear perspective on porn. Most of us will have gone through a process of convincing ourselves that sex was not 'dirty' but 'wonderful' and that porn, since it is about sex, was not revolting. Now that we have the best of political reasons for being revolted we have to climb back into the fight. The aims of the Festival of Light are not our aims. They seek to reinforce the nuclear family and the oppression of women within it. Therefore they attack particularly, those forms of porn which threaten this structure, e.g. Poem in Gay News** and not normal sexist images of women in advertising which bolster up the status quo. The fear of being associated with Mary Whitehouse and her ilk just because they attack porn, though we reject and are actively struggling against everything else they stand for, must not hold us back.

On Censorship

When we became, or were brought up as, 'liberals', 'no censorship' was one of the ideals we learnt, like no hanging, no flogging, gay rights, even the right to abortion. To launch an attack on porn we have to make a stand, to say that it is not the god-given right of any ruling group with money and power to plaster the environment with their sadistic, dehumanising and degrading view of a less powerful section of society. If this is to advocate censorship, then that is what we must do. There already exists an example of grounds on which censorship can be reasonably demanded: in the area of race relations. In as much as magazines devoted to the brutal dehumanisation of blacks would be regarded as 'incitement to racial hatred' so we must demand that porn be prohibited on the grounds that it is an 'incitement to sexual hatred', in fact a clear incitement to rape and murder, as well as to the general inferiorisation of women.

We do not seek to change the law towards increased censorship. We could not advocate any increase in the repressive activities of the institution (the state) which males use to legitimise their control of us. By enforcing legislation against porn, the male ruling class tries to make itself respectable, and by pretending to curb its worst excesses, validates the sexploitation of women, e.g. state legislation would never outlaw Playboy. We are censored in that we do not even have the right to object to and destroy that which offends us. We must demand that right, as more than half the population, to clean up the streets and shops so we can walk in them with pride.

Liberal arguments on porn

Reports and Royal Commissions looking into porn have been concluding for some years now that it has no dangerous or harmful effects, e.g. 'The Presidential Commission on Obscenity and Pornography', U.S. 1970:

'If a case is to be made against 'pornography' in 1970, it will have to be made on grounds other than demonstrated effects of a damaging personal or social nature. Empirical research designed to clarify the question has found no reliable evidence to date that exposure to explicit sexual materials plays a significant role in the causation of delinquent or criminal sexual behaviour among youth or adults.'

President Nixon rejected the report outright, with an interesting comment:

'The Commission contends that the proliferation of filthy books and plays has no lasting effects on a man's character. If that were true, it must also be true that great books, great paintings and great plays have no ennobling effects on a man's conduct. Centuries of civilisation and ten minutes of common sense tell us otherwise.'

There is in fact evidence to suggest a strong connection between pornography and crimes of sexual violence, e.g. the Cambridge rapist and Son of Sam both had vast stocks of pornographic material. However the real weakness of the reports is that they do not even look for the kinds of effects that we consider important, but only for 'abnormal' effects, such as delinquent behaviour. How then could they notice the 'normal' effects, the 'normal' run of male aggression, contempt and hatred towards women?

How is it possible to study the effects of total immersion from birth in a pornographic society, on every male, not just on individuals. Also the effects of pornography on *women* are totally ignored.

The reports come up with all kinds of good and constructive purposes that they believe porn to serve, the most common of which are:

(a) Catharsis, providing a safety valve for those people whose sexual urges might otherwise explode and harm others.

(b) The provision of sex information.

It is far more possible that porn provides the opposite of catharsis, that is a desire for a model to try things out on. The leader of a gang of youths who savagely attacked and raped a 14 year old girl for several hours, had a large stock of pornographic material at home detailing every one of the practices that the boys carried out on her. (It is significant that these boys are reported to have shown no consciousness of having done anything wrong at their trial.) If porn provides sex information, this must mean information on a male-defined sexuality, that women are passive objects to be humiliated, abused, etc., and this purpose it seems to fulfil very well.

What is the real purpose of pornography?
One Socialist analysis, via Marcuse, is that the liberalisation of the sexual climate and marketing of sex as a product is a way of making people falsely believe that they are free and that they live in a new golden age of liberty. Their revolutionary fervour is defused, they do not recognise the important freedoms they have not got, they can't see the wood of repression for the sexual trees.

What is wrong with this analysis is that it sees porn and sexual revolution as just elements in class struggle, that is as weapons against the working class (meaning men) instead of as part of the sex war. It confuses and obscures an issue which is potentially a consciousness-raiser for women in seeing themselves as women as a class vis-a-vis men. Another thing that is wrong with this analysis is that it sees the sexual revolution and porn as being about a thing called sex, when they are in fact about power over women.

It is not sex that is being handed out like bread and circuses to keep the masses quiet, but women to men, by the ruling group in the ruling class that is men. As sex becomes less and less of a panacea, as discontent spreads against the failure of the 'affluent' society, so it is against women that the anger will be directed for not coming up with the goods. The reaction of women to being given away like plastic daffodils is the Women's Liberation Movement and the fight for feminist revolution which will eventually bring down the whole of the male ruling class.

**Poem in Gay News suggesting that Christ was a homosexual. Also, Festival of Light was a group of Christian fanatics who support SPUC among other things.

Written for the London Revolutionary Feminist Conference in February 1978 by: Maria Katyachild, Sheila Jeffreys, Sandra McNeill, Jan Winterlake and one other woman.

This paper was written by the first anti-porn group in the UK Women's Liberation Movement. Right from our inception in the summer of 1977, we encountered hostility and opposition from within the WLM. 'We can't be seen to be against porn, we'll be associated with Mary Whitehouse'. 'Let men have their porn; it's their right; I just don't want to see it or know about it'. These were things we had felt also — but wanted to work through and get beyond. We met weekly for over a year and mostly what we did was consciousness raising about porn and about our sexuality. The paper was written very early on, and has enormous gaps — particularly there is no discussion of the effects of porn on women.

As well as doing CR and giving talks and running workshops we participated in and initiated a number of actions.

We were part of the planning group for the first Reclaim the Night March in London, which went through Soho.

Along with members of the London Rape Action Group, we organised a defence/publicity campaign for two women, one from each group, who were caught spraying and stickering posters in London Tubes, with the message, 'This Violates Women'.

Again jointly with the Rape Action Group we did the first ever picket of a shop for selling porn. Beforehand we put notices in Local and National Newsletters suggesting that other women's groups do the same that day — none did. And in spite of our brave words we went out that grey morning in some trepidation. We returned elated, bowled-over, by the positive response from women. The rest is herstory.

Sandra McNeill, April 1983

Here is the leaflet we used that day — jointly written by the porn group and the rape action group:

HOW DO MEN SEE YOU?
(A leaflet for women about porn)

Martin's stock porn. Porn is the way men like to see women — submissive, obedient, helpless, naked, open and available, longing to be violated. It encourages men to see women as bodies which exist solely for their pleasure; bodies to be leered at, groped, assaulted and raped — used and thrown away.

While porn makes men feel powerful and confident, how does it make us feel? What effects does it have on our lives?

Do you know a man who has never looked at porn — your father, husband, son, brother, boyfriend, doctor, schoolteacher? How can they look at it and respect women — How can they look at it and respect you?

Men say they have the right to look at porn, what about our rights? Why should we be assaulted by these images whenever we go into a newsagents'?

It is becoming harder for us to object as porn becomes 'respectable' — no longer just in Soho but flooding into our family newsagents' such as Martin's.

Let them know it is not acceptable to women. Sign our petition. Go in and object now!

(September 1978)

FIGHTING PORN

Porn is one of the most obvious ways men have of showing their hatred of women. It points out very clearly just how they see us — sexually available, open, submissive, nothing more than just playthings, objects for men's titillation and the victims of their sadistic fantasies. In the past ten years

19

porn has come out from under the counter and is now openly available in most newsagents'. While it continues to be so overt men feel justified and encouraged in seeing all women as theirs for the taking. Porn is one thing which incites men to rape, assault and beat us and to perpetuate the myth that it is our fault, that we have asked for it!

Like prostitution, porn uses women to fulfil men's obscene 'kinks'. It is not the women who are to blame and we must therefore always make our attacks very clear, to avoid being seen as anti women who pose for porn or who work as prostitutes (or strippers, etc.). We want fighting porn to be a unifying issue not a divisive one. It is absolutely in the interests of the male ruling class for women to see themselves as passive sex objects. In this way we are intimidated, sapped of self-confidence and self-respect and men remain in power and get stronger. Porn is therefore an important issue to be fighting against as we need to be angry together and thus hopefully to raise the sex-class consciousness of all women.

Because we believe this and we had become extremely angry at the increasing amounts of porn on display in newsagents everywhere, a group of us in London decided (two years ago) to picket a W.H. Smith's branch. The reasons we chose a chain of family newsagents' was, (1) because we wanted to show our opposition to the fact that porn was becoming 'respectablized' and, (2) we hoped that other women would take similar action and picket W.H. Smith's elsewhere. However, after going to several W.H. Smith's branches we found that stocks of porn we had previously seen had been removed, leaving only Mayfair, Playboy and Penthouse. So we looked in Martin's, a similar chain, and discovered a lot of porn still on sale. We decided to picket a branch in a shopping centre in Wandsworth.

Despite one or two difficulties such as being moved out to one of the outside entrances in the rain, by shopping centre security guards, we continued picketing undeterred and collected a hundred and ninety women's signatures in an hour and a half, on a petition objecting to the porn on sale in Martin's. We had written a leaflet to give to women which was about how men see us and what that does and we had placards saying 'Men use porn to violate women', 'Porn shows men's hatred of women' and one or two fairly typical centre spreads with the caption 'Is this how your man sees you?'. The response from women was amazing. They were pleased that we were demonstrating against porn as they felt angry about it too and welcomed the chance to say so. Some women were surprised that we were picketing *against* porn, and some young women of 12—14 who had never seen porn rushed to sign our petition after looking at examples on the picket. It would perhaps be more immediately clear to have a prominent placard saying 'Sign our petition AGAINST porn' to avoid confusion. Even women who were with men stopped to agree with us and sign the petition, while their men hung around looking superfluous!

Porn has been and by and large remains a 'contentious' issue, both 'out there' and in the Women's Liberation Movement (WLM). This is largely due to the fact that many of us have been through the 'sexual revolution' of the sixties, which in reality benefited no one but men. The 'love and peace' mentality meant that women were more frequently coerced into sex with men and had to be freely available in order not to be considered frigid or sexually hung-up. If we refused we were asked 'What's wrong with your head, baby?'. Unfortunately, the feeling that if-we-don't-have-sex-often-with-men-there-is-something-wrong-with-us lingers; not a million miles from the WLM there is still the idea that sexual 'repression' is to be avoided.

We are certainly repressed by men, but in a different way. We are intimidated and terrorized and harassed if we 'dare' to go out alone (without men) always afraid that we may not escape assault — we feel lucky to reach our destination alive or without being raped or attacked. And for those women who live with or relate to men there is always the danger of being attacked at home too. And everywhere we go the advertising hoardings and porn in the newsagents remind us that we are purely objects for men's use — simulated lesbian porn and child porn, using young girls, is now freely available as well as hard-core blue movies (not as freely available but still on sale in some porn shops). At every step men are reminded that they are in power and that we are 'at their mercy'.

Another reason porn is not being taken up by feminists as an issue to fight against is the concern over being associated with the 'Festival of Light', as their reasons for wanting a 'clean-up' of porn totally contradict many other beliefs we hold about woman's place in the family' and so on. However, we should not be afraid to raise the issue of porn and fight against it from a feminist perspective. It is crucial to our understanding of male power.

(With thanks to other Revolutionary Feminists)

Maria Katyachild, November 1980

SHOULD WE BAN THESE FILMS AS INCITEMENT TO VIOLENCE AGAINST WOMEN?

Horror films are fashionable and have shed their B-movie image.

The latest films from Stanley Kubrik and Brian de Palma — directors whose films have found critical respect — while they thrill and terrify us, also legitimise male violence against women, arousing and titillating male sexuality in a vicious, sadistic way.

The Shining*
The British opening of *The Shining*, Stanley Kubrick's new film has been greeted with all the usual display of media excess reserved for Great Directors.

The reviewers who glorify in cinematic conspicuous consumption have carefully noted the time and money spent (three years, with over a hundred takes for some shots), while gently panning the film for its over-acting, dubious plot and incoherent narrative.

What these reviews have ignored is that *The Shining* is not simply the work of a past master who has lost his edge but also a grossly exploitative and sadistic film. It must be discussed in terms of its role in legitimising the victimisation of women rather than the hushed and respectable phrases of *auteur* criticism.

The plot, briefly, is that a blocked writer turned caretaker (Jack Nicholson) takes his wife (Shelley Duvall) and son (Danny Lloyd) to a vast and empty hotel in the Rocky Mountains for the winter knowing that his predecessor hacked his wife and children into small pieces with an axe. Within fifteen minutes we realise that Nicholson and son are beset by 'traces' of the atrocity, and thereafter the film slavishly follows the possessed Nicholson's attempt to duplicate the crime.

This simple plot can be read as an almost classical lesson in the ways that films can oppress women, as the audience in a highly suggestible state of near-panic, is subtly manipulated into believing that women are stupid, pathetic and deserve what comes to them.

Throughout the film Mrs. Torrence (Shelley Duvall) provokes aggression with her passivity as she cringes and snivels, clutching a wet handkerchief. She has no job, no interests (except ghost stories) and has been transported into the middle of nowhere to resuscitate her husband's career. Under pressure she becomes a non-person, a cipher for the abject fear which produces incapacity — the type of terror most of us could exhibit but which in most films is always shown as a specifically female response. The gains she does make are almost always presented as the result of accident or her male child, who becomes amazingly resourceful in the same situations.

Against Duvall's realistically acted horror is the Mr. Hyde Nicholson, a larger than life Grand Guignol stereotype complete with Quasimodo limp and maniacal cackle. Kubrick has also made him amusing, encouraging us to release our tension by laughing with him *at her*. The audience convulses at his baby-talk imitation of her stuttering terror. She is annoying and weak, while he is terrible with theatrical panache.

The plot structure further encourages us to dismiss her (and by extension all women) by tricking us into feeling that Mrs. Torrence is profoundly ignorant. At a particularly crucial moment drama is provided by her forgetting how to open a door — rather than the door sticking as it might for a male character. The reasons for her husband's madness are obvious to the child and to us in the audience, but not to the unfortunate Mrs. Torrence, who is continually placed in the position of not understanding what we have known for several minutes. From our privileged position we know what she must do, where she must go and why her actions are tantamount to suicide. Strung with tension we want to hiss

"God, NO, you stupid bitch, THINK" just as the man next to me did. At the woman's expense we are given the thrill of being right, of knowing more, of having male power, since Kubrick's move, like Hitchcock's art, operates by gratifying our expectations rather than playing off and with them.

As the camera follows her tortuous steps into blind alleys we castigate her rather than her husband who has been transformed into an irresponsible killing machine. She becomes the one we blame for everything, just as woman is the enemy for Torrence and his ghostly cohorts.

· · · · · ·

It is hardly new to see women presented as a pathetic but spiteful stereotype. What is disturbing however, is that Kubrick's position as respectable director has closed people's minds to the noxious elements that are mercifully recognised in exploitation flicks like *Texas Chain Saw Massacre* (a film to which *The Shining* bears more than a passing resemblance.)

In our society violence against women is not just conducted by unknown lunatics in dark streets — it is institutionalised and normalised, even by such supposedly 'neutral' areas as film making technique. Sanctified by BBC-2, *The Shining* contributes to the ritualisation of subordination at least as much as snuff movies and sadomasochistic pornography.

Jane Root

*Film Review from The Leveller, Oct. 29 — Nov. 11, 1980

TOWARDS A REVOLUTIONARY
FEMINIST ANALYSIS OF RAPE

It is essential for the Women's Liberation Movement to fully develop a feminist theory of rape, to expose rape for what it is — 'a conscious process of intimidation by which all men keep all women in a state of fear.' (Susan Brownmiller, *Against Our Will*, New York, Bantam, 1976.) The fear of rape is always with us. It affects our lives in countless ways — not only in that we are afraid to walk the streets late at night, but in all our dealings with men, however superficial these might be.

Men's images of our bodies are thrust upon us wherever we go — in magazines, on advertising hoardings, on the tube, in the newspapers, in films, etc. etc. This makes us self-conscious about our bodies, the way we sit and stand and walk — when was the last time you saw a woman sit sprawled across a bus seat the way men do all the time? We keep our knees together, our legs crossed, our faces neutral. Somewhere in our minds we are always aware that any man — every man — can, if he wants to, use the weapon of rape against us.

And men know it too. The man who mutters obscenities at us in the street knows it, the local greengrocer who insists on calling us love (although we have objected) knows it, the wolf-whistling building workers know it, the man reading page three on the tube and grinning at us knows it. At one point on Reclaim The Night in Soho, we were confronted by a large group of men shouting "We're on the rapist's side — we're with the rapist." They didn't really need to tell us. We already knew.

Rape has nothing to do with an uncontrollable sexual urge — rape is an expression of power and hate. Men rape to cause fear and pain and to prove their superiority. Read any woman's account of being raped.

Male myths about rape abound, naturally, for in a society controlled by men, they have the power to spread their propaganda effectively. Many women are confused by these lies — it is really important that we work on understanding what rape actually is and that we share our ideas and experience with each other.

Rapes have been documented from very early times, but until the end of the 13th century, in Britain at any rate, they were not treated in law as crimes against women, but as violations of male property. In early Hebrew law virgins were sold into marriage by their fathers for 50 pieces of silver. A man who raped a virgin outside the walls of the city had to pay the bride-price to her father and they were commanded to marry. If, however, the rape took place within the walls of the city, both rapist and victim were stoned to death, the argument being that if the woman had screamed she would have been heard and rescued. Under Assyrian law, the father of a raped virgin was allowed in return to violate the rapist's wife.

During the early Middle Ages in England, the rape of an heiress became a common method of men of power to extend their wealth and property. On the continent, meanwhile, a manorial lord had the right to take the virginity of the bride of any of his serfs (the jus primae noctis), unless the bride and groom paid a certain fee.

From the time of Potiphar's wife, men have perpetuated the myth that women are prone to making false accusations of rape. This myth has been so thoroughly absorbed by male culture that warnings of women's tendencies to lie are handed out regularly at Police colleges and sometimes even in instructions to juries.

Men usually deny their responsibility for rape, and disassociate themselves from rapists, by either blaming the victim for her provocative behaviour, or, when that is impossible, placing the rapists in some special category: pervert, lunatic, etc. However, in war, men admit that rape is an act of power when committed by the enemy (the rape of the Hun), but the act of an uncontrollable urge when committed by themselves: "That's an everyday affair . . . the guys are human, man." (American squad leader in Vietnam, quoted by Susan Brownmiller.)

The threat of rape is a weapon men use to perpetuate their dominance of women. The ways in which it is used in Western 'civilised' society are less obvious than in some of the primitive cultures studied by anthropologists, where rape was customarily a punishment for women who were sexually demanding, disobedient to their husbands, quarrelsome, or simply without a male protector. There is no law in Britain which forbids women to be independent, live alone or with other women, to go out alone at night, to refuse to relate to men sexually or emotionally, yet in so many cases of reported rapes the behaviour of the victim is cited as provocation. She was hitch-hiking (she asked for it). She was wearing a low cut dress (she asked for it). She left her door open (she asked for it). She seemed friendly in the pub. She

came up for a coffee. I only wanted to talk to her and
she told me to fuck off. She's a lesbian. She's a prostitute.
She's had two abortions. SHE HAD TO BE PUNISHED.
Feminists; bitter, frigid, man-haters: what you need is a
good fuck. The point being of course to keep woman isolated
from her sisters, the protected property of one man, who has
exclusive sexual rights over her body. It is not a crime for a
man to rape his wife.

A man can force sexual intercourse on a woman without
the fact of his forcing her spoiling his enjoyment. Obviously,
in most cases of rape, what the man is getting off on is the
woman's fear, pain and humiliation, and so we can say that
rape is not a sexual crime — that's true in that it is about male
power and is therefore political. But it is important to
consider this fact, that very often the willingness and pleasure
of the woman are quite unnecessary and irrelevant to the
man. Many women say that they have never ever enjoyed sex
with their husbands, but they have existed through years of
married life 'letting' their husbands 'exercise their marital
rights' when they couldn't put them off with one of the
excuses women have been using over the centuries to deter
their spouse from raping them.

Since in patriarchal society man is considered to be the
hunter/doer/seducer/instigator, the one-who-goes-out-and . . .
it is considered quite O.K. and normal for a man to try to
persuade a woman to have sexual intercourse. He asks her
to dance, she accepts. (She wants to, or she doesn't want to
but she's afraid of hurting his feelings, she's afraid of making
him angry, she wants a man to dance with.) He asks her out,
she accepts. (She wants to, or she doesn't want to, but all
her friends have got blokes, she's afraid of making him angry,
he might feel hurt, she can't go out if she's on her own.)
He kisses her. He puts his hand on her leg, her breast, her
cunt. He wants to see how far he can go. She lets him. (She
wants to or she doesn't want to but he's taken her out after
all, and spent money on her, she needs a lift home, she
doesn't want to seem a prude, he might be angry.) He asks
her to sleep with him. She accepts. (She wants to, or she
doesn't want to but she thinks she might as well, she can't
back off now, it might be O.K., she's flattered that he wants
her, he might be angry.)

Or she refuses. He tries to persuade her. He tells her he

27

loves her. He says she doesn't love him. He calls her a prude, immature, frigid. He says he 'needs' sex, so if she won't come across, he'll have to find a girl who will. Each time they meet he carries on a bit further, a bit further. (Why not go all the way?) He buys durex to demonstrate his sense of responsibility. Each time she finally tells him to stop, breaks away, he gets angry, he rages, he sulks; he tells her how bad it is for men to be left 'excited' (Prick-teaser!) He teaches her to suck him off. He works toward his goal, which is her vagina. He means to have, to possess this woman.

This isn't rape, this is normal everyday stuff. The magazines call it young love.

So if this is normal and acceptable no wonder the rape laws in this country are ambiguous. If a man believes, however erroneously, that the woman he is fucking has consented to being fucked, he is not guilty of rape. So if a woman shows any signs of reluctance, that's not to say she doesn't really want to. She needs talking round, she's playing hard to get, she needs turning on, she likes a rough time.

In heterosexual relationships it is the man's desire which comes first and which is necessary. Then it is up to him to make the woman want sex as well. But if she doesn't, he can go ahead anyway. He has his penis. He has his erection. There's the woman, there's the vagina. So what is rape? And what, exactly, is 'consent'?

Some women would argue that a top priority must be the reform of the law on rape and a new legal definition of rape, one much broader than the current definition of perpetration of an act of sexual intercourse on the body of a woman not one's wife, longer jail sentences for rapists, etc. While such reforms might have some good effects, we think that this perspective ignores a very important area — the administration of the law. Without radical changes in the attitudes of the police, judges, juries, etc., any changes in the law will come as small comfort to rape victims. In general women who have been raped receive appalling treatment both by the police and the courts — if indeed they get as far as the courts. The police accuse them of lying, of being prostitutes who didn't get paid, etc. In court a woman's past sexual history may be brought up at the discretion of the judge (the rapist's may not) — the result of this is that in many cases the *woman* ends up being on trial for 'promiscuity', the assumption being that if she has previously had an active sexual life then she no longer has the right to refuse a man!

Whatever improvements may be made to the law on rape, so long as it is 'enforced' by misogynists (men), we can see of no way it can be used to women's advantage.

So what is the answer? Shall we have a national campaign against rape, People Against Rape, the initials indicating the essential equality of sisters and brothers in struggle, mixed marches, Men Against Rape groups, Trade Unions passing anti-rape resolutions, etc? Or shall we fight every step of the way against de-radicalisation of rape, against rape being amalgamated into the liberal consciousness along with abortion? In the same way that the radical meaning of 'a woman's right to choose', a woman's right to control her own body, has been watered down and lost, shall we sit back and let hoards of self-congratulatory men say "of course I'm against rape"? For many men will flock to do so to disassociate themselves from those awful men who rape women.

We must be clear — *all* men are potential rapists.

Reprinted from FAST No. 1, written for the Bristol Conference on Rape in 1978 by 3 women who have been working together in a rape group for more than a year, London Rape Action Group.

This paper was first published in *On the Problem of Men:* Friedman (Scarlet), Sarah (Elizabeth), eds., The Women's Press, U.K., 1982. Reprinted with permission.

BLAMING THE SYSTEM

We all know about blaming the victim of sexual crimes for having invited the offence, but in this paper I want to look at another way of avoiding the issue — that is by blaming the system. Most liberal-oriented social agencies use this as their main mechanism for attributing blame — and everyone wants to lay the blame for sexual crimes *somewhere*.

Blaming the system is rationalised through marxist theories of alienation, amongst others. It goes something like this — the industrial worker (male) is exploited by the capitalist system. He becomes alienated from the fruits of his labour. He is powerless vis-a-vis the process of production, so he acts out his alienation on those over whom he still retains a measure of control — ie. — women and children. So it's the system which has screwed him up.

Unlike those who blame the *victim*, those who blame the system are opposed to the existing state of affairs — they are critical of the way things are and want to change it. But blaming the system effectively takes away from men any measure of individual responsibility for their actions. It denies that men attack women because they choose to take a course of action which results in women's suffering. It provides a rationale for the denial of responsibility through its emphasis on external factors (overcrowding, slum housing, unemployment, boozing, undesirable parenting, etc). Both the sexual offender and the liberal agencies which act for him are able to argue that the offender was *acted upon* by these external factors — that his behaviour was socially determined (not biologically determined, as psychoanalysis argues).

Not only this. Blaming the system legitimises the argument that it is only working-class men who are violent to women. But women working in refuges and rape crisis centres tell us that men from all classes attack women. Solicitors, doctors and judges are not supposed to be alienated or to lack power, yet they, like working-class males support the ideology that women ask to be attacked, and thus they hold women in contempt whatever their objective socio-economic class.

Of course, if we take an uncritical look at criminal statistics we will find that the working-class of both sexes feature in larger numbers than do men or women from the middle and upper classes. That should surprise no one. The agencies of control are there to control working-class people (and I mean people — it's not a slip of the type-writer). So working-class males feature as offenders, and working-class females feature as victims in official statistics — but they are grossly misleading. The extent of middle-class violence from men to women never emerges in the figures, and this is very convenient for the dominant ideology.

Blaming the system to the exclusion of all else provides an ideological escape route for ignoring the universality of male violence to women. It cannot be explained away by seeing it as the cause of the environment since sexual violence is one of those phenomena which transcend time and space. Furthermore, blaming the system acts in the interests of men for while men are excused from responsibility for their actions, women are still held to be responsible for theirs.

Of course there are structural constraints which affect the way men behave towards women — there are material and ideological limits to free choice in actions. I don't think that anyone has totally free choice but some have a great deal more than others, and that availability of choice depends on the power that a person has to impose his will on others. Men have that power over women, certainly on an individual basis. To this extent they are responsible for their actions and should be seen to be so. The ideology of blaming the system provides an escape route from responsibility for men. For women, — well — they have only themselves to blame, after all . . .

Sue Rodmel, 1978

Reprinted from Scarlet Woman 10, Dec. 1979.

HOW ALL MEN BENEFIT FROM RAPE

Working in a Rape Crisis Centre, we are confronted by the reality of rape all the time through its effects on individual women. These effects are devastating. We also have to deal with these effects on ourselves of this constant reminder of male violence. Some of us try, and partially succeed, in hiding the truth from ourselves in order to function in the world. Other women, particularly after an attack, cannot do this — and a constant fear and tension seems to surround them even in their dreams. A helpless inertia may follow an attack — work, sleep, social-life become impossible and interaction with others is dominated by constant thoughts — either about a particular experience which cannot be explained or accepted, or about one's whole life that seems meaningless against this threat of invasion and devastation by male violence. Very heavy — very real — few of us can cope alone with these experiences.

Why is nothing done? — Why does it happen at all? — Why did it happen to me? All society's answers include criticism of the woman. Always we did something wrong. It may be something that we have done before without causing much of a stir, like:—

- inviting an acquaintance in for a drink;
- going to the chip shop wearing a skirt;
- refusing to have sex with an ex-lover after a chance meeting it turns out he has engineered.

Or our behaviour is not so 'innocent' — we did want company, love, affection — why not? Does this mean we want to be battered or threatened into submission and raped?

I don't really know the answer to the question 'why do men rape?'; all I know is that men do little to prevent rape and a lot to excuse it and to encourage each other's violent and negative feelings towards women. I also know that rape succeeds as a control on women's lives — a threat we cannot afford to risk being carried out on us and yet we cannot avoid it either. And this control relates to others in the complex structure of male dominance which pervades our lives. There isn't a clear line between rape and other pressures on us to submit and behave for men. The law pretends to define rape very strictly in two sentences:—

"A man commits rape if:
(1) he has unlawful sexual intercourse with a woman who at that times does not consent to it; and
(2) at that time he knows that she does not consent to the intercourse or he is reckless as to whether she consents to it."

In reality very few rapes can be conclusively proven with this law. Consent is meaningless to men when they are used to over-riding women's feelings most of the time anyway. Always the judgements in court are made using all the prejudices of sexist, racist, classist, ageist, etc society, and these prejudices have already decided what kind of women are raped and what kind of women are lying or guilty of 'provocation'. Also intercourse means penetration of the vagina by the penis which limits the crime a good deal. With obvious reference to women as men's property (valuable if virginal) and an equally obvious exclusion of any reference to the woman's experience of the rape/attack which can be just as traumatic without penetration.

We are taught to believe that men don't want rape to happen. Many men make it clear that they are horrified and upset by other men's violence. Men have made rape a serious crime, haven't they? Yes they have officially, and men have always condemned other men for 'violating' their own mothers and daughters. But who are the men that rape then? We know they are somebody's fathers, brothers, sons, and they even rape their own female relatives. Men laugh at jokes about rape, cover up and excuse other men's violence and punish women for daring to suggest that they have been raped. *These are all the same men* — not a minority of sex-starved maniacs.

The minority are those who do try to disassociate themselves from acts of violence, heterosexuality, sexist humour etc., but men that are doing this are still given relatively more power, freedom and wealth than women, and they will and do use this when they are pushed hard enough. In terms of rape, all men can use this threat to their advantage. At the time of the 'ripper murders' in Yorkshire women students in Bradford (and no doubt elsewhere) were finding that men were offering to see them home and then expecting to have sex as some kind of reward for giving their protection. How many of us have know this situation? It is just part of life for most women without a permanent male companion. If we have a husband we are legally bound to have sex with him. If we don't belong to a man we are expected to submit to all men if they want us or be punished with jokes, insults and sometimes rape.

If men really thought rape was so bad then the other men who get involved in dealing with rape would not behave as they do. Here I mean police, doctors, judges, etc. They would not punish us with cruel jokes, humiliating medical examinations, and refusals to believe our story. They wouldn't pass judgement on a woman's behaviour, life-style, clothes and sexuality if they did not in some way want to prove her guilt and his innocence.

The effect of rape, battering and all male violence serves to remind us that men have physical as well as economic and social power. Rape is the special one — ultimate proof of men's power and women's insignificance. That is why it is such a heavy traumatic experience — it is meant to be and it works (as I tried to show at the beginning). And rape continues to happen unchecked by laws, police and high sounding moral codes.

Of course there are some rapes that are condemned very strongly — the higher the social status of the woman the greater the outcry in the press: the rape of a prostitute is completely ignored. The overall picture is very confused precisely because there is this apparent horror of rapes that are 'undeserved' (because the woman is pure and another man's property) whilst women get no sympathy and can be raped at any time whoever we are.

Men control the whole situation from the rape itself to the final judgement in court. For a crime specifically committed against women this may seem surprising if we didn't know how male supremacy operates.

Women, too, often agree with men's judgements about rape. Always we are taught to 'understand' men, forgive them their 'mistakes', their aggression, and lots more. This is not unrelated; it is the price we pay for 'protection'. If we are working so hard for male approval then surely there are some women who don't merit that approval. So in our survival struggles we are forced to adopt men's standards — or are we? The protection is still not there because many of us are raped by those very men we are looking to for protection/love/security.

Women don't always sympathise with each other and we remain divided, sometimes completely alone after an attack. All men benefit from this because the fact of male violence is obscured with questions about women. They all benefit because they exploit our fear, and we work for their protection. They all benefit because rape is just a part of male dominance and control over women.

What we do about rape must take this into account — not treat rape as a strange isolated event involving two individuals.

Rachel Adams

PATRIARCHAL JUSTICE AND THE THREAT OF RAPE

The leftist press has started a violent anti-women campaign on the issue of rape: 'Since it is well known that prison is not a deterrent, to ask for the indictment of rapists is a reactionary demand which strengthens bourgeois juistice.' To ask that rape be exempt from legal consequences because punishment does not deter offenders is 1) to make a serious mistake and what is more 2) to make a confusion in very bad faith.

1. It confuses two quite distinct issues: the punishment applied or the forms of repression on the one hand, and the principle of indictment and the designation of an act as criminal on the other. Indictment determines that act as a crime, but it does not determine the form of repression. The very fact that rape is prosecuted shows that it is a crime. Not to punish one crime when all the others are punished does not call into question the principle of repression: it simply results in this act being seen as legal and permissible. This is what happens with rape.

Whether *or not* one agrees with their form of punishment in this society, no one asks that murderers go free.

2. Left wing political groups understand this very well and make the distinction for every crime except rape. When one approves of a boss being charged and placed in preventive detention, one is not supporting the principle of preventive detention, but that bosses should be treated as criminals, so that one fine day it will be acknowledged that workers do not die from inevitable and natural 'accidents', but because of the criminal negligence of their employers.

It is the left that has decided that to be 'against repression' is also to be 'against indictment', they must state that no one must be indicted, including murderers and employers, and that from now on you can throw workers off the scaffolding by the dozen with a clear conscience. If they continue to say that rape is an 'act of revolt against capitalism' and that it is in the same category as crimes against property, they must recognise that they are thereby saying that women are *possessions*. If their whining, contradictory and hypocritical attitude ('rape is a crime that mustn't be punished') reveals that rape is certainly a crime against the people, they must admit frankly that in this one instance they are on the side of power and not of the people, and that their sole aim — and the only explanation of their position — is to protect their interests as oppressors: their right to rape us with complete impunity.

As the left knows and practises the use of the judicial system to denounce crimes against the people, *far from reinforcing bougeois justice*, is an extraordinary effective means of *ideological struggle*.

1. It can show that supposedly natural 'accidents' are in fact the result of criminal acts committed by the class in power. This is the reason for indicting the company directors responsible for industrial accidents.
   This is why we want to bring the rapist to court.

2. The reaction of those in power and the press can demonstrate that the 'law' exists to protect and not to punish bourgeois criminals. For example, the outcry that followed the detention of an employer for three days after a fatal accident and the intervention of the Minister of Justice himself to secure his release, did more to demonstrate the bourgeois nature of Justice and the role of the State in the class struggle than years and years of classic agit-prop.
   Similarly, the way in which rape trials are conducted and their outcomes show better than any long arguments that the law exists to protect not the woman but the rapist. The use of the law in this case does not reinforce the law but on the contrary *unmasks* it.
   This is why we use the law: to make clear to all women the PATRIARCHAL-nature of Justice and the State it represents.

If indictment allows us to show the criminal and illicit nature of rape, the way in which the trial unfolds — the whole game of 'extenuating circumstances' (for the rapist) — serves to show the nature of rape and also the patriarchal nature of the legal system.

The fact of rape itself reveals first that a certain number

of activities are in fact forbidden to women: that a woman who is not 'protected' by a man (who doesn't have a protector/pimp), cannot move freely. She cannot go to the cinema, for a walk, camping, hitch-hiking or out in the evenings without the 'risk' of being raped. Lesser sanctions against these independent acts by women are endless questioning, catcalls and demands that she justify being alone in these places by men who try to pick her up. These are the inquisitors, the cops, the wardens of the patriarchal system, who want us to be 'protected' and sanction us if we are not.

In theory and according to the letter of the law (with the exception of marriage laws) NOTHING is specifically forbidden to women. But in fact and in jurisprudence, society has a 'risk of rape' which increases with the woman's independence of behaviour. That this risk has been socially established and measured is not accidental. It is part of the whole rewards and punishments which make up the system of control of women. This system ensures that women stay in their place in the patriarchal order. Violent sexual aggression represents the extreme on the continuum of punishments: the penal (physical and violent) sanction *par excellence*. Social control of women thus includes *the threat of rape*.

Further, the response of the police and what happens in court shows that these activities are not merely forbidden in fact. By treating the autonomous behaviour of women as incitements or proof of consent to rape, the law absolves rapists and legalises rape. It affirms that women do not have the *right* to carry out certain activities and penalises them *by law* by acquitting the rapist.

The NCCL (National Council for Civil Liberties) in its pamphlet on rape sets out a list of questions to which the victim cannot answer 'yes' without the rapist being systematically acquitted (even when the non-consent of the woman has been proved).

There are two main kinds of questions on their list which reveal the patriarchal nature of the judicial system:

1. Questions which establish if the woman 'ran the risk of being raped', that is if she engaged in activities which made rape materially i.e. *socially* possible – such as living alone, wearing 'indecent' clothes, talking or having

37

a drink with the rapist before the rape.

All these activities are not seen as simply making rape easy or possible, but as justifications which absolve the rapist — even when non-consent is proved. It is *thus* not rape which is judged, but its circumstances: only a married woman, locked in her home, in company and decently clothed can be recognised as a victim. That is to say, when rape is not only physically impossible, but above all *socially unjustified* from the point of view of the patriarchy.

This coincidence of what is dangerous for the woman and what justifies the man's action clearly reveals the legal, and at the same time punitive nature of rape.

2. There are also questions on the list concerning actions which establish the *autonomy* of the woman (such as being unmarried, divorced, an adultress, having had an abortion, having an illegitimate child, having a lover etc.) but which are all absolutely irrelevant to the act of rape itself, (since the rapist does not know these facts).

We can see that what is important here is how well founded the risk of rape was, since if the victim is a 'loose' woman the rapist is absolved: he did well to rape this woman.

The second kind of 'extenuating circumstances' illuminates the first and proves to us that the material danger which is in question in the first set of circumstances was indeed not physical but social. How can one explain that a crime can be justified by the ease with which it can be committed unless it is precisely because this ease is *evidence* of reprehensible behaviour in the victim? This is why the independence of the woman is enough to get the rapist acquitted even if the victim can answer 'no' to the questions about her attitude which could have been perceived by the rapist, and even if he knows nothing of the victim's independence.

. . . . . .

Everything concurs to show that it is not the rape which is judged:

— because the rape is *a priori* justified by the fact that it was possible, the very fact of rape incriminates the woman;

— because the life style of the victim takes the place of 'extenuating circumstances', although it has nothing to do with the fact of rape.

What then is judged is this:

1. the right of the victim to complain or not: only circumstances rendering rape 'impossible' give her this right;

2. the legitimacy of the rape/punishment which has in fact been inflicted. If the man is acquitted it is because the woman has committed acts which ran the risk of rape. If by some extraordinary chance that rapist is found guilty, it is because he has gone beyond his duties as a policeman.

What rape cases and their outcome reveal is that judges and rapists are on the same side of the fence; the side of those who repress and penalise women in practice (rape) and in law (by legalising rape *a posteriori*). Far from being the accused or the repressed, rapists are the real snipers, the private militia of the patriarchal justice and the State it represents.

What these cases show us is that women are up against guerilla warfare led by the patriarchal state. In the struggle between men and women this state has a role of maintaining the oppression of women by men through its judicial framework, its official police and its private police (rapists).

These cases teach us at one and the same time that we cannot depend on the legal processes of the patriarchal state to defend us against the private militia of the same state, and that we, women, must overthrow this state.

des Feministes Revolutionnaires

Feministes Revolutionnaires, originally set up in 1970, was the first Radical Feminist Group in the French Women's Movement. This paper was distributed as a leaflet at the launching of a public anti-rape campaign in Paris, 1976. It was reprinted in 'FOIE-A-FEMMES', Alternative Paris, 1977.

SEXUAL INITIATION AS RAPE

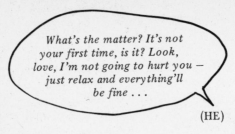

*What's the matter? It's not
your first time, is it? Look,
love, I'm not going to hurt you —
just relax and everything'll
be fine . . .*

(HE)

How do you feel about your sexual initiation? (At the end of this paper are accounts of how three women experienced it.)

Was the loss of virginity seen as significant to you at the time? Have you thought about it since? Too often the experience is filed away in dusty crevices of the mind and forgotten. I wish to argue, however, that it is a crucial moment in securing our oppression, and that there are reasons for our amnesia.

Penetration changes us, both in our relation to men and to ourselves. I will explain how by analogy. Invaded peoples often lose their self-respect, the land no longer belongs to them. Women, once colonised by the penis lose their right to self-determination. Once we have said 'yes', in men's heads resides the belief that we no longer have the right to say 'no', as exemplified by a woman's past sexual history being brought in at a rape trial.

The first penetration is like a rite of passage for the young woman. It is her initiation into heterosexuality, which in this patriarchal society is the only socially accepted framework for sexual activity. Penetration is, of course, the standard practice (the myth of the mutual orgasm — synchronically timed, ecstatic union and all that). Anything other is deemed perverse or at best a deviation from the 'Real Thing'. Moreover, the heterosexual couple is the structure whereby each woman has her own individual oppressor. Sexual initiation therefore becomes an important issue as the point at which she loses her selfhood as free, autonomous being, and becomes a sexual servicer to the male. (This isn't extreme. Look at how the mature virgin is hated by men.)

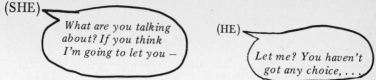

(SHE) *What are you talking about? If you think I'm going to let you —*

(HE) *Let me? You haven't got any choice, . . .*

Simone de Beauvoir argues that sexual initiation for the young girl "always constitutes a kind of violation" and goes on to say: "Formerly it was by a real or simulated rape that a woman was torn from her childhood universe and hurled into wifehood; it remains an act of violence that changes a girl into a woman; we still speak of 'taking' a girl's virginity. . . This defloration is not the gradually accomplished outcome of a continuous evolution, it is an abrupt rupture with the past, the beginning of a new cycle."[1] Reluctance on the part of the female virgin is therefore understandable. Even in these post-sexual revolutionary times, heterosexual sex is seen as a submission on her part. She is caught in a double bind. If she yields to coercion, she's a slut; if she refuses to submit she stands accused of 'playing hard to get' or being frigid or sexually repressed. Man, confronted by a virgin has a wish to conquer. *He* knows how important her 'first time' is. The male virgin gains credibility, acceptance as a 'man', once he has fucked a woman. He gains status in the eyes of men. Following the logic through then, woman must lose, and her resistance springs from an intimation of this. She is forced into a position of defence. What sexual inclinations she has get swamped under outright male aggression.

De Beauvoir calls her reluctance a problem![2] "Here we come to the crucial problem of feminine eroticism; at the beginning of a woman's erotic life her surrender is not compensated for by a keen and certain enjoyment. She would sacrifice her modesty and her pride much more readily if in so doing she opened the gates of paradise. But defloration as we have seen is not an agreeable feature of young love . . ."

I would be tempted to call it self-protection. Words like 'surrender' and 'sacrifice' indicate the inequality in terms of power — an imbalance that carries into subsequent relationships as well. Under present conditions feminine eroticism is constructed to be dependent on the male, thereby securing woman's consent in her domination.

41

I am not saying, however, that women do not learn how to 'get into' penetration sex. Only that there must be something very wrong with contemporary heterosexual practice for woman's initiation to be so frequently tantamount to rape.

What do we forget from our past, as we strive to assume our right to enjoy heterosexual sex and make our own demands and take the initiative?

How did we relate to our bodies before they were colonized by men?

What cannot be forgotten is that men want penetration, and that there are structures in present society to facilitate its instigation. There are material reasons for woman's less enthusiastic approach, — unwanted pregnancy is a real fear. So man develops the pill, the coil, the cap. Apart from the damage they do to woman's health, contraceptive methods ensure that her reaction to the possibility of unwanted pregnancy does not become an excuse for sexual abstinence. Young girls go on the pill at 14. It is presumed that they will have intercourse with boys. They harm their bodies in order to be 'safe' sperm recipients. We do not realise, especially at that age, that our bodies belong to us; that we need them; that a sick body is not much fun or use to its owner. Is this swallowing of hormones not alienating? Is it not against our interests?

I am not proposing that penetration sex is inherently evil, but that with present technology it is dangerous, and that under male supremacy there is no way that we can see it outside of a dominant/submissive power relationship. Our sexual initiation is not for our benefit. The hierarchy exists before we screw; and in so doing we get sealed into place as the oppressed. And if we don't consent . . .

"What very often happens in all circles and classes is for the virgin to be abruptly taken by an egotistic lover who is primarily interested in his own pleasure . . ."[3]

. . . in other words, sexual initiation as rape.

Annie Smith, 11 November, 1980

1 Simone de Beauvoir, *The Second Sex.*
2 Ditto.
3 Ditto.

The speech bubbles are from a picture story in Jackie Magazine under the 'A Reader's True Experience' section, in which the heroine/reader suffers an attempted rape by her boyfriend. First he tries to buy her acquiesence by a present, then he tries blackmail. She escapes before he uses violence, but not without attendant feelings of guilt and shame.

Sexual Initiation — Three women speak

I was 16, 5 feet tall and anorexic, weighing 6st. 2lbs. instead of 7st. 8lbs. or so — that says something about my attitude at that time towards sexuality. He was 17, 6ft. and weighed about 12st.

I'd always thought of him as a friend, a 'mate'; we knocked around together during the day, sometimes along with two other blokes. In the evenings we had different circles of friends, went to different pubs. Mine were weekend hippy/aspiring intellectuals, his were right-on trendies. In retrospect, his attitude towards women boiled down to "does she go?"

One conversation with him on the subject of sex sticks in my mind. The question was, why was I 16 and still a virgin? My answer, that when I had penetration sex for the first time I wanted it to be with someone who loved me and whom I loved. I'd fallen hook, line and sinker for the idea of sex as a sacrament "the highest form of communion" between lovers.

So much for the background. Except that I had been infatuated with him for about 2 years, but had rejected his advances about a year before, dealing a severe blow to his pride. Anyway . . .

Five or six of us had gone back to his parents' house on New Year's Eve (the parents were out!) I was the only female. My jeans were torn so I went upstairs to sew them up.

10 minutes or so later, he came up "to see how I was going on". Banter about how I'd think I was fat if I ate a peanut developed into kissing and petting and then started to get heavy. As far as sexual initiation goes I'd describe it as semi-rape. He was twice my weight, on top of me and forcing my legs apart. I was too shy/embarrassed to scream to the others downstairs.

He withdrew to ejaculate and I didn't quite realise that penetration had taken place until the following morning when I noticed some spotting of blood and considerable soreness. I was quite literally sick with worry and with *guilt* until my next period when the worry subsided but the guilt remained. There are still odd times now, 7 years later, when guilt says 'you could have struggled more'.

Just a word or two on his attitude. The following year I saw him at a New Year's Party. "Remember what we were doing this time last year?" were his words. About 5 months later he brought it up again: "I'm sorry, I didn't realise it was your first time". I think that says it all.

. . . . . .

My first lover was called Ron, and it happened when I was 21. But before I talk of him I must mention the boyfriend before. Bob and I had gone steady for about a year. I probably would have gone the whole way with him — we often slept together — but he also believed sex came after marriage. He wanted to marry me. We got along well enough. What saved me was my dreams of romance. 'Is this all there is going to be' I thought. 'Just me and Bob and settling down in the Welsh Valleys?' I was still waiting for the big romance as in the movies.

And I found it with Ron.

I finally gave in to him, in a hotel room in Paris, after weeks of heavy pressure. (You don't love me. We need to find out if we are sexually compatible before we marry. Veiled threats that if I didn't do it he'd find someone who would etc. etc.) I can't blame it all on Ron. I mean the setting, April in Paris. It certainly fitted the backdrop to the big event. That had a lot to do with it too.

The actual experience was zero, absolutely zilch. 'Is that all there is?' I wondered. It didn't seem worth all the fuss. There I was a non-virgin. (Maybe men on the Metro could tell by looking at me, yet I felt no different). But it had a big effect on me. I became like Ron's slave. The why not take all of me syndrome you could call it. For after all if this was not 'special' what had I been and gone and done it for? As my sexual enjoyment in bed grew, I was ever so grateful to him. And I told him so.

One day, some 3 weeks after the big event, I met him by the fountain as usual. But he looked very glum and serious. 'What's wrong?' (How have I displeased you). 'I have something to tell you S—. . . I can never marry you . . . I can never marry a woman I have slept with . . . but I still want you . . . I want us to be lovers at least as long as we are in Strasbourg'. 'Oh Ron, I'm yours as long as you want me'.

. . . . . .

Various girlfriends at school had been trying to pair me off with one boy or another and eventually I gave in and went out with one of them. Autumn. I was 15, he 18. It was, for both of us, our first heterosexual relationship, and in many respects just like a normal friendship. We went swimming, rode bicycles, played snooker at the local youth club, walked the dog, with the addition of a kiss goodnight/goodbye at the end of the day.

He experimented at the pictures. First an arm snaked round my shoulders. (I remember it well. I was in a thick turquoise jumper and jeans, my daily apparel, not having much else in the way of clothing at the time). Having established the arm was still in position, the hand attached moved over to examine my left breast. In all this I watched the movie, Somebody Smith, a western with Steve McQueen, and tried to pretend it wasn't happening; not in the least bit sure what I was supposed to do about the situation. It wasn't particularly pleasurable; my dominant emotion was confusion. If I removed the hand he might get angry; if I didn't he might think I was encouraging it. I didn't touch him, and it didn't occur to me to ask what he was up to. I just endured in good stoic faith.

Things developed to heavy petting. We used to go to a hay barn with dog, torch and radio. (It was mid-winter by now.) The subject of Sexual Intercourse constantly arose. He wanted it. I didn't. (Memories of painful times with a tampax because I insisted on going swimming at all times of the month.)

The pressure got progressively heavier. I was threatened with termination of the friendship, and by then I was quite involved. I was used to having him around. He employed all the old arguments. "If you loved me you'd let me make love to you . . . It's the testing ground of the relationship". So I gave in. I also knew I'd have to go through with it sometime and reasoned I might as well get it over with. Penetration was painful. I remember thinking; hell it lasts a long time, and do I have to put up with this regularly?

After the ordeal he picked up the torch and inspected his penis. Me, perplexed, asked why. He was looking for blood. Not finding any he got angry and accused me of not being a virgin. I felt dreadful. Realisation dawned, but I didn't want to talk about the tampax episode as menstruation wasn't considered something to be discussed with boys. And besides I felt shamed. My body had become his property (and I allowed it to), and he was therefore upset because he felt ripped off by the hymen not being intact.

By the way I married this guy.

IN STEERING WOMEN WHO HAVE BEEN RAPED TO SEX THERAPISTS WE ARE PERFORMING A FUNCTION FOR MEN, AND GLUEING OVER A CRACK IN MALE SUPREMACY.

The New Sex Therapy by Helen Singer Kaplan[1] is the most complete and widely used account of sex therapy (it is the standard text used in Health Education in UK). Descriptions and quotes below are from this book, unless otherwise stated.

The Origins of Sex Therapy
Sex Therapy developed from the studies of Masters and Johnson[2] and most of the research and spreading of information on it comes from the Marriage Guidance Council[3]. This is because sex therapy serves to cement a couple's relationship — serves to keep the woman more bound to the man. Before sex therapy, the only 'treatment' for couples not getting on in bed was psychoanalysis. This, with long one-to-one sessions where psychiatrists delve into people's pasts, is very costly. Sex Therapy evolved in the second half of the sixties to bring 'treatment' to the masses. It ignores unresolved Oedipal complexes, other marital problems, and concentrates on 'getting things right in bed'. Most of the work is done at home, with your partner or on your own. Its proponents claim that in most cases once the sex is right other problems disappear.

The sexual arena, 'the bedroom', is seen as a place separate from the rest of life, a sort of neutral territory. It is a place of 'mutual pleasure and trust' and the rest of the world 'must be left outside'. Kaplan keeps stressing the fact that many women use sex — the bedroom — as a battleground (I mean they may for example want to talk about money problems or the kids when he wants to screw). Under sex therapy women must give prime importance to what should go on in the bedroom, and leave all other problems outside.

While no outside problem can be brought into the bedroom what happens there is seen as affecting the rest of life. 'Often it is possible to bypass marital problems. Nodal points of trouble are identified and the couple is charged with the responsibility of "keeping them out the bedroom". Once this is achieved and the sexual harmony restored, other problems resolve themselves.' Kaplan gives no examples of this. Brown and Faulder[4] do. 'Dorothy had been urging John for the past three years to move house and the pressures had increased since he had been made a foreman'. After successful sex therapy 'They decided not to move house and instead they bought a new car.' (Presumably what John had been wanting all along).

What goes on in this neutral territory has nothing neutral about it. Sex therapy functions to keep women tied more securely to men, and within that relationship keeps the man dominant.

What is Sexual Disharmony?
Before we can talk of sexual disharmony, or as Kaplan calls it 'dysfunction' we need to see what the therapists call sex. 'Sexual dysfunctions ... make it impossible for the individual to have and/or enjoy coitus' ... 'The patient does not enjoy sexual intercourse'. Homosexuality is dismissed as a perversion and the aim of therapy is to help him get it up, keep it up, and ejaculate in the vagina: to get her to open up and enjoy it.

There are 2 kinds of dysfunction. The first affects the male: impotence, premature ejaculation etc. The woman is made responsible for curing these, turning her into a 'servicer of his penis'. Meanwhile he is encouraged to 'take advantage of his morning erections and commence rapidly with intercourse without trying to stimulate his sleepy wife'.

The second kind affects the woman, and is generally termed 'frigidity'.

Frigidity
What this means is she does not like it/does not want it/does not want it as often as he does/does not have orgasms.

There are 2 main causes of this. One is that he simply does not know what to do — so he is provided with techniques. The other is that she is 'refusing him' or 'refusing him her pleasure'. She is 'in rebellion against men'. Psychoanalytic explanations for this include of course 'penis envy'. Kaplan admits there are 'more rational hypotheses which seek to explain the anger and envy some women harbour toward men' due to the 'repressed, insecure and exploited role of females in our society'. (Have you noticed how men are oppressed and exploited by other men, but women have a repressed and exploited role?)

Frigidity as Rebellion

This is variously described by Kaplan as the woman 'refusing to abandon herself' and the woman 'refusing to let go'. She stresses that 'the wife must learn to trust her husband'.

'For a woman, a feeling of trust that the partner will meet her needs, particularly dependency needs, and a feeling that her spouse will take care of her, will take responsibility for her, will not abandon her and will be loyal to her seems necessary in order to enable her to abandon herself to sexual pleasure.' So these feelings of trust (note feelings of, we are not talking about the reality of them) must be developed. She is *not* talking about just in bed. She does mean the 'marriage contract' whereby he provides for all the outside needs of the woman — is her intermediary with the world — and is rewarded by her providing for all his needs within the couple. The woman must think herself into this frame of mind to be able to abandon herself to sexual pleasure. Remember the crux of sex therapy is that getting the sex right will solve other problems in the marriage/relationship. While they insist nothing from life outside be brought into the bedroom, what goes on in the bedroom they do see as having an effect outside it.

Since what should go on in the bedroom — for successful sex therapy, in this culture — is either the woman becoming the man's sexual slave, in the case of male sexual dysfunctions, or the woman thinking herself into total dependence on the man, to overcome her sexual dysfunction, this activity is not neutral. Thus it can only have a reinforcing effect on the power imbalance between men and women, individually and collectively, outside the bedroom. That is, it will solve the power struggle between men and women as it has always been solved. Men win, women lose.

Extreme Frigidity — Vaginismus

Vaginismus is the name given to extreme cases of 'frigidity'. 'Whenever penetration is attempted, the vagina . . . snaps shut.' Further attempts to penetrate cause great pain. Women with vaginismus are *not* asexual. 'They may be orgasmic on clitoral stimulation, enjoy sexual play, and seek sexual contact — as long as this does not lead to intercourse'.

Leaving aside psychoanalytic explanations for this — penis envy (fear and hatred of men) again — Kaplan cites either physical causes, eg. pelvic inflamatory disease, or actual nasty experiences with men. *'Others were raped . . . or had been subjected to brutal sexual experiences'*. Masters and Johnson also cite *'rape experiences'* as a prime cause of this.

The treatment is horrific. So before describing it Kaplan reminds us how serious an ill, vaginismus is. 'Because this disorder makes intercourse impossible, vaginismus is seldom tolerated lightly'. Before the sex therapy cure for it evolved surgery was often resorted to. While these operations — cutting the woman open and disabling the muscles — made intercourse possible, they usually 'adversely affected the patient's sexual responsiveness'. She mentions the case of a woman, once orgasmic, who had surgery (she had 75 stitches) and as a result no longer could achieve orgasm. Having given us that background, Kaplan describes the treatment.

Sex therapy treatment consists of introducing first small then larger objects into the vagina. You start with a small plastic penis, then force in larger and larger ones, till you fit the size of your partner's penis (a process similar to that in countries where women are castrated and sewn up; before marriage they must accustom themselves to a clay model of the husband's penis). Sometimes instead of the plastic penises the woman's or her husband's fingers are used. You force one in then two and so on. This is painful. Kaplan refers to women having to 'stay with the pain' for up to 10 minutes, and 'bearing down on the pain'. 'Sexual intercourse is not attempted until the insertion of objects in the vagina can be tolerated without discomfort'. There are two alternative 'therapeutic' techniques to go with this. One is 'systematic desensitisation'. While enduring the pain, the woman 'fantasises the sexual situation she fears in a gradual manner' starting with imagining her husband's approach, then him lying beside her, then him approaching with an erection, and so on. The other method is called 'flooding'. With this method the woman starts by imagining the worst possible. She is asked to imagine 'that she is being ripped apart by her husband's penis, on the theory that once she can tolerate this fantasy, which is her unconscious expectation, she will be able to tolerate actual intercourse'. Just in case we get freaked out by all this talk of pain and being ripped apart, Kaplan reminds us that the alternative is surgery, 'or vaginal entry is forcibly attained' (rape by husband).

The woman who stays with her feelings of fear and her pain has her 'behaviour reinforced by the therapist's approval and by her husband's pleasure as well'. Good Girl.

Rape and Sex Therapy

Rape was noted as a cause of vaginismus. It also causes 'frigidity'.

This is a reasonable response to rape/brutal sexual experiences, but it is not one approved of by society — ie men. Rape functions effectively as part of the way men control women and maintain dominance — all men benefit from the act of the rapist (see paper on rape).* But if all women raped went off intercourse for life this would be an unfortunate side effect, for men. Sex therapy, however can now 'cure' such side effects, with the above treatment. The woman must live and relive the rape experience till she can tolerate it.

The London Rape Crisis Centre offers sex therapy to raped women, but only they say 'to women who ask for it'. The woman who had surgery for vaginismus also 'asked for it'. If we can't comply with male demands we often seek treatment ourselves, like Cinderella's Ugly Sister cutting off part of her foot to fit the shoe. But it is men who are setting the demands and insisting we comply, albeit indirectly. Of course it can be more direct. Man and Woman Magazine[5] had an article on rape which told men they could send their wives for sex therapy. The London Rape Crisis Centre number was given, so they could get their wives to ring and ask for it.

Sex Therapy evolved to bond women more closely to men at a time when older patriarchal forms of control weakened. Divorce plus even limited access to jobs and education meant more chance of freedom for women. Only when women began to fight for such rights did men begin to talk of women's right to sexual pleasure. Only when we began to win them were we told that the ultimate in sex equality was to find a man who could satisfy us in bed, and to that end should we work.

It therefore should come as no surprise that sex therapy is called on to solve, for men, the problem of women who are raped becoming 'frigid'. Or even worse starting to consider the nature of the relationship between the sexes, particularly with rape on the increase.

What is a woman told by the sex therapist? That the problem of rape is her reaction to it. That bad treatment from some men should not put her off others. So even if she is abused by men she will still trust others, and if she can't she will blame herself.

In steering women who have been raped to sex therapists we are performing a function for men, and glueing over a crack in male supremacy.

Sandra McNeill, 7 November 1980

1 Kaplan (Helen Singer) The New Sex Therapy. Penguin 1974
2 Masters (William) Johnson (Virginia) Human Sexual Response. Churchill 1966.
3 Brown (Paul) Faulder (Caroline) Treat Yourself to Sex. Dent 1978.
4 Brown and Faulder, as above.
5 Man and Woman Magazine: Part 3. Dec 79/Jan 80.
* How All Men Benefit From Rape. Conference paper by Rachel Adams.

The **LONDON RAPE CRISIS CENTRE** would like to make it clear that we do not offer or encourage women to have 'sex therapy'. We believe that sex therapy is yet another way in which men gain access to women's bodies and much of our work is about enabling women to control that access.

We have in the past considered referring women for all kinds of therapy, if they wanted that. We considered ourselves to be a resource for all women to use as they wished. We have gained experience over the years however, and now know that to refer women to sex therapy is not helpful and in fact negates our work of trying to help women to survive and fight against the male violence we all face every day.

London RCC, May 1983

SEX THERAPY

The theories underlying every sort of therapy I've come across are based on male ideas. Men use psychology to prove their superiority and they use therapy to make us conform to their ideas of what we should be. Some of this therapy comes in the form of advice, or as saying things that put women down, directly or as comments on other women. Some is in the form of "professional" advice. As we grow and change we develop survival tactics, ways of living with as little pain as possible in a hostile world. These tactics are described as neurotic by psychological theories, that is, by traditional psychological theories which are based on the idea that men are normal and healthy and if you haven't got a penis you must have a complex about it. Trendier theories reject that but still are prick-biased and based on men's ideas of what we are or should be. The old theories are based on the idea that some people are normal and some aren't and their therapy is to make us conform to whatever the theory defines as normal. The alternative theories say that we've been damaged by the wicked world and their therapies are designed to get rid of what they define as damage. So both want us to get rid of whatever survival tactics we've learnt and to get rid of the protective wall we've built up around us. I think we may need to develop ways of getting rid of survival methods that are no longer any use to us. I know that when I lived with men I found ways of avoiding being hurt that I shouldn't need now that I live with women and that may be damaging to the women that live around me but I don't need men and any of their grand theories to tell me when and how I should get rid of them.

When a woman is raped or beaten by men they want to make sure that she doesn't learn anything that might be to her advantage in dealing with them. They try to prevent her finding ways of behaving towards all men that are good for her and other women rather than making their lives easier and more pleasant. So they blame her for their violence and say she should be "cured" of anything she's learnt. She should have therapy so that she can continue to conform to their ideas of what a "normal" woman should be like.

These ideas are thrown at us in a more or less disguised

or watered down version from time to time in our everyday lives. They are built up out of the everyday experience of men, "proved" true by various "scientific" methods and filtered back down to us by TV magazines newspapers and by our family friends, neighbours and workmates. They reinforce male supremacy and make our lives and experience of less importance to us. They make our own experience seem unreal, make it seem like each of us is different, feels differently from other women.

This has been experienced by women in the drive to get women back to the home and family after the war, in the 50's, when men backed up their desire to trap women into being 24 hour a day slaves and concubines with Bowlby's theories that children needed their mothers 24 hours a day — and the children referred to are always "he". Then in the sixties we suffered from the drive for sexual "freedom", when women were told how to enjoy sex with men and that we were abnormal if we didn't. There were articles telling us how to fake orgasms as well as telling us how many we should be having with how many men and in what contortionate positions. It seems amazing that with all this advice on how to enjoy — or pretend so they wouldn't guess — having sex with men, that so few women realised that they didn't and might as well stop and that they weren't doing these things for themselves but for men. From the Hite report it looks as if nothing's changed, except for those few women who've accepted or thought out for themselves a feminist analysis of what's happening.

It's very enlightening to compare modern Western ideas of what women's sexual feelings and behaviour are — or should be — with those of other times and places. Or even with those of different men at the same time and place. They're always backed up by indisputable authority — by religion in the case of puritanism, catholicism or Islam, by science with psychological theories or pop psychology, or by politics in fascism. And they all tell us how we should feel or behave. I think the ones that tell us how we should feel as well as how we should act are the most dangerous now and are a reaction to our attempts to free ourselves of male dominance. Here's an example of advice given to a woman who isn't managing to conform to men's ideas of how she should feel. The advice is given by a woman, as so many of men's ideas have been filtered down to us through women, from our mothers and sisters on.

From the letters page of Women's Voice — with comments from the York WIRES women:

Sex problems

Dear Women's Voice, my baby is now 6 months old and since his birth I haven't wanted to make love to my husband at all. I am really getting worried in case I am frigid even though I enjoyed sex very much before I had my baby. My husband is getting fed up and it is causing a lot of arguments.   Anon.

Dear sister,
First of all try not to worry, worrying will only make it worse and lots of women experience exactly what you are going through either during or after pregnancy. One of the big problems is the fact that many women with young babies don't get a decent night's sleep for months and there is nothing worse than being really tired to put you off sex. You may also be concentrating all your energy and affection on the baby which leaves you little time for other people.

Tut tut, there's nothing to worry about — lots of women feel like that so it doesn't matter.

No suggestion that hubbie helps with baby.

It's not a matter of 'concentrating' on the baby so there's no time and energy for other people. Babies need lots of attention and make lots of work — and what about time for herself?

If you had a painful childbirth perhaps fear of another pregnancy is putting you off sex. This depends of course on the contraceptive you use.

This implies that a bad choice of contraception is her fault. But there's no 100% reliable harmless form of contraception, except avoiding penetration and of course if we don't want that we're frigid.

You could try to talk to some of your women friends with babies and you will probably find that they had similar problems. Getting something off your chest to a good friend could make you feel a lot better. If you can't talk to your friends then you could go to your local Family Planning Association and ask them to help you. They would probably refer you to someone who could help you.

i.e. get support from your women friends so you don't have to tell him how you feel and can go on screwing and supporting him.

Refer you to who? An 'expert'? Psychiatrist? It's saying it's all her own fault again, like saying she's frigid which is a term she's used herself and is being controlled by.

One way of solving the problem with your husband is to find other ways of satisfying him sexually.

i.e. pull up your socks and pull down your knickers — after all

This would take some of the pressure off you and you might find that you get turned on too. I hope this helps.
Women's Voice

women exist to service men. If you can't satisfy him like he wants it try something else.

This is just one example of the crap women are fed every day of their lives, in lots of different ways, some shovel it in, some wrap it in sugar first. Well let's start spitting it back and hope it chokes them.

Lesley H.

PS   I've generalised about psychological theories but there's not time to criticise them all one at a time and I don't think academic criticism is relevant.

The comments on the advice letter are condensed from those in WIRES 74 which were made by some of the York WIRES collective including me and those I could contact said it was OK to use it.

WHY I LIKED SCREWING? OR, IS HETEROSEXUAL ENJOYMENT BASED ON SEXUAL VIOLENCE?

When I was 5 I played doctors and patients with my little girl friends. The *male* doctor, played by the eldest girl, "made" the rest of us take our knickers off and bend down while she "tortured" us. At 8, I played gypsy girl; dressed only in a skirt I fantasized nameless horrors forced on me by some lord of the manor. A friend aged 7 fantasized herself as a Roman Slave in the Market Place; naked and chained with legs wide apart for men to see.

In 1969, aged 22, I read "Story of O" and my horror and disgust was deepened by the then unspoken-for-many-years, ultra-guilty realisation that reading of O's total degradation was to me — a *turn on*. Passages from the book came unbidden to my mind when my boyfriend penetrated me and however fast I banished them they *worked* — I *did* enjoy it more.

Never did I speak of this, even when women in sexuality

55

c-r groups revealed their own hated masochistic fantasies and dreams — how in order to come they had to think of the man in the raincoat who'd flashed at them in the woods when they were 15; how images of rape, beating, bondage came to their minds when masturbating. It's only recently I've been able to get away from thinking I'm a bit of a pervert and it's all my fault, mainly through realising the power of male supremacy in our lives.

Our sexuality has been constructed by male-dominated society. We are brought up to kow-tow to men in every area of our lives, accept a generally lousy deal in jobs, pay, etc. etc. . . How can our sexuality possibly escape? We have to *fight* to begin to define it for ourselves, just as we have to fight for everything else that's ours that has been taken away from us, or never allowed growth or expression in the first place — control over our bodies, our fertility, our right to do any sort of paid work, a culture of our own . . .

Sexuality is too often talked about in the Women's Liberation Movement as something untouched, separate, as if it grows in us free and unfettered. But in a non-male-dominated society, would I have identified with degraded images of women and found them erotic? Would I have put up with faking orgasms and feigning headaches for 2 years of monogamous heterosexuality accepting that it was *my* fault and that I must be frigid? Would it have taken me *4 years* of bisexuality with feminists to finally push the last man out of my bed (with much guilt and fear) and say "I'm a lesbian"?

I'm not saying I never enjoyed sex with men. I did. But I suspect I enjoyed it most when I was most "on the bottom", most "giving", not being apparently in control bouncing around on top getting sore, but *being screwed* (provided he didn't go on and on and on, mind you). As I grew more feminist I couldn't let that happen with men I saw as "equal" or "superior" to me in age, status, education etc. so I chose a much younger and less educated "pretty boy". With him I could abandon myself in the missionary position and think (*never* say!) things like "He's my master". But as time went on even that became impossible (how could such a relationship ever last? Anyway he oppressed me as much as a man as all the others did), and I turned away more and more from men, towards women.

Relating sexually to women, or being a celibate lesbian, I still sometimes have masochistic fantasies. I *hate* them and fight to accept I'm not alone, nor a pervert. I *don't* believe the answer is to welcome and revel in them as "natural", I don't think they come from my own self-definition of my sexuality. I think they were planted and grew there as I grew up as a means of adapting my sexuality to the demands of a heterosexist society where men are supremely in control.

I don't recall being a victim of incest. My father was jealous of my boyfriends but this seems true of a lot of women I know. My mother was the dominant parent within the 4 walls of our home. But I don't think my particular family background is relevant to all this.

The stirrings of our own self-defined sexuality challenge male supremacy at its *roots*. But until we have ended male supremacy, we won't have a truly self-defined sexuality, full control over our bodies and our lives. It's fighting for this that will *end* male supremacy. Yes, I think we have to get out of men's beds as part of achieving this — but no, I'm not advocating going to bed with a woman "for political reasons", or "to further the revolution" — would any woman do so anyway? Saying lesbianism can be and is a political as well as a personal choice doesn't imply that, does it?

So — my sexuality, and that of many many other women, was twisted into masochism, which came out most strongly in my fantasies, which made me enjoy being screwed, which gave me an extra thrill. Many women have been turned on by "Story of O". Many of us have carried our fantasies into reality, have put up with or indeed initiated extremely humiliating sexual practices with men, like kneeling before him to suck him off, asking to be tied to the bed, or being fucked by two male 'lovers' simultaneously, one vaginally, one anally. What about the way this humiliation carries over into everyday life with men, how we allow ourselves to be treated like slaves, insulted, joked about? Who could "enjoy being a girl" with all that implies now, unless she was helped along by masochism?

Not *every* battered woman has nowhere else to go: not all are financially dependent on their man, or have children. Among hippies for instance it was/is, common enough for a woman to support a man out of *her* S.S., let him live in *her* accommodation, score his drugs herself and basically mother him, while getting beaten up and betrayed by him through-out. And she'll say she has no choice, but to stay, because she loves him. And here enters that other aspect of women's oppression, Romantic Love: two artificially constructed, grafted and carefully fostered mechanisms of social control of women by men —

masochism + romantic love = slavish emotional dependence.

As a woman in one of the sexual violence conference's papers says (in *Sexual Initiation — Three Women Speak*), just after her initiator has been really insulting to her — "I'm yours as long as you want me, Ron".

For a long time it's been impossible to speak about masochism in the Women's Liberation Movement because of the way this idea has been used against us, by men. "Women like being beaten by their husbands, that's why they stay, they're masochists" they say, as an excuse for doing nothing and letting the situation go on. No, that's not true, we say, we aren't masochists — fair enough — but it stops any further discussion. To raise the topic at all must be anti-feminist.

But it must be said a lot of women are influenced to be masochists, from a very young age, so that we'll become heterosexual and "enjoy" it. In a world where all men have power over all women maintained by the use or threat or ever-present possibility of sexual violence, isn't it inevitable that our sexual dealings with men should be filled with such things? And this in itself is a form of sexual violence against women.

A Fantasy: a stimulus to sexual arousal, that is, a necessary or helpful accompaniment to masturbation or sexual activity with another person. Physical arousal would be impossible, or more difficult, without the fantasy. But a fantasy can be less deliberate, conscious than this. Sexually stimulating thoughts and images that come unbidden to your mind when masturbating or making love are a form of fantasy, whether you banish them immediately or let them develop. So are erotic dreams. The people in the fantasy may be faceless, or engage in sexual activity which is outside the fantasiser's actual experience.

Many women have fantasies which entirely consist of, or have elements of, sado-masochism, bestiality, rape, being passive, looked at, tied up etc. etc. In discussion with women in Leeds it turned out that the two in the group who had *always known* they were lesbians did not have, and never had had, any of these sort of sexual fantasies. The rest of us had had. Obviously we can't generalise anything from so small a sample — but it is *interesting*, nevertheless.

Without masochism and the rest, would we get into "I'm yours as long as you want me, Ron"? Would we, indeed, ever get into Ron at all?

Justine Jones

With many thanks for discussion and help to revolutionary feminists and other women in Leeds.

This paper was included in the collection, "Love your enemy?, the debate between heterosexual feminism and political lesbianism," U.K. Onlywomen Press 1981.

PROSTITUTION

Prostitution and the women's liberation movement
There has been little discussion in the WLM about prostitution and less action. So far the issue has been aired mainly by Helen Buckingham and the English Collective of Prostitutes. It has been posed as the need to protect prostitutes from police harassment and persecution by unjust laws, a need which it would be impossible to deny. Yet there has been little response from feminists, little support for imprisoned prostitutes or for prostitute groups campaigning to change the law. Why is this? One reason seems to be an uneasiness about supporting prostitutes against victimisation in a way which offers no real threat to male power and no room to criticise the institution of prostitution itself and its effects on women. Another reason may be that the issue of prostitution raises uncomfortable questions about sexual relationships with men in general and all our past experience of them.

It became clear to me from discussing this paper with

many other women that it could be used to support a deeply felt prejudice against women who work as prostitutes, which is quite the opposite of what was intended. There is a great need for us to examine our feelings about prostitution whether they be betrayal, moral outrage, unease or bravado. It is in the interests of men that women are divided into groups whose interests are apparently opposed. 'Good' women have been encouraged to turn their anxiety at their precarious position into anger at prostitutes who can appear to threaten the married woman's home and security, to undermine her efforts to control her man and his sexual demands. Or we are told that prostitution is necessary to protect the married woman's security. Neither is true, as I hope to show. It is vital to male supremacy that women be divided into the 'pure' and the 'fallen' so that we may not pool our knowledge and engage together in the fight against male sexuality as social control of women. It is vital to us that we break through this division. I hoped that this paper would help to shift the discussion from the question of why women work as prostitutes to focus on why men require prostitution. I still hope it will but I recognise that we also need to do a great deal of consciousness-raising on the subject and it would be fatal to try to leap straight into theory about men and prostitution without talking about ourselves.

Explanations for prostitution based on why women do it
The experts often claim to be explaining the existence of prostitution by looking at why individual women begin to work as prostitutes. Even the ECP seems to fall into this trap:

> 'we are forced into prostitution by poverty, we are also fighting poverty through prostitution. Getting money for sex is one of the few ways open for women to make some money of our own and be financially independent from men. It's a way to have better control over our lives and dictate what kinds of relationships we want and on which terms. Many of us go on in the game in order to be able to live as lesbians.' (Scarlet Woman 10 p.20)

Not all women who become prostitutes do so because they are poor and the study of women's motivations does not help us to understand the function of prostitution. It is interesting to know why women choose that particular way of making a living but it will not help us to explain why prostitution exists. Those seeking to explain prostitution in the past and sociologists today have taken this tack. They cite poverty, women being oversexed (?), women being lesbians. Present day sociologists follow the life histories of women, fascinated to discover why they got into prostitution and the details of their lifestyles once in it. The poverty explanation leads to such absurdities as the proclamation by the infant USSR that prostitution was a class problem and would be eliminated with the destruction of the economic class system and a little retraining, probably compulsory. (N. Haire ed., "Sexual Reform Congress", 1930)

Studying prostitutes to explain prostitution is as useful as examining the motives of factory workers to explain the existence of capitalism. We must ask who benefits and in whose interests the institution is maintained. Only examining the motives of the ruling class can tell us this.

Who uses prostitutes?

Who uses prostitutes? Our husbands, brothers, sons, male lovers, fathers, male friends and supposed comrades. A few prostitutes can service a great many men and we must assume that a great many men use prostitutes. This is difficult to stomach, of course. It is so much easier to think of men who use prostitutes as somehow different or exceptions. It is harder to think of men who use as exceptions when they shove it under your nose.

But there is a conspiracy of silence going on about prostitution. How many women know that the men attached to them use prostitutes? I had to think about it because a male friend, a man I knew well and had lived with as a lover, who had been a charming hippy, told me in an unburdening moment about his use of women prostitutes. He went to them to be whipped. Knowing that your male lover used prostitutes would be, I imagine, a very disquieting and disorientating experience. Knowing how he could use other women, your sisters, knowing, undeniably at last, how fundamentally different his experience of sexuality was, must affect your ability to relate to him sexually. Men know that — hence the conspiracy of silence. We may think about prostitutes but not about their clients. There is no way to explain prostitution without working out why men use prostitutes.

Why do men use prostitutes — the experts' views

Most work on prostitution assumes a biological difference between male and female sexuality. One speaker at the progressive Sexual Reform Congress in 1929 was very open about this. He said the reason for prostitution was *'sex'* and explained that there was a naturally polygamous instinct in men which required expression through prostitution. (Robinson, Norman Haire ed., "Sexual Reform Congress", 1930)

There are very few studies of the men who use prostitutes. One English study divides the users into seven main types:

1. young men for their first sexual experience
2. young married men — maybe away from home
3. homosexuals who become compulsive clients of women to prove they are not homosexual
4. elderly men worried about their potency
5. alcoholics
6. vulnerable professions — sailors, lorry drivers, etc.
7. generally promiscuous men who are like criminals in personality.

When looked at closely the study turns out not to be a study of why men use prostitutes at all but an attempt to blame women again for the existence of prostitution. (T.C.N. Gibbens, "The Clients of Prostitutes", 1962) One third of the clients were married and most said their marriage was 'satisfactory', their wives 'were very good to them and so on'. Gibbens doesn't believe this,

> 'Later, it would sometimes emerge that no *outside observer* (sic) would agree with this, that the wives sounded possessive and neurotic, retiring into illness if they could not get their way or creating hysterical scenes. In other cases there seemed indeed little wrong except that the husband felt displaced by the wife's preoccupation with the children. This passive attitude to marriage, unable to admit difficulties, but secretly acting as if there were difficulties, was characteristic.'

Alternatively Gibbens suggested, there would be a 'dominant and rather possessive mother' in the background. So according to Gibbens women cause men to use prostitutes. The explanations are astonishingly similar to those given by other male apologists for male exhibitionism, rape, sexual murder and other forms of sexual terrorism. Putting the blame on women hides male responsibility.

Mary McIntosh presents us with an excellent demolition of the idea that men visit prostitutes because they have some biologically different sexuality but her explanation is not totally satisfactory either.

> 'The question of different sexuality, the question 'who wants sex, and of what sort?' can thus be seen as a sociological one and not a biological one. Its answer is rooted in specific social structures. The ideology of male sexual needs both supports and is supported by the structures of male dominance, male privilege and monogamy.' (Smart and Smart, "Women, Sexuality and Social Control", 1978)

Her analysis unfortunately shows no understanding of the crucial function of male sexuality under male supremacy. But before we get further into that I want to approach the objection that a rejection of prostitution is a form of moralism and not political.

Is it moralistic to object to prostitution?

The sexual liberals would argue that prostitution is simply the provision of sexual services for money. The sexual liberals don't often bother to try to explain why women don't use prostitutes though if they did they might say that we don't use prostitutes because we are sexually 'repressed' and because we don't have enough money to provide a reasonable market. There is nothing apparently wrong with the buying of sex in and of itself. So, based on the idea that women can and will use male and female prostitutes in the glorious egalitarian future, the sexual liberal argument runs as follows:

People have sexual urges which they can't necessarily satisfy in their sexual relationships. Either because they have sexual problems, their partners don't want to do it, they have no time or energy for prolonged sexual involvements, or they are very ugly and can't get sexual partners. Therefore, the argument goes, prostitution serves a very useful function in our society. A logical extension of the idea is that of Lars Ullerstam who recommends that there should be state and private brothels for everyone, heterosexuals and male and female homosexuals, as well as travelling brothels for the old and the handicapped, and special state subsidies to enable impoverished adolescent boys to attend brothels. (Lars Ullerstam, 'The Erotic Minorities', 1964) The NCCL takes much the same line in its recommendation that there should be regulated brothels run like G.P.s' group practices. (See NCCL report on sex offences, 1976)

I think it's important to remember when men talk of women being able to use prostitutes too that this is not realistic and only an attempt to justify what they wish to go on doing only more easily. I will suggest that the 'necessity' for prostitution arises from the tailoring of male sexuality as a weapon for the social control of women. The exploitation of women in prostitution is only possible whilst women can be treated as an alien group, have little power of self-determination, unequal economic opportunities and an inferior status in law.

Prostitution is not just a job like any other. At present women who work as prostitutes suffer from isolation from other women and family from the necessity to keep the nature of their work secret, from the harrassment of police and legal penalties and the exploitation of pimps and from less protection in law with regard to rape, murder, custody of children, etc. Even if soliciting was decriminalised prostitution would not be like any other job. When our bodies are used sexually, not for our own pleasure, but that of a man, whether money is exchanged or not, it affects the way we feel about ourselves, our bodies and our sexuality. As feminists we have campaigned to wear what we like, and not what men like, for the right to control and develop our own sexual experience, against the sexual abuse of women in childhood, in marriage, in rape, from an understanding of the devastating effects of alienation from our bodies on our whole lives. Through receiving payment, women working as prostitutes gain some recompense for what is happening to them but it does not make the experience of alienation, constant invasion of their bodies, harmless and acceptable. Prostitution harms the women who work in it just as the need to conform our bodies to the perverse tastes and desires of men and to perform sexual servicing out of obligation, fear or pressure rather than desire, has harmed us all.

'J' in the 'Prostitution Papers' (Kate Millet, Paladin, 1975) describes the effects of prostitution thus:

> 'But what they're buying, in a way, is power. You're supposed to please them, follow orders. Even in the case of masochists who like to follow orders themselves, you're still following his orders to give him orders. Prostitution not merely puts down women, but it puts down sex — it really puts down sex . . . The worst part about prostitution is that you're obliged to sell not sex only, but your dignity. That's the worst part of it: that what you're selling is your human dignity. Not really so much in bed, but in accepting the agreement — in becoming a bought person. When I really felt like a whore was when I had to talk to them, fucking up to them really while only talking . . . having to agree with them all the time because you're bought.'

Of the effect on her sexuality she said, 'Now I guess I'm sort of neuter.'

Prostitution and marriage

One explanation for the existence of prostitution is that it is the inevitable counterpart of the institution of monogamous marriage. Inevitable for men only we note. Monogamous marriage and prostitution don't inevitably go together. If they did the elimination of monogamous marriage would lead to the elimination of prostitution. But the so-called sexual revolution did not eliminate prostitution: it thrives. There is a connection though. Men need the form of relationship with women which I shall call the emotional/domestic/sexual servicing relationship. They want their bodily desires to be fulfilled and their comforts attended to, and loving ego support for free, and many wish to be 'fathers' of children. This form of relationship, the basic heterosexual relationship, also has other advantages for male supremacy as a whole. It separates women from one another by attaching them to individual men and ensures that each woman is controlled by an individual man. At the same time and precisely because of the need for the e/d/s relationship, men must have prostitution available. Some men are able to express their true sexual interests and all their contempt and hatred of women to the e/d/s woman but most have to conceal it for fear the woman might object or get out or not be prepared to pour as much devotion and support into the man as he wants. So both forms of relationship are vitally important to the interests of men.

The exchange of money in prostitution

Many feminists say that marriage is really just a form of prostitution and there is very little difference between the two. This obscures the crucial importance of payment and doesn't allow us to work out the precise function of prostitution. Money doesn't just benefit the women who receive it, but the client. The exchange of money apparently legitimates the activity since the woman appears to give consent. Through payment men gain power over the woman for a period of time. They can avoid the dangers of emotional attachment by either party. Payment allows them to use the woman without guilt. Payment reduces the woman to a bought object. It reduces the threat to their primary servicing relationships because the women in them are unlikely to find out. Only in such a directly pecuniary relationship can they fully express themselves, their contempt and hostility and sexual quirks because the woman and her feelings do not count.

Male sexuality as social control of women and prostitution

Male dominance over women is both expressed through and maintained by sexual control. Why is male sexuality so important to the maintenance of control over women? Women like other oppressed groups are controlled through economic dependence, brute force, poor education and many other factors. But unlike other groups we experience sexual control. It is specific to the oppression of women. Male sexuality as social control of women is almost invisible because it is made to seem natural. The injustice of unequal pay can be spotted but the crippling effects upon women of the exercise of male sexuality are still looked on as something to do with 'sexuality'. This is like speaking only of economics and not recognising the existence of capitalism.

'Sexuality' is a value-free term, male sexuality as social control of women is the reality within which 'sexuality' for men and women is structured and played out.

The ways in which the exercise of male sexuality cripples women's lives are many. Sexual harassment at work and on the street control the way we act, where we go and constantly remind us of our inferior status and of male power. Sexual abuse in childhood teaches us to be afraid and teaches us that our bodies are not ours to control. Rape and unwanted sexual intercourse alienate us from our bodies and leave us feeling out of control of our environment and of our lives. The objectification and fetishisation of women through perverse male desire lead to women being crippled by restrictive clothing, shoes, makeup. The male obsession with penetration leads to women having to damage their bodies with dangerous forms of contraception, with sterilisation, abortion or unwanted childbearing, to damaging infections and cervical cancer. The portrayal of women in porn. and advertising pollute our environment with woman-hating images which undermine our self-respect and confidence. Meanwhile all these aspects of the exercise of male sexuality strengthen men, making them feel confident and powerful over women. The pattern of male dominance and female submission is mediated through 'sex' into every facet of our lives, at work, on the street, and on television. Sex is not and cannot be neutral. The exercise of male sexuality contributes to the systematic weakening and restriction of women which is necessary to the maintenance of male control.

The form taken by male sexuality is perfectly tailored to fulfil the social control of women in all these ways. The dominant form of male sexuality as we have all experienced it takes the form of aggression, objectification, supposed uncontrollability, obsession with penetration, the ability to separate 'sex' from emotion, affection or sensuality. None of this is accidental. The form taken by male sexuality is not the result of male biology, nor a mere reflection of the fact that men have power. Male sexuality has evolved and is constantly reproduced to take the form best suited to controlling women. It does not just reflect the fact that men have power, it is a vital support to that power.

Male sexuality as a perversion

Male sexuality is a perversion because its primary motivation is not pleasure, individual or mutual, or the enhancement of personal relationships, but control of and power over women. Because it requires our objectification, women are fetishised by male sexuality. Our footwear, make-up, clothing, and posture are developed to facilitate the perverse form of male sexual delight. Thus what is commonly called fetishism, such as glove fetishism whose exponent can only ejaculate into a woman's glove, is not a perversion in itself, but only an exaggerated form of the perversion that is male sexuality. Thus sado-masochism is not a perversion but only the exaggerated form of the power relationships intrinsic to heterosexuality. The analysts reveal, though they never comment upon it, that what they call the 'perversions' are practised only by men, such as coprophilia, urolagnia, fetishism, transvestism. All can be understood in terms of the perverted nature of the sexuality which is male sexuality as social control of women and of which the 'perversions' are only an exaggerated form. Men often need to visit prostitutes in order to practice these exaggerations of male sexuality.

The function of prostitution

Men cannot express their sexuality as they would wish in relation to the women they know and 'love'. It would shock the women attached to them and perhaps change the nature of the relationship. Moreover men need practice and must hone the valuable weapon of sexual aggression and contempt which is needed for the job of social control of women. Men need the reinforcement of their woman-hatred if they are to be effective. There are also the casualties of the system. Men whose ability to gain any sensual pleasure at all has been damaged by their attempts to direct their sexuality totally into the control of women. Such men can only perform with prostitutes and in certain selected situations. Prostitution then, serves as a *guerilla training camp and rehabilitation centre for sexual terrorists.*

Why individual men visit prostitutes, a summary

- they are able to totally objectify the woman through payment.

- they are able to show the hatred they feel and degrade the woman in ways which might endanger their e/d/s servicing relationships.
- they are able to indulge in the exaggerated forms of the perversion which is male sexuality as social control which other women they relate to might find alarming such as woman-hating language, a practice for 'obscene' telephone calling.
- they are able to express themselves towards women without the restrictions of emotion, guilt, etc.
- they are able to feel more powerful over all women by abusing one.
- they are able to indulge in homosexual bonding through the sharing of women.
- they may fuck a woman in another man's sperm either symbolically or literally. Prostitutes have in previous ages been called 'common women' meaning that they are held in common by men, like the common land. Such sharing helps form bonds of unity between those who share.

Conclusion

Prostitution is vital to the use of male sexuality as social control of women, not merely as a guerilla training camp and rehabilitation centre. It serves to conceal from the majority of women what men and male sexuality are all about at the expense of splitting women into two groups, the pure and the fallen so that the knowledge cannot be pooled. If women who work as prostitutes were not separated from other women the system would break down. We must fight the division of the class of women. This paper is not meant to be a strategy paper but simply to help in defining the problem. The main question seems to be how we can both support women who work as prostitutes whilst working to eliminate the institution of prostitution. As feminists we understand that marriage is not in women's interests but an institution designed to shore up male power which has dire disadvantages for women. We consider it vital to fight discrimination against women on the grounds of marriage, in law and in practice but we do not consider that getting married is a revolutionary act for a woman. Similarly I do not support the argument that working as a prostitute is a revolutionary activity. Marriage, prostitution and heterosexuality in general are designed to strengthen the male ruling class at the expense of women. We have to work out ways in which to attack the institution of prostitution as we attack all other ways in which male supremacy is supported, whilst positively supporting women who work as prostitutes against unjust laws, the police and pimps. When women who work as prostitutes are imprisoned they are political prisoners in the war between men and women. They are scapegoated to conceal the reality of male sexuality as social control of women.

Sheila Jeffreys

Thanks to other Revolutionary Feminists in Leeds and members of the Patriarchy Study Group for ideas and suggestions.

This paper was printed in Revolutionary and Radical Feminist Newsletter No. 6, Spring 1981. Available from RRF, c/o 17 Kensington Terrace, Leeds.

PROSTITUTION – TOWARDS A FEMINIST ANALYSIS AND STRATEGY

The first part of this paper is intended as a contribution towards an analysis of why prostitution exists as an institution. There is very little room in a conference paper to discuss contradictions and qualify or explain generalisations. It's intended as a springboard for discussion, not a definitive statement. The second part consists of suggestions for strategies. Again, this is intended as a basis for discussion. I think that workable feminist strategies around prostitution can only come out of dialogue between women who work as prostitutes and women who don't. The first step towards any strategy has to be an attempt to break down the divisions between women which men have created through the institution of prostitution.

Why Prostitution?

Prostitution cannot be understood except as part of the whole structure of male sexual aggression in which *all* women are sexual property to be bought and sold, or taken by force. In all societies men's power over women is maintained by the use of sexual violence and its threat. Men's sexual violence takes many forms — verbal assault, rape and other sexual assault against women and female children, battering (which is usually accompanied by sexual abuse), sexual mutilation and murder. The various forms of direct sexual assault against women form the bars of a cage within which most women are forced to become the sexual property of men. For the majority of women, the bars are reinforced by economic powerlessness. Most women become private sexual property within the institution of marriage; many women become public sexual property within the institution of prostitution.

Men's sexual violence is not indiscriminate. If it were, the institution of marriage would be impossible. Marriage gives an individual man control over a woman's sexuality, her ability to reproduce and her labour. Most of her energies and skills are channelled into him/used for his benefit. To make this possible a woman must, in effect, become the private sexual property of her husband. To ensure that she does, it is necessary that *some* men direct their sexual aggression indiscriminately. This keeps women in constant fear of men while, at the same time, obscuring the real extent of men's sexual violence.

Myths about strangers in dark alleys are part of a network of pressures (usually including economic pressures) which force women to seek the protection of one man against the rest. In doing so, a woman becomes extremely vulnerable to *his* sexual violence (25% of violent crime is woman battering, and this probably represents only a tiny proportion of the real extent of battering. Rape within marriage is not even legally recognised as such). The protection he offers her is part of a massive con — a protection racket.

If this protection racket is to work male sexual violence must take different forms and it must be controlled to some extent — it must operate through specific institutions. Women must be prevented from seeing the relationships between different form of sexual violence — one form of sexual violence must cloak another and divisions between women must be created.

The institution of marriage necessitates some collective male control over men's sexual violence towards women. Men punish other men for sexual assault in order to protect male private property in women. Rape was originally seen as a crime against *men* — initially the woman's father (if she was a virgin and therefore marriageable property) and later, her husband.

This attitude is still implicit in legal practice — only "respectable" women are given any protection from sexual assault. A fully respectable woman is one who is the exclusive sexual property of a man (husband) who has the legal right to rape her. (Even in countries where this is not the case e.g. Sweden, for a woman to prove a charge of rape against her husband is virtually impossible in practice.) In general, women who "belong" to men who have power over other men i.e. members of a dominant economic class and race, are more likely to be treated as "respectable".

The contradictions created by men's need to maintain their private property in women and, at the same time, to express their sexual hostility towards all women, leads to the male created dichotomy between the "wife" and the "whore". A "wife" is private sexual property. A "whore" is public sexual property. Not only women who work as prostitutes are treated as "whores". A woman may be treated as a "whore" because she is a member of a dominated economic class or race. This tendency exists in most societies and takes more obvious forms in some. For example, in some Southern states of the U.S. it is almost impossible for a black woman to prove a charge of rape against a white man.

However, all women who work as prostitutes are treated as the legitimate prey of male sexual violence. The institution of prostitution creates a group of women who are social outcasts, whom all men can freely abuse and degrade. It is virtually impossible for a man to be convicted for sexually assaulting a woman who works as a prostitute. She is expected to sexually service all men, and is extremely vulnerable to sexual attacks, particularly if she works on the streets.

For clients, a woman is degraded and robbed of personal autonomy because she has been bought.

"But there's a special indignity in prostitution, as if sex were dirty and men can only do it with someone *low*. It involves a kind of contempt, a kind of disdain, and a kind of triumph over another human being. Guys who can't do it with their wives can do it with whores. They have to pay for it. For some of them *paying* for it is very important." ('J', *The Prostitution Papers*, p.36)

Prostitution is an expression of men's power not only over the woman involved but over all women, and helps to maintain that power by creating a division between "whores" and "respectable" women.

This division partially hides their real status as sexual property from women who are supposedly "respectable", whose attitude towards women who work as prostitutes is often one of hostility and contempt. This arises partially out of an attempt to deny that men see all women in essentially the same way as they see women who work as prostitutes — to deny that we are all seen as 'cunt'.

While prostitution obscures this, at the same time, the more open sexual abuse which women working as prostitutes are subjected to acts as a warning to other women and helps to keep them in line.

An example of this is the police and media presentation of the murders of women by the Yorkshire 'Ripper'. We are told that he hates not women, but prostitutes. He has been described on T.V. as carrying out a "moral crusade" against prostitution. When he has killed women who have not worked as prostitutes, they, and only they, have been described as "innocent" victims. So while fear of the 'Ripper' helps to control all women, his hatred of women is obscured by the pretence that his motivation is moral outrage against a distinct group of women. There is also an implication that the murder of women who work as prostitutes is not important; that they deserve what they get. By extension, any woman who does not conform to "respectable" behaviour deserves what she gets, or at least asks for it.

Pimping

The women interviewed in the *Prostitution Papers* say that most women involved in prostitution work for pimps. The English Collective of Prostitutes (E.C.P.) in *Prostitutes — our*

Life, suggest that only a minority do so. This is impossible to prove conclusively since pimps do not advertise their activities, and women who work for pimps are far less likely than other women working as prostitutes to be able to organise collectively with other women.

On the basis of what evidence there is, I would say that most prostitution is controlled by pimps, and that it is mostly men, not women, who make money from prostitution. In the area where I grew up, which was then the main centre of street prostitution in Birmingham, most women worked for pimps, who took most of their money. Women who worked for themselves were exceptional, and had often started out working for a pimp. Kathleen Barry's *Female Sexual Slavery*, brings together evidence that much prostitution is controlled by organised criminal syndicates and that slave trading (literally) in women is widespread and international. The forms pimping take range from loose networks of pimps who help each other control their "stables", to tightly organised gangs and syndicates involved in other forms of organised crime, from whom it is often impossible for a woman to escape.

Women are often effectively imprisoned in brothels, unable to refuse any client, and making nothing except their keep. This is common in Third World countries, where massive unemployment and poverty created by imperialist exploitation leave women no choices but prostitution or starvation. In many countries, child prostitution is widespread, as it was in Britain before the development of the Welfare State, and before feminist campaigns against child prostitution during the nineteenth and early twentieth centuries.

Although poverty forces many women, particularly in the Third World, into prostitution, it is mostly men who profit from it. At Subic Bay in the Philippines, for example, a highly organised prostitution industry has been built up to sexually service American men stationed at the naval base there. The economy of the whole area depends on prostitution. Those who make least money from it are the women who work as prostitutes. (See ISIS no. 13 *Tourism and Prostitution*.)

For many women the pressures which force them into prostitution are more subtle; based on relationships with men who control them by a combination of psychological manipulation and violence. A favourite target of pimps are teenage girls who have run away from home, and are broke and alone in a strange place. He offers her "help" and she ends up working for him.

Whatever the pressures forcing women into working for pimps, for those who do, prostitution is a form of slavery. The pimp takes her money, controls her movements and usually gives her little or no protection from violent clients.

> "They gamble, they drink, they beat you up. They ride around in their cadillacs. They look pretty... Pimps don't do a damn thing for you. They spend all your money. That's what they do for you. They'll bail you out of jail only cause you're their money. But you can bail yourself out of jail and you can keep your own money. You don't need a pimp." ('J', *Prostitution Papers*, p.45)

What can we do?
As Karen Lindsey says "Prostitution will not end until the social structures that surround it end... our goal cannot be to abolish prostitution in particular; we must instead build the movement that will destroy all institutions that oppress us." (ISIS no. 13 p.5) In the meantime, we can attempt to work out strategies to reduce the coercion of women into prostitution, to prevent harassment/punishment by the State of women who work as prostitutes, and to break down the divisions between women created by prostitution. Discussion between women who have direct experience of prostitution and other women, is the only basis on which we can begin to work out strategies and find ways of putting them into practice.

These are some suggested strategies for discussion at the conference:

Support for the decriminalisation of prostitution
The E.C.P. and PROS. (an organisation of women who work as prostitutes and some probation officers, lawyers etc. who are opposed to the criminalisation of prostitution) are already campaigning for de-criminalisation. The WLM should support the demand for the abolition of laws directed against

women working as prostitutes, such as the loitering and soliciting laws, the labelling of women as "common prostitutes", and the use of the laws on brothel keeping to prevent women living together.

Women should not be punished by the State and labelled criminals for participating in an institution which is created by men and which works in men's interests.

The criminalisation of prostitution forces women who work as prostitutes further underground and therefore makes them more vulnerable to exploitation by pimps, club-owners etc. (In the U.S. hotel owners who profit from prostitution have opposed its de-criminalisation because it would mean loss of profit for them.)

Opposition to State regulation of prostitution

State regulation of prostitution has been proposed in this country by Southampton City Council. They have argued for the ghettoisation of women working as prostitutes in a non-residential area set aside for this purpose. Similar forms of State regulation have already happened in other countries, such as West Germany. Their effect is to limit the freedom of movement of women working as prostitutes, to force them into brothels where their working conditions are strictly controlled, and their earnings are creamed off by male brothel owners (in addition to pimps).

Any form of State regulation of prostitution can only further institutionalise prostitution, increase the stigma attached to it, and deepen the divisions it creates between women. This will make it more difficult for women who want to get out.

Provision of refuges

Kathleen Barry suggests setting up refuges and crisis lines for women who are or may be forced into prostitution as well as providing economic alternatives. She suggests that the money now spent by governments in enforcing laws against women working as prostitutes could be used for this by feminists.

If possible, I think that such refuges should not be separate from those provided for any woman trying to escape male violence. Our strategies should try to break down, not mirror, the divisions between us which men have created. We need refuges for women and girls from all male violence, whatever its form.

Support enforcement laws against pimps

The E.C.P. argue for abolition of the laws against pimping on the grounds that they are used to harass women working as prostitutes. We should oppose this use of these laws (and it would be more difficult to use them in this way if prostitution itself were de-criminalised), but we cannot support the legalisation of the direct coercion of women into prostitution and we must recognise that this goes on.

The laws against pimping do give women some protection against abuse and exploitation by men. If pimping were legalised, this exploitation would increase and young women in particular would become more vulnerable to pimps. (Given the extent of child prostitution in countries where girls have less protection from it, the combined effects of the legalisation of pimping and the proposed lowering of the age of consent laws in Britain are potentially horrific.)

We should combine our demands for the de-criminalisation of prostitution with demands for the use of the pimping laws against pimps, not against women who work as prostitutes.

It has been suggested that we demand that soliciting of women by men be made illegal. This has been done in New York, where its main effect seems to be to drive women working as prostitutes further underground and increase their vulnerability to pimps. As this law is specifically directed at prostitution, I doubt whether it has much effect in reducing general street harassment of women by men. I am not sure what the effect of a general law on such harrassment — similar to the laws on homosexual importuning — would be. A law against male soliciting of women used to exist in Britain. It would be useful to find out what, if any, effect this had, and whether its removal has made any practical difference.

Publicity

As with rape we should try to publicise the realities of prostitution as widely as possible and to eliminate the myths surrounding it, (e.g. that women working as prostitutes are "nymphomaniacs" who enjoy their work, that prostitution results from sexual "repression" etc.). In particular, we should try to get across to as many women as possible that prostitution is about the oppression of all of us by men.

Maureen O'Hara, November 1980

MAIN REFERENCES
Much of this paper is based on an earlier one; *Heterosexuality as Protection Racket*, printed in Rev/Rad Newsletter 4. Other references are listed there. I now disagree with much of what I said there about the relationship between marriage and prostitution, as it implicitly minimizes sexual violence in marriage. Thanks to Vicky Webb for pointing this out, and for other criticisms.
1. Kathleen Barry, *Female Sexual Slavery*, Prentice Hall, 1979.
2. ISIS Bulletin, No. 13 *Tourism and Prostitution*
3. Claude Jaget (ed), *Prostitutes — Our Life*, Falling Wall Press, 1980.
4. Kate Millet, *The Prostitution Papers,* Paladin, 1975.
5. Alison Plowden, *The Case of Eliza Armstrong: a child of 13 bought for £5*, London BBC, 1974.
6. *Second Class, Working Class*, November 1979, People's Translation Service.

Notes re Paper on Prostitution

I now want to qualify parts of the sections in this paper on the position of refuges and the laws on pimping. While I still think that creating refuges specifically for women working as prostitutes raises problems because it would mirror divisions between women created by men; I now think that we should try to set up such refuges because they would be more accessible to women who want to get away from pimps/get out of prostitution. Women in this position would be more likely to come to a refuge specifically set up for them, where there would be mutual support between women who shared similar experiences. Setting up refuges specifically for women working as prostitutes would also make it easier to publicise the refuges in ways which would reach the women they would be set up for.

The section on pimping laws over-simplifies the English Collective of Prostitutes' position on such laws, and I want to correct this. While the E.C.P. wants all laws which relate specifically to prostitution abolished, they also suggest finding ways of using other existing laws against pimps. For example, they suggest that the laws against kidnapping and extortion could be used to prosecute pimps, and that these laws could be strengthened in ways which would make this possible. The E.C.P. point out that many of the existing laws against pimping such as the law on "living on immoral earnings", would be unworkable without the laws which operate against women who work as prostitutes. For example, a charge against a man living on immoral earnings can only be proved, if it is also proved that he is living with or receiving money from a woman who is working as a prostitute. Proving the latter would involve police harassment of women.

Because the laws against women who work as prostitutes and many laws against pimping are closely intertwined, we need to think out very carefully the ways in which we can decriminalise prostitution for women while at the same time giving women as much protection as possible from pimps. I am concerned that total abolition of pimping laws as such would make pimping even more invisible than it already is, and therefore more difficult to prosecute in practice. If all present laws were abolished, pimps could not generally be prosecuted unless women brought charges against them, which most women are obviously not in a position to do. Young women could be put in a particularly vulnerable position if this were the case. We need much more discussion within the Women's Liberation Movement about the ways in which we can demand the decriminalisation of prostitution for women, and at the same time make more visible the sexual enslavement by pimps which much prostitution involves, and give women protection from such enslavement.

Maureen O'Hara, January 1983

INDECENT EXPOSURE

Exhibitionism accounts for 1/3rd of all reported sexual offences. According to Kinsey 52% of all sexual offences against young girls by adult males are of exhibitionism. The reporting rate is probably very low. I only reported one of the half dozen flashers who threatened me. As a child you do not know why you are worried, and as an adult you feel you should not be. Is it something harmless that we should learn to laugh at?

Well what is flashing?
It is the unlawful exposure of the penis and commonly takes place in such diverse places as streets, trains, office buildings,

department stores, laundromats and churches, but usually outdoors and in daylight. The commonest times are when children are going to and from school i.e. 8-9 am and 3-5 pm by adult males only and the victims are almost exclusively female, either children or adults, a heterosexual offence. Offenders usually masturbate during or after the event. Many are silent, some make remarks such as, "Have you ever seen one so big?" "Hi, girl, I've got more hair here than I have on my head," or in my case and well remembered from when I was eight, "Stroke my little pet." Exhibitionists are usually younger and brighter than average sex offenders. One in ten will at some time rape or attempt to rape. They have definite "beats", can recognise others of their kind and will often inform on them to reduce the competition.

Why does it happen?

Offender explanations: These vary from drunkenness, amnesia, drugs, a desire to urinate, to zipper trouble, "My zipper comes undone sometimes and things pop out," split pants, physical illness such as heat rash or stomach-ache, to unusual emergencies such as cigarette ash down pants to adjusting underwear when they get their equipment in a tangle, mistaken identity, e.g. it was really a pop bottle, to trying to seduce a girl. Few offenders actually admit to indecent exposure.

Explanations of psychologists and sexologists

Fascinating these are. Best to get Freud out of the way fast, "exhibitionists ... display their genitals in order to get a sight of the person's genitals in return." Apparently this is because they worry about castration and want girls to display the fact that they do have penises really and it is not possible to lose them. Guttmacher suggests that women don't do it because they want to conceal their lack or injury, not reveal it? The same man explains that there are fewer black exhibitionists because black men have longer penises anyway and so they know that they are superior without showing it off. Lots of friendly unbiased reporting here.

Is it something to do with phallus worship? Apparently, according to MacDonald, early Jews made oaths by placing their hands on or under each other's penises, not being able to think of a more holy object. The penis is translated as thigh in our version of the Bible.

Then there are popular views that the mothers or wives of exhibitionists are to blame really.

Mothers of Exhibitionists
MacDonald in his recent book, *Indecent Exposure*, U.S.A., 1973, quotes verbatim chapter entitled as above from a much earlier book by Rickles (1955). Clearly his very favourite theory, Rickles writes, "To understand the exhibitionist one must first understand the woman of his life — the Mother." Blameworthy mothers are "Extremely narcissistic women, unconsciously motivated by strong penis envy." Both of these attributes are apparently quite normal in women if kept within bounds. These women try to relive their lives through their son whose male organ they secretly covet. So the boy exposes to break the identification with his mother "to cut the cord that binds him to her so tightly, to affirm himself as a separate, masculine individual." Rickles describes two types, either masculine in appearance and apt to be "strong willed, aggressive and openly hostile to all males" or "clinging vines". Mothers of schizophrenics are very much the same apparently. Some dominate openly, some are subtle about it. Some 'curry favour' with their sons which seems to mean being generally helpful. Some deliberately develop serious illnesses in order to obligate their sons, such as diabetes. One mother wore "mannish clothes with an oversize hat" and spoke in a "brusque voice with deep overtones". So loving mothers, ill mothers and mothers with a dress sense that the author does not approve of, aggressive mothers and dominant mothers all turn their sons into exhibitionists. It seems to me that all we can conclude is that men are exhibitionists because they are born of women, any women, and that might be indeed near the truth.

Wives of exhibitionists
You guessed it! If it's not the mothers, it's the wives. Men exhibit because their wives are dominating. The Maudsley Hospital, among others, goes as far as to treat the wives of exhibitionists. The wives and husbands together are helped to understand "what has been developing between them and how to adjust with one another". Or they may be treated in groups with other wives. It is important, apparently, that the

wife understands that she is involved and needs help because that makes the husband feel better. However the wife often becomes depressed during this treatment while the husband improves. Not surprisingly, really, since the responsibility for his offence has now been laid at her door. Her depression is considered dangerous because the wife might try to escape it by 'again asserting her dominance, so that the husband would be likely to repeat the pattern'. So if all women were cheerfully subservient, but not clinging (i.e. demanding affection and having needs) there might be no need for men to flash?

The effects of exhibitionism

Writers on the subject seem determined that there are either no adverse effects on the victims of exhibitionism, or that these effects are very slight. Kinsey's helpful contribution is to suggest that children are only upset at having their genitals fondled by adults and being flashed at, in the same way as they worry about spiders, as a result of adverse cultural conditioning. He considered, like many other writers that what worried children was not the offence but the reactions of parents and police when told about it. It is clear that they were simply not looking for the effects we would consider important. In fact the effects that we would consider disastrous they are able to think desirable. This is clear from the comments of Anthony Storr in his book *Sexual Deviations*. About women who are repeatedly exposed to he says "These repeated shocks, however, do not have the effect of deterring them from taking solitary walks on heaths and commons where exhibitionists are known to lurk; and the woman who complains that this experience often happens to her can generally be justly accused of seeking it out."

The effects of flashing then, are expected to be a restriction of the freedom of women. The legacy of flashing in childhood is anxiety and fear, of strange men, of open spaces. In adulthood the message is the same. Flashing is far more common than rape and teaches women that the streets and all the areas outside the home are the territory of men. Women live in a colonised land, where they may walk on the streets only on sufferance having no right to do so and there are men constantly prepared to remind them of this.

Why do they really do it?

The penis is the symbol of the male ruling class. By exposing to a woman the man expects to provoke fear or awe through his demonstration of power and this gives him sexual as well as ego gratification. The 'aweful' aspect is illustrated by this charming quote from a flasher who haunted French churches around the turn of the century,

> "Why do I like to go to churches? I cannot say, but I know it is only there that my act takes on its full importance, the woman is in an attitude of devotion and she must see that such an act in such a place is not a joke, indication of bad taste or obscenity. If I go there it is not for fun. It is far more serious than that. I watch the effect produced on the faces of the women to whom I expose my organ. I hope to hear them exclaim, "How impressive is nature when one sees it in these circumstances!"'

One explanation by Macdonald may come near the truth. He suggests that "the emergence of women from domestic slavery", is threatening to the male and this is causing an increase in flashing. He also suggests that anger, contempt and hostility are often the reason and with this we would agree. He quotes a middle-aged Chinese cook who had been locked out and made fun of by the waitresses who later exposed himself to them while they were sitting having a meal with the manager as saying, "Who is the boss? Me? Here's the boss."

A researcher called Spitz did a thematic apperception test (you show subjects pictures of scenes with people in them and get them to weave stories around the cards) with 20 exhibitionsts and 45% of responses involved open aggression toward women with murder and rape as predominant themes.

Flashing as sexual terrorism

Sexologists pretend that exhibitionism shocks women because it is about nudity or sex and as women become more liberated they will cease to report it. Many lawyers as well as psychologists would like it to be removed from the statute book. An American judge in 1968 when refusing to commit an exhibitionist argued that the offence was not dangerous, ' There was no evidence of any actual harm to adult women from appelant's past exhibitionism ... very seclusive, shy, withdrawn, sensitive women are in a minority. While the law must and does protect them like other citizens, there are limits on the extent to which the law can sweep the streets clean of all possible sources of occasional distress to women.' I think that we are called upon to prove that we are not seclusive and not a minority! Halleck, the psychiatrist, proclaims that, 'similar considerations (lack of harmfulness) apply to other sexual behaviours such as homosexual relations between consenting postpubertal partners, voyeurism and exhibitionism. Such behaviours do not inflict physical harm on anyone. There are serious questions as to whether they even inflict enough psychological harm to warrant unusual attention on the part of society.'

Well, flashing is not about nudity. When I walk into the Gents toilet by mistake I may feel a frisson of distaste but I do not experience fear. No one in the toilet is being deliberately threatening. Flashing is a crude way of showing authority, like wearing a prefects tie or flashing your identity card might be if you were a policeman. But at the same time it is the clearest and simplest way of demonstrating power under male supremacy. A flasher's message is simple, 'I rule because I have a penis'. Now we can see why flashing is an almost exclusively heterosexual offence and why women cannot do it. A woman who revealed her genitalia would not be threatening and she would not be showing a symbol of authority but the badge of her oppression.

We must make it clear that we see flashing as an act of aggression and threat. An act of sexual terrorism. We must fight every attempt to make it appear acceptable or harmless. At the same time other aspects of sexual terrorism about which some of the same arguments are used must be brought into focus such as obscene telephone calls and voyeurism. The obscene phone call brings the threatening presence of a policeman of the male ruling class into our homes and our most relaxed moments. Voyeurism, an offence linked with rape since a rapist has to reconnoitre for a victim, is deeply disturbing in its own right. Have you ever looked up to see a face pressed up to the window late at night while you are alone?

Indecent exposure is not a joke, it's an act of war.

Sheila Jeffreys

Reprinted from FAST newsletter No. 1.

SEXUAL HARASSMENT AT WORK

At a recent workshop on 'women and work' in Leeds we discovered we had all suffered from this, plumbers or University lecturers. As woman after woman cited incidents we breathed out a sigh of relief. We had (almost all) been so isolated. Felt nutty almost in complaining, blamed ourselves for reactions we 'had provoked', or suffered in confused silence. Now we knew it was a *common problem*.

We need to go on from there.

Yes, if there is a group of us at work, we can do something. Even individuals can learn from how the others handled it. But most of us are pretty isolated — sexual harassment needs to be *recognised* as a problem before it will be taken seriously. 'When did you last beat your wife?' was a joke before Women's Aid. We need to organise about sexual harassment at work — so no one will joke about it the way the papers did recently over a failed appeal to the sex-discrimination tribunal.

Does your boss demand sexual services from you/lay hands on you? Do your co-workers make remarks about cunts/tits in front of you? Do your pupils bring in pornography and show it off? This is being done to keep us in our place! This should not be dismissed as part of 'normal working conditions' something we just have to put up with. We must begin to *collectively fight back*.

Sandra McNeill, 19 October 1980

There are two books out on how women in USA have organised around this. I am not sure how relevant their experience is to our situation but they are interesting.

Farley (Lin), *Sexual Shakedown,* Warner Books, USA, 1978. This book is a bit anecdotal, but gives an idea of the extent and variety of sexual harassment. She notes that it is used 'to keep women in line' 'keep us down' but implies that this is purely to exploit us economically.

MacKinnon (Catherine A), *Sexual Harassment of Working Women*. MacKinnon is a lawyer and a lot of the book is details of sex harassment cases, how they have been fought and suggestions for the best approaches. Her analysis is more complex showing that sexual harassment keeps us down economically but also that economic exploitation serves to keep us vulnerable to sexual exploitation. The men gain both ways. Yale University Press, 1979.

While I worked in marketing at Ford Motor Company headquarters the men began to put pornography on the walls. It began with page 3 type pin-ups but soon pictures from porn mags joined them. The men in one office made a 'collage' of bits of women. You can imagine what bits — no faces. The men in another office used a 'pin-up' as a dartboard — throwing the darts at her tits.

At first I played it straight. I objected to them. When that brought no change I objected to personnel. They issued a memo asking for all 'girlie' pictures to come down. It was by and large ignored, so I went back to personnel. Meanwhile the guy in charge had changed. From a rather po-faced quiet geezer to a real smarmy type. He said he would ensure the 'obscene' pictures came down. But most of them were not 'obscene' — after all they were taken from the daily papers so I could hardly object to them. And anyway I didn't need to look!

Why was I objecting? Those pictures were serving to remind the men of their power over women, all day, boosting their confidence. It was quite direct. The man at the next desk to mine looked at a 'page 3' then said 'You know I could never have a woman boss. I don't respect women.' No way is it just pretty pictures to cheer them up — have you heard a group of men discuss a pin-up? It's all 'ugh, look at her fat thighs' 'she sags' 'shame about the face' but it always ends up with 'mind you, if I had to I could still get a leg over I suppose. I could still manage to waaahr'.

And what effect do these pictures have on women? We know it is us up there — bits of us on display. It serves to remind us of our powerlessness, it undermines our confidence. One night at home I caught a glimpse of my own breasts reflected in a mirror. I instinctively covered myself up. It seemed an obscene object, my own body.

So what did I do? I arranged to do overtime when no one was around and took all the porn down. Nothing happened the next day but the day after I sensed a different atmosphere. (Maybe it took them a day to unite and organise.) I went to the loo and when I came back my daily paper was torn and in the bin. My coffee was spilled over my chair. Then bits of my work went missing. When the supervisor was out of the room one man refused to give me information that I needed for the job. I threatened to go to the boss. 'Go, I'll deny it'. He also put up 'page 3' — I took it down. The open war was on.

It was a war I could not win. My health began to suffer, nervous complaints — the worst being recurrent cystitis. The supervisor wrote a bad 'performance report' on me commenting on my 'inability to get on with others which was hindering office work'.

This was not the only reason that I left Fords. But it was part of it. My co-workers were clearly saying 'you put up with porn or we will drive you out'. Had I not been isolated, had there been others of us perhaps we could have done something. But on my own I could not.

Sandra McNeill, August 1980

(With thanks to the sisters at the July women-work workshop in Leeds, which helped me to see this experience in perspective.)

MIXED WARDS — A FORM OF SEXUAL VIOLENCE AGAINST WOMEN

We are familiar with women's sufferings at the hands of a male-dominated medical profession. Rough internal examinations, interference with childbirth, humiliation in the abortion and ante-natal clinics, the impossibility of coming out as a lesbian to health workers and the consequences this may have for your recovery, the dismissal of thrush as a side-effect of antibiotics, dangerous contraceptives, doctors who pass comments on your body or mess about with you in examination . . . well all this has been written up and discussed in the Movement many a time.

But, unless I've missed it, mixed wards haven't. Yet

these innovations, fast gaining in popularity with a cut health service, go right against the wishes of many many women.

When you are very ill, you don't notice. Mixed casualty is not a problem.

When you're less ill, you do notice. And it's horrible. I spent 3½ weeks on a surgical ward, arranged in bays; one bay was for men. Only 4 of them, yet they made their presence felt. It was necessary for many women to pass the bay on their way to the toilet. One man would call out comments as we staggered by, hobbling with our drips and drain bags: right up to *the half-hour before his death* he was evaluating our bodies — "like your knockers" and the like. We hated it.

All but the sickest ate in the day-room. The women, all ages from 16 to 70, would stagger down and fill up all the tables before they'd take a seat at the one the only man well enough to sit at table, was seated at. (Apart from anything else, this can't have been very nice for *him;* but I'm not concerned about that aspect here.) None of the women felt that we could hold our own with men, wanted anything to do with men, when we were in nighties and dressing gowns, ill, unable to lock the lavatory door for fear of collapsing in there and needing help, same with the bathroom, etc. You can cut off from the doctors as men as far as possible — you have to. But you can't cut off from your fellow patients.

The trouble was, the women felt their dislike was due to "old fashioned attitudes". All the women drew the curtains over the windows that interlinked the men's bay with ours. Yet they'd do so apologetically, quite often. No one complained, of course. (You don't complain when you're in hospital and ill and weak and at their mercy. Anyway it's free, you should be grateful. Anyway, doctors know best.)

Elderly patients, on geriatric long-stay wards, have to put up with this more and more frequently. The old are treated pretty badly in hospital as it is, seen as idiots and pushed about. Curtains aren't drawn for washing, bedpans, as they are for younger women. This causes elderly women extreme distress when they are in women-only wards — imagine how they feel in mixed ones. Several of the bedridden women I talked to really hated it — "but don't say anything dear, don't make a fuss".

The focus of feminist activity around health and hospitals has been what affects (mainly heterosexual) women only — maternity, abortion, gynaecological problems, contraception — and up to a point, what affects our children. Obviously mixed wards don't arise much in all this. We need to oppose them actively, and also, see them for what they are — not just a money-saving reaction to cuts and recession, but the interjection of men and male control into every area of our lives, every enclave where we as women previously had space from them. One London hospital boasts of its mixed ward policy as "reproducing normality; providing an environment closer to that of the family". And who is *that* likely to benefit?

Al Garthwaite

GYNAECOLOGY, OBSTETRICS —
a refined form of violence?

I don't want to make this a long paper but simply to open up a discussion about the violence against women which we all encounter in our dealings with the medical services (sic!). Of course there are many other grounds for objection to medicine apart from the violence it uses: as a broad subject we could discuss the coercion which medical people use to get us to use their services on their terms — their drugs, their institutions, regimes, etc. But for this conference I just want to narrow the area of debate to the actual use of violence and to looking at ways of counteracting it.

Many of us have felt a vague unease, perhaps growing as we come into contact with the gynaecological/obstetric profession more often. Since we became 'women' we have been encouraged to allow examinations of our bodies, often culminating in a full internal examination. This has often been so nerve-wracking, painful and humiliating that we have striven to reassure ourselves that it was a medical, not a sexual, encounter, and that it was clinically necessary. Can we all call to mind an occasion on which the bounds of propriety were overstepped? What about my sister, examined internally when still a virgin at about 14, because she had migraine? What about the friend of another sister, 'examined' internally by a male nurse at the age of eleven? (When she told her parents they said she was filthy.) What about the time when I had a 'retroverted' uterus (that's how they described it though it's not troubling me now) and went to a temporary doctor, nearly passing out with pain. He 'examined' me for 15 minutes, asking questions about sexual activity while he was doing it. I had gone to him for help in an emergency. What about the time I went to have a tiny (benign) cyst removed from my clitoris, and six students came to look, exclaiming in surprise when I used the word 'clitoris'.

Well, if we thought it was all in our heads, we only have to turn to the writings of gynaecologists. One Professor Rhodes, now in Newcastle, but then at St. Thomas' Hospital, London, addressed the 'Third International Congress of Psychosomatic Medicine in Obstetrics and Gynaecology'(!) in 1971 on the subject of 'Sex and the gynaecologist'. In this he advocated that "gynaecologists in an age of sexual revolution must now work more in the field of psychosexual problems than they have ever done before". The general idea is that women who come with "apparently physical" problems probably have a "specifically sexual" problem which naturally they will not present. "It is here that he (!) must display insight and avoid taking the patient at her own valuation". The first phase of therapy involves complex tests designed to prove to a woman that nothing is wrong physically. I simply want to quote the rest of his paper:

> "A decision is now required by the gynaecologist as to how far he will pursue psychological and psychophysical therapy himself. This will depend upon his aptitude and his workload. His expertise is often mainly in surgical and medical therapy and therefore, he may wish to hand on psychosexual disorders to other specialists. But if he decides to continue with the management of his patient he is very favourably placed. He has been the first to recognise the problem and by the intimate nature of the physical examination he establishes a rapport with the patient, based on contact, which is denied to other practitioners. He also has the chance to 'listen' to non-verbal communications such as the racing pulse, the

tender abdomen, the tender pelvis and above all the reaction to vaginal examination with its obvious sexual overtones. Women who have difficulty in talking about sexual matters may be much more forthcoming about their problems if careful questions are posed as the vaginal examination is being made. Moreover, as anatomical areas are touched there is no doubt as to what is being referred to, for many women do not fully understand the meaning of the words the doctor may use ... Many tender pelves have a psychosexual basis which should not be ignored. They may at least show some of the patient's attitudes to her body, in the direction of narcissism. During the vaginal examination the response may point to an overt sexual problem. There may be undue anxiety with muscular spasm or such easy relaxation as to suggest sexual anaesthesia, but it must be remembered that physiotherapists and ballet dancers learn such muscle control that interpretation of the psychological state from physical signs needs great care."

I don't think I need to elaborate much on the main assumptions here — sex = heterosex, (he actually states that earlier), women lie back and think of England — women respond to a gynaecologist as they do to a lover!

If you're still in any doubt read the sub-chapter 'Gynaecology as Psychotherapy' on pp284-253 of Ehrenreich and English's book *For her own good*. PLEASE TRY and read this if you're coming to this workshop because the quotes are too many and too hairy for me to cope with on paper! But I would refer just to the idea that the gynaecologist breaks women in to marriage and femininity by a vaginal examination which they 'undergo without resentment', before marriage. Did you think 'droit de seigneur' was dead?

The other area is of course obstetrics. Just when we are really up against it, giving birth, we are not only coerced to accept obstetric practice but treated like pieces of meat on a slab. One issue of the radical midwives journal has a picture of a woman tied down like Gulliver with a wire or tube coming out of every possible place. I would like us to talk about this as another manifestation of violence against women, done in hatred and contempt. Apart from making labour dangerous where it need not be, obstetricians are affecting our personalities, our sexuality, our relationships, and everything in our lives, by the way they treat us in childbirth. Many of the implements used unnecessarily — the foetal scalp monitor, the 'sweep' (an examination where the doctor goes inside the cervix and which is extremely painful, especially as women are not warned it is to be done), the forceps used to break the waters, all have rape-like qualities. When phrases like 'women in labour are not very feminine', 'some women resent intervention because they have been told that birth is a natural physiological event' etc. are being bandied about, it is easy for the labouring woman to be degraded and oppressed just at the peak of her power.

I hope the workshop can discuss how to enable us all to articulate our fury about our treatment at the hands of these professionals and how we can counteract their violence.

Anna Briggs, 6 November 1980

WOMEN AND MEDICAL PRACTICE NEWSLETTER
(Nottingham Report)

We are in the process of helping 'campaign' for divorce from an absconding wife-battering/raping husband, and child beating father. (Who was aided and abetted of course by the mediKILL 'profession' and the 'LAW'. See Newsletter No.1. 'Ardent Feminist')

The following is a quick herstory of the woman's experience with her G.P. . . . .

After suffering for YEARS from husband's extreme physical violence and downright mental cruelty, I found that this G.P.'s attitude to me was consistent with my husband's cruelty.

The first time I tentatively approached him for 'help' was after the birth of my first son. It had been an extremely difficult birth and I was very badly bruised and torn (25 stitches). For over a year I was unable to sit, stand, or walk for more than a few minutes at a time without causing a lot of pain and discomfort. My husband had absolutely no understanding of this, and his sexual demands never ceased. When I refused, he'd get angry and punch or squeeze my arm hard. (I now realise this violence would have been a great deal worse if we had not been living with my family at the time.) However, on relating to my G.P. my fear that if I didn't 'satisfy' my husband he would kill me (in the hope he would offer to 'explain' to husband) the reply I got was . . . "I don't blame him!"

Although I continued attending this man for physical complaints both for myself and my children, it was a long time before I felt able to broach the subject of 'battering husband' with him again, and only did so from sheer desperation.

This next occasion on which I approached my G.P. on the 'battering husband syndrome' was some years later after yet another extremely bad attack in which I was bruised so badly the right side of my body was black from knee to armpit. By this time, my physical and mental health had suffered so badly after years of putting up with this sort of violence, I was on the verge of both a physical and mental breakdown. I hadn't had a SLEEP for YEARS. My husband also used to keep me awake at night by mauling me, sometimes even in his sleep. Between that, and having to get up to attend to crying children etc. the only 'sleep' I was able to have in years was 'dropping off' in the chair for 15/30 minutes at a time. On the occasions I felt so desperate and was crying from lack of rest and made a bed for myself elsewhere, 'Hubby' would drag me by the hair back in to his bed telling me that was where I belonged. That's what I was there for. On occasions he'd commence to prove this to me by RAPING me. Sometimes he'd twist my arms up my back using real hard force (he weighed 13 st. at that time, and I by then had gone down to under 6 st.). Sometimes he'd kneel on them, depending on his NEEDS on that instance. If he was demanding 'oral' intercourse he'd kneel on my upper arms and try to force his penis into my mouth. I'd clench my teeth so tight this was impossible for him, so he'd rub his penis all over my face, enjoying the disgust and horror I felt when he ejaculated on me. If he was demanding 'regular' intercourse, he'd slap and punch me round 'a little', twist my arms up my back. On one occasion he also put a pillow over my head.

Usually when he'd finished he'd call me a whore or prostitute, and tell me no 'decent' woman would 'let' a man do that to her. (This is the 'man' who now wants things done in a 'civilised' manner. This is the 'man' I only married because of my 'Moral Upbringing' ... He'd RAPED me, and I felt 'soiled', 'unclean' ... Unable to go to a 'decent' man!!! This is the 'man' whose daughter was 'assaulted' by his father and refused to discuss it.) Anyway, back to the drawing board ... On this 'visiting' occasion to my G.P. I was in a dreadful state. Physically and mentally battered, and having gone without PROPER rest or SLEEP for YEARS, I felt my most important priority was SLEEP. I 'explained' quickly and embarrassedly about THAT night's violence, TRYING to 'get it over' that 'THAT' had been my life for YEARS, and that if only I could get some SLEEP/REST it would help me regain some of my strength and I would be able to 'fight back' a little ... PLEASE, would 'doctor' help me do this? His reply was to take a few slow puffs at his pipe whilst glowering at me over the top of his glasses, then taking the pipe out his mouth long enough to say in a very patronising/superchilious manner ... "And just what GOOD do you think THAT would do you?" and I was dismissed.

The next occasion was an even longer time later. It was the FIRST time my husband tried to strangle me, and left me lying unconscious on the floor. For nearly three weeks I had no voice, and found it impossible to eat. The pain was excruciating, and the bruising on my throat and neck so bad I went about all the time with a scarf round my neck. The G.P. 'diagnosed' tonsillitis, and 'treated' me for such.

It took me a long time to suss out that my doctor was just as big a woman-hater as my husband. It took me a long time and a great many experiences with him to realise that my 'doctor' had so many 'hang ups' that he was a danger to ALL his patients, not just his female ones. Unfortunately, I didn't come to this conclusion until quite some time after my mother had died in agony under the 'auspices' of this General Pricktition(h)er.

However, it didn't take me quite so long to realise I was NOT getting 'proper' MEDICAL treatment for *physical* complaints. At first I put this down to the G.P. not being a very good diagnostician, but feeling that at least he tried. And who was I to put anyone down for trying? I kept putting his abrupt, arrogant manner down to the fact that perhaps he was a bit 'shy' and wasn't able to communicate very well with people. After all, he was a 'good Christian' who attended and was an Elder in a local Kirk, and was a member of the 'Rotary' Club. So . . . I kept politely trying to 'get through' to this man. (How naive can we women be?) My politeness to him got me nowhere. As long as I continued being 'polite and respectful' to him, his attitude to me continued to be patronising and supercilious and I got NO medical treatment.

At the beginning of my 'marriage' I lost 4 st. in weight in three months. Feeling pretty ill I visited a temporary doctor in London. This doctor diagnosed the onset of thyrotoxicosis. (The shock of 'marriage' and the violence it brought with it?) She wrote to my G.P. recommending I be sent for investigation/treatment. My G.P. NEVER DID THIS. It was some years later when my oldest child was about 5/6 and he'd fallen and broken his arm and I had to take him to the surgery, that the 'junior partner' I saw on that occasion took one look at ME and wrote a letter to the hospital. So began my 'treatment' for thyrotoxicosis. Years after its onset.

One of the first occasions I really began to question my G:P.'s attitude to me, was after having been on 'THE PILL' for a number of years, and having suffered continual and various 'side' effects i.e. nausea, tiredness, lethargy, breast lumps, etc. etc. and having spent a great deal of time and energy running up and down to the clinic complaining of these things only to find that most of the time my G.P. did not take these symptoms seriously. It was only when I managed to see another G.P. that I would be given a change of pill to 'try'. Eventually I began to show signs of 'arthritis', pains, stiffening and swelling of joints, I was finding it more and more difficult to cope with housework and children. By this time too, my mother was very ill and I was also nursing her. All this, on top of still trying to cope with a husband who was still givimg me a rough time, and by now had also got in to 'thieving' from his employers. These signs and symptoms continued for so long, that eventually I began to get angry with my G.P. for not taking them seriously. Each visit I made to him, or each time I had to call him out, his irriation at my 'neurosis' became more apparent.

By now I was finding it physically impossible to cope properly with housework, children, sick mother, *and* husband. I had also developed over fifty large almost black bruises all over my legs. My finger-nails were so hollow I could use them as teaspoons. I was feeling extremely physically tired all the time.

This physical condition was also causing a lot of mental frustration. My ANGER against these two 'men' who were using or abusing me was becoming very great. I was becoming more angry with my G.P.'s complete disregard for my physical condition, and becoming more frustrated that this physical condition was preventing me from doing something about my anger . . . My G.P. decided I was DEPRESSED, and suggested giving me anti-depressants. I told him this was rubbish. I was no more depressed than 'fly in the air'. I was ANGRY. "NO", he said, "you are depressed", but 'seemed' to agree not to give anti-depressants. He gave me a prescription for tablets, one of which I took that afternoon. I began to feel very agitated, but did not connect it with the tablet. Early evening I took another tablet, and by 8/9 o'clock that night I was feeling murderous. This time I *did* realise it was the tablets, and did *not* take any more.

A couple of days later the G.P. arrived and asked me how I was getting on with the tablets. I told him they had made me feel very, very, agitated, and I thought it would be better if I didn't take any more. The G.P. INSISTED it would be better if I *continued* taking them. At this, I demanded to be told exactly what the tablets were for, and he admitted they were 'anti'-depressants. (Just how arrogant can these ?????? be when they continue to insist, and persist with the attitude that they know better than the patient, just exactly how SHE feels? *He* had completely ignored what I had told him, and decided HE knew better.) I put his 'anti'-depressants down the loo where they belonged, wishing I could flush 'him' down with them. But, so much for my 'physical' condition. This never was treated by my G.P. I *began* 'it' myself by taking myself straight off 'THE PILL', and putting myself in the hands of a Homeopathic doctor.

It was about this stage I began to have 'serious' suspicions about my G.P.'s real attitude to me both as a patient and a woman. This 'suspicion' was borne out some time later when my youngest child became ill with violent vomiting and diarrhoea. For over six weeks I tried to get my G.P. to 'do something'. He just kept saying there was nothing *wrong*, 'just an upset tummy'. I was being a bit over-protective, and 'over-reactive'. (I guess it must have been this 'over' active thyroid which he didn't believe I had.) In the end I was so worried about the child that I went to see his teacher. She too said she had been worried about him, and had been going to contact me. When I explained the 'situation' to her she said she would contact the school doctor. Two days later a paediatrician examined my child and had him admitted to hospital right away. SO YOU SEE ... IF YOUR G.P. THINKS YOU ARE JUST ANOTHER 'NEUROTIC FEMALE', HE WON'T EVEN TAKE YOUR CHILD'S ILLNESS SERIOUSLY.

Another occasion which was *extremely* distressful to me was when my mother died. She had been ill for a number of years, and had spent most of that time in a great deal of pain. This was SO bad just a couple of nights just before she died that I had to call my G.P. out. He left a prescription which I sent my oldest child to collect. The child arrived home quite upset, and said the chemist had spoken to the police about the 'medicine' so I'd better keep it in a safe place. Faithfully I gave my mother her prescribed doses of this 'medicine' having been led by the doctor to believe it would help her pain. Faithfully I kept this 'medicine' in a safe place out of the reach of my children. He (the G.P.) had also prescribed a suppository for my mother saying this would help relieve some of her pain by emptying the bowel a little. (I believe it was this which caused my mother such an *agonising* death ... She had an obstruction of the bowel.)

The night she died the pain was so bad she was SCREAMING in agony. I had to phone the duty doctor (a 'Doctor' Henderson). It took me 20 minutes on the 'phone to talk him into coming out. When he did he was so rude to both my mother and me ... Brushing past me in the hall, and going straight upstairs demanding to know "Which room?". Took a syringe from his case, gave my mother an injection, then handed me a form saying "Sign this," (for payment of night call). Hours later I was still waiting for this injection to give my mother relief from her pain. I phoned one of our local nurses and asked her to come as I needed help. Over the phone she could hear my mother screaming, and said she would be there in ten minutes. She was. She walked into the bedroom and stopped dead . . . "Jesus Christ, did HE leave your mother in this condition?" She picked up the vial which had contained the injected drug and said "This isn't even a bloody pain killer. It's a sleep inducing drug which would have absolutely NO effect on a person in *this* amount of pain." At approximately 5am that morning I had to phone another doctor. My mother died at about 7am . . . I thanked 'god' for her release. (During all of this time my 'loving' husband was in bed sound asleep while his children cried in the next room. He got up at about six o'clock when I went in and asked him to.)

He went to work that day (just the same as he did on the day my father died). He "HAD TO" he said, he "had the office keys."

However in the process of cleaning up and preparing my mother's bedroom, I came across the 'medicine' prescribed by my G.P. Remembering what my son had said, I phoned the chemist explaining, and asking if I should return this bottle to him or pour it out. "Oh! Don't worry about that" he said, "your son has got mixed up. I was on the 'phone to the police about a prescription, but it wasn't that one. That's just a 'SENILITY' bottle. Just pour it out."

After the funeral, I wrote to the local medical authority and complained. Some time later my G.P. arrived asking me to withdraw the complaint. He said it was extremely difficult to get young doctors to join the practice, and when they did get a 'good' one they just couldn't afford to lose him. Little did I know there had already been dozens of complaints against this doctor, and that our local G.P.s were protecting him.

Another occasion was when I took ill with a 'chest complaint'. I was working at a local hospital and was sent home due to chest pains and a high temperature. I phoned the clinic, but the receptionist refused to give me an appointment sooner than 10 days later. She said I could come and see the nurse, and she would "tell me if I NEEDED a doctor." (Standard procedure at this clinic. Patients were always complaining.) I went to the clinic and sat 1½ hours waiting to see the nurse, who told me I was ill, and needed to see a doctor. I waited well over another hour to see the doctor, and in the end told the receptionist to phone a taxi to take me home as I felt too ill to 'hang about' any longer. She said she would send me in next.

When I went in to the doctor he glanced up from his desk and said, "Oh! And what's supposed to be wrong with you this time?" I told him I was feeling very weak and that my legs felt as if they wouldn't hold me up much longer, and that I had a pain in my chest. "Tracheitis" he said, and told me to go home and go to bed. When I then told him I was also 'burning up', he leaned over his desk to feel my forehead with the back of his hand. "So you are", he said. "Go home and go to bed, and come back and see me next Wednesday."

It took over three weeks to convince my G.P. I really was ill, despite a nightly temperature over 105. I was in bed for over eight months with a lung 'infection' of which I was given 3 different diagnoses (Pneumonia, Psittacosis, Bronchitis), and all together I was off work for over a year. The first three months of this time were spent in delirium, and by the end of the rest of the time I'd been so ill I weighed 3½ st. Despite this, no home help had been organised, and no nurse organised even to give me a bed-bath. I was alone in the house all day except when my son came home from school. It was left completely to an eleven year old child to look after me, and see to his young brother, getting him out to school etc. My 'husband' refused to take time off work, and also decided he needed his rest so moved in to the other room. One night, needing help and too weak to shout, I tried to waken my husband by attempting to throw my bottles of tablets at the bedroom door. This did not work, and as there was an extension 'phone by the bed I had to phone the operator for help.

Another occasion during this time was when I was needing to go to the toilet. Being so physically weak this was only possible by 'allowing' myself to 'fall' out of bed and crawling to the top of the stairs, lying on my stomach and letting myself slide downstairs feet first. Arriving at the bottom of the stairs I discovered that the entrance hall was flooded. The toilet bowl in the bathroom just off the hall had fallen on its side, and water was pouring everywhere. I was far too weak to start mopping all that water up, but just managed to get back upstairs in order to phone a plumber.

It was *after* 'this' incident, and during another less traumatic one that I phoned my husband at work and told him it was time he realised he DID have a certain amount of responsibility to a wife AND children, and it was about time he started shouldering them, and stopped leaving them to an eleven year old boy, or anyone else he was able to palm them off on. My 'husband' did come home, but not before he phoned the G.P. The next thing I knew was that the G.P. was in the middle of my living room asking me "Do you realise your husband has a job to do, and can't just keep taking time off to suit you?' And if you don't behave yourself, I'm going to put you on tranquilisers." When I asked him if he put his own wife on tranquilisers when she got angry, he said "NO!" "Then" said I, "you're not bloody well putting me on them. Because when I get angry you can bet your boots it is well justified."

The G.P. did not like this reply. It was after this he wrote the letter to the optician saying I was an 'ardent feminist', and gave the 'sanity' 'insanity' report to my insurance company.

These are only a few of the incidents I have 'lived' through with my G.P. AND my husband. If I wrote it all, I would be writing volumes.

During these years of mal-treatment from both G.P. and 'husband', I consulted lawyers on no less than four occasions with a view to divorce, only to be told I hadn't a hope in hell. I needed 'EYE WITNESSES' to my husband's behaviour.

Despite this I left my husband on at least three occasions because of HIS mental condition (sick), only to be 'forced' back to him thanks to the 'LAW' of the male orientated society which dominated my life, life-style, including my financial and housing prospects first as a WOMBAN, then as 'a WIFE'.

Now, this very same 'law' which made it almost impossible for me to leave HIM, have now made it possible for him to leave me, and telling me that by providing me with less to keep myself and two children on, than my husband has for 'pin' money (plus all the 'perks' (???) of his job), that my husband is being 'very *civilised*'.

SO MUCH FOR THE REWARDS OF 30 YEARS ENFORCED, AND RE-ENFORCED 'MARITAL' ABUSE.

MALE 'LAW' CONDONING MALE VIOLENCE ????

addendum 1983:
After suffering many more years of this sort of USE/ABUSE from both the 'husband' and G.P. the woman eventually began to fight back. *This* was when SHE was threatened with being 'committed' for what the 'doctor' called 'her' *aggression*, ie. shouting back at him and 'demanding' PROPER medical treatment and reminding him how 'USE-LESS' he'd been in the past.

He said "If *You* don't 'Behave' yourself, I'll have *you* committed. I have the form in my bag and all it takes is MY signature. I'll sign it RIGHT NOW if you like" . . .

WOMEN AND MEDIKILL PRACTICE NEWSLETTER (NOTTINGHAM REPORT)

WILL ANY WOMAN WISHING A COPY OF THIS RATHER 'HIM!MATURE?' NEWSLETTER PLEASE WRITE ENCLOSING SMALL DONATION TO COVER COST OF PRINTING AND POSTAGE. (Is 50p too much?) ALSO, PLEASE STATE WHETHER YOU REQUIRE COPY No. 1 or 2.
NOTTINGHAM IS NOW BADLY IN NEED OF FUNDS TO KEEP OUR CAMPAIGN GOING, SO ANY DONATION TO THE FUNDS WOULD ALSO BE EXTREMELY WELCOME.
PLEASE SEND DONATIONS/ REQUESTS FOR NEWSLETTER TO:
   W.A.M.P.
   c/o The Women's Centre
   32A Shakespeare Street
   Nottingham
   (Phone 819166)

```
┌─────────────────────────┐
│         ONLY            │
│   WHEN WOMEN TAKE       │
│      THE 'LAW'          │
│   OUT OF THE HANDS OF   │
│         MEN             │
│   WILL WOMEN GET        │
│      'JUSTICE'          │
└─────────────────────────┘
```

PSYCHIATRY AS MALE VIOLENCE

In Britain, 1 in nine women, as compared with 1 in 12 men, will spend some time in a psychiatric hospital. A similar proportion, but even greater in number, will be prescribed tranquillisers and anti-depressants. The vast majority of psychiatric patients are working class. Working class and black women, who are forced to cope with capitalist and racist oppression in addition to patriarchy, are much more likely to be diagnosed as mentally ill.

Yet, psychiatric illness as a phenomenon of individual or biochemical origin simply does not exist. Psychiatry is a powerful and effective means by which patriarchal society controls those whom it is unable to persuade or destroy. It cannot cure because it treats only the symptoms and not the social and political causes of behaviour which is a response, whether conscious or unconscious, to oppression. Society sets the criteria by which mental health is judged. Psychiatry is only one of the means used to confirm and reinforce the norms and values of that given society. To dissent from its definition of mental health is to commit a political crime for which we are presumed guilty (ill) until proved innocent (health). In much the same way that women are blamed for their lot, so psychiatric patients are blamed for their illness.

To become "Healthy", we must suffer violation by hospital confinement, therapy, drugs, ECT and even be given psychosurgery until we readjust and conform. Even then we are never fully forgiven for having dissented. With a psychiatric record, we are punished for life by never being permitted to play a "normal" role in a society which we are obliged even more strongly to uphold.

It is tempting to romanticise this form of political reaction to our position. It implies that there are millions of women in this country who are at least passively aligned with the feminist cause. Their potential is enormous, and brings up the importance of consciousness raising as a way of increasing awareness and uniting women for action, but has so far hardly been awakened. We must help to turn "illness" into anger, and to direct this anger towards the destruction of a system which is insidiously destroying us.

Psychiatric illness is usually a sign of powerlessness, rather than revolutionary strength and activity. We may be in pieces, and unwilling to operate on society's terms, or in ways in which even those of us who are opposed to it are able to understand. For example, when we are unable or unwilling to think or articulate in a socially acceptable way or even give up talking altogether, we are accused of "thought disorder" and "Mutism" because we are not using language according to certain prescribed rules. Our feelings and behaviour weaken and confuse us, while psychiatric treatment inhibits our capacity to struggle.

The real crisis is not so much in the individual woman as in society and its institutions, particularly marriage and the family. We must struggle against these forms of external oppression, but also against the internalised ideology of a male dominated world. We need liberation from the mystification and normalisation of this oppression by psychiatry and all the other agents of patriarchal society, from religion to social work.

The psychiatric patient has been used as a scapegoat in our society, in the way that witches and heretics were in the past. When a psychiatrist is unable to understand a woman, he will blame, punish and chide her for breaking society's norms. She may be hospitalised: imprisoned without trial. If she claims not to be ill, this will be regarded as yet more concrete proof that she is, indeed, mad.

Only if she cooperates and admits that she is ill will there be any possibility of her being regarded as "cured", leaving hospital and being allowed off drugs. Healthy women are those who accept an inferior role, even though they despise it: to be "normal" is to be repressed.

103

We would not deny that women experience depression, anxiety and confusion. But it is not these feelings that determine our lives, it is the circumstances of our lives which bring about these feelings. If we react in a way which can be considered frightening, it may very well be because we, ourselves, have been frightened. So-called "paranoia" and "hearing voices" can demonstrate heightened awareness and insight. Our voices may tell us that it is men who lie. We are not suffering from delusion or a persecution complex. We are truly being persecuted for our feelings, conscious or unconscious, that it is male dominated society, and not ourselves, which is sick.

Greater tolerance is usually shown to women seeking help and showing distress, but only if they do so in an acceptably passive way: by becoming upset. If we display conventionally male traits of anger, assertion and independence, we are regarded as the serious threat which indeed we are. Like the lesbians and sexually active unmarried women who have been incarcerated for life in psychiatric hospitals in the past, we, too, will be "treated" for rejecting the female role, as defined by men.

As daughters, wives and mothers, we are expected to give unceasingly. If men are in need, we will sacrifice ourselves in order to nurture them. Refuse to live within them, we may be rejected by society for failing to act like a 'normal woman'. Women may get into the position when they are no longer able to give and indeed need men to give to them. These are two common reasons why it is usually the female members of a family who end up in hospital, where the caring image of medication and therapy can appeal to their sense of deprivation. Psychiatric treatment is offered as a means by which women may regain their capacity to cope. But in order to cope mechanically with this society, we must give up the freedom to use our own capacities and capabilities.

The family and marriage institutionalise the inferior position of women, yet if we refuse to live within them we are totally rejected by society. While a large proportion of women work, we are also expected to take the major responsibility for housework and childcare as well. Sometimes we are unable to cope with this triple burden, but this is seen as an individual failing. We are blamed, often by ourselves too, for not being able to handle all the contradictions of our role: from mother to sex object to drudge. Whether we conform or drop out, we will either be driven or be labelled mad.

A psychiatric hospital gives little relief to female patients apart from the opportunity to escape from our families. We are given drugs which might dull our pain, but which also affect our memory and concentration and may make us restless and unable to coordinate our movements. The effects of strong tranquillisers, ECT and psycho-surgery can be permanent. Most of all, psychiatric hospitalisation and treatment removes our control over our own bodies and minds and renders us incapable of helping ourselves. We are made to feel guilty both for failing to cope with our role and for having to resort to treatment.

Psychiatry violates and humilates. It perpetuates an oppressive social system by punishing those who dissent in a way which appears to be doing them a favour. It holds the threat of punishment and ostracism over each and every one of us. Like freedom, mental health can only exist if it exists for everyone. Psychiatric illness is not an individual problem — it is the responsibility of us all. Its prevention and care is neither physiological or psychological — it is political.

Ginny Cook — Women and Medical Practice

SEX LAW — ENGLAND AND WALES

This is a fairly brief outline of the main points of English and Welsh Sex Law relating to heterosexuality (Scottish law differs in some respects). There isn't room here to discuss the ways in which the laws work in practice. For more detailed coverage in non-legal language see Tony Honore, *Sex Law*, published by Duckworth, 1978 (available from many public libraries). More technical coverage is given in Archibold, *Criminal Pleading, Evidence and Practice*, edited by Buther and Garcia — this is a standard text on criminal law. The Criminal Law Revision Committee, of the Home Office is currently undertaking a review of all the law relating to sex offences, and they will issue several 'Working Papers' with suggested changes, on which they invite comments from the public (us). These are available from HMSO.

Rape

Rape is legally defined as sexual intercourse with a woman without her consent where the woman is not the man's wife. The judiciary's definition of 'without her consent' has varied and the current working definition is 'if he has sexual intercourse with a woman who at the time does not consent to it, and he knows she does not consent or is reckless as to whether she consents'. Only penetration of the vagina by the penis is legally rape. A male under 14 cannot be convicted of rape.

Maximum penalty: life imprisonment.

For attempted rape: 7 years.

In practice a convicted rapist is likely to get less than 2 years unless the rape is accompanied by other violence.

Sodomy/Buggery

In law anal intercourse between a man and a woman is a crime whether or not it involves consent, and whether or not it occurs within marriage.

If a woman is deemed to have consented to buggery, she is liable to prosecution as well as the man.

Maximum penalty: life imprisonment.

For attempted buggery: 10 years.

Indecent Assault

This term covers forms of sexual assault which don't involve penetration of the vagina by the penis. It includes 'touching up', penetration of the vagina with an object, forced oral intercourse, forcing a woman to masturbate a man, any sexual touching without consent. Honore comments "It is not necessary that the force used should be great, or indeed anything which the ordinary person would call force". However it is not an offence if he persuades the woman to masturbate him, without use of physical force. To cover cases like this involving young women/children, a specific Act was passed in 1960, 'Gross Indecency with Children Act'.

The principal offender in a charge of indecent assault can be a male under 14 or a woman.

Maximum penalty for indecent assault on a woman: 2 years. (For indecent assault on a man, by another man: 10 years.)

Incest
It is an offence for any male over 14 to have sexual intercourse with his daughter, grand-daughter, mother, grandmother, sister or half-sister.

If the woman is over 16, she is also liable to prosecution if she is thought to have consented.
Maximum penalty: 7 years.
For attempted incest: 2 years.

If the incest is with a girl under 13 the maximum penalties are life imprisonment for incest and 7 years for attempted incest.

Sexual assaults not involving penetration of the vagina by the penis are not covered by the incest laws.

Age of Consent
Several laws come under this category.

Act of Gross Indecency
This law forbids any 'act of gross indecency' towards a woman under 14, or incitement of a woman under 14 to commit an 'act of gross indecency'. The main offence in this category is when a man exposes his penis and asks the girl to touch it. But it covers any act involving the man touching her genitals or 'asking' her to touch his genitals.
Maximum penalty: 2 years.

Unlawful Sexual Intercourse (USI)
If she is under 13 — Maximum penalty: life imprisonment. Attempt: 7 years.
If she is under 16 — 2 years.

A woman under 16 cannot legally consent to sexual intercourse. In theory for a man to argue that she consented is no defence to the charge. It often is in practice, particularly if she is over 13. Whether or not she is deemed to have consented of course affects sentencing. Many charges of USI are in fact 'plea-bargains' for rape ie. the man will be charged with USI where a rape was actually committed, but he has agreed to plead guilty to USI in order to get a reduced sentence.

The man must be over 14. In practice males over 14 but under 18 are not prosecuted, unless a young child was involved.

If a man is under 24 and has not previously been charged with USI or attempted USI, no offence is committed if he 'reasonably' thought the woman was over 16.

If the assault or sexual act does not involve penetration of the vagina by the penis the charge can be Indecent Assault, as defined above. In theory consent is no defence, although it does affect sentencing. Maximum penalty: 2 years.

Sex with Women Regarded as Defective

A defective is defined as someone with 'severe subnormality' who cannot look after themselves. There are 5 offences designed to protect women defectives and one is USI.

USI with a defective. Maximum penalty: 2 years.

It is not an offence for a man to have sexual intercourse with a woman defective if he is married to her.

It is not an offence if the man did not know that the woman was defective and had no reason to suspect it. The test is not whether an ordinary person would know that the woman was defective, or have reason to suppose it, but whether the man himself knew or suspected it.

Laws relating to Prostitution

It is an offence for a woman to loiter or solicit in a public place for the purposes of prostitution. 'Loitering' means standing on the street — for the purposes of prostitution, it is an offence even if the woman is not soliciting. Soliciting is defined as any form of "actively inviting" customers, whether by words or gesture.

A public place includes a street, doorway, or sitting in a window.

Before being taken to court a woman thought by the police to be 'soliciting or loitering' is given 2 cautions. The third time she is taken to court and the fact that she is a known "common prostitute" is read out in the court as she is charged. Once defined as a "common prostitute" all that is necessary in practice to get a conviction for loitering or soliciting is to prove (usually on the word of a policeman) that she has been standing or walking in an area known for prostitution.

Penalties: For the first 2 court appearances, fines only.
For third and subsequent convictions, fines and imprisonment.
If 2 or more women who work as prostitutes live together they can be charged with keeping a brothel.
Maximum penalty: 3 months imprisonment plus fine for first offence. Up to six months imprisonment plus fine on re-conviction.

Living off Prostitution — Pimping and Procuring
It is an offence for a man to live wholly or partly on the earnings of prostitution.
Maximum penalty: 7 years.
This takes 3 forms in law.
1. Where the man receives the money a woman earns from prostitution, either directly from the client or from the woman (*pimping*).
2. Providing goods or services for the purposes of prostitution, e.g. advertising.
3. Overcharging a woman for goods or services because he knows she works as a prostitute, e.g. charging higher rent for living accommodation than with other tentants.
   A woman cannot be charged with this offence but can be charged with '*controlling prostitutes for gain*'.
Maximum penalty: 7 years.

Procuring
It is an offence for anyone to 'procure a woman to become a prostitute in any part of the world'.
Maximum penalty: 2 years.
   This law is directed against international slave trading in women. Legally the term 'procuring' implies 'persuasion' and implies that the woman would not have done what she did without persuasion.
   There are several other offences designed to give extra protection to young women, particularly those under 16, from enforced prostitution. These laws are additional to the Age of Consent laws.
   There are also several other offences relating to other forms of profiting from prostitution.

Indecent Exposure
Section 4 of the Vagrancy Act 1824 makes it an offence for

a person 'wilfully, openly, lewdly and obscenely, to expose his person with intent to insult any female'. It has been established in law that 'person' means 'genital organ'. It is limited to exposure by a male to a female and requires specific 'intent to insult' so does not include 'accidental' exposure, e.g. taking a piss/split trousers.

The wording of the act may seem 'Victorian' but it works well in practice to distinguish between nudity and exhibitionism.

Maximum sentence for first offence: £100 fine or 3 months in prison.

On repetition the offender can be sentenced to 1 year in prison. Most offenders, even repeaters, are fined.

Obscene Phone Callers

Section 78 of the Post Office Act 1969 makes it an offence for a person to send a message or matter that is 'grossly offensive ... or of an indecent obscene or menacing character'.

It is also an offence if someone 'persistently makes use of the phone for the purposes of causing annoyance, inconvenience or needless anxiety'.

Maximum Penalty: £50 fine.

The only point of passing this Act in 1969 was to repeal a previous Act which allowed for imprisonment.

Peeping/Voyeurism

This is not a specific offence in English Law. But anyone doing it can be prosecuted under the old (1361) 'Breach of the Peace' law.

Men Soliciting Women/Kerb Crawlers

A 1956 Act made it an offence for a man 'persistently to solicit or importune in a public place for immoral purposes'. In 1966 a man challenged his conviction on the grounds that heterosexual sex was not 'an immoral purpose' and he won. So this act has been invalid ever since. Men can solicit women with no fear of prosecution.

Leeds Womens Liberation Sex Law Group

SOME PROPOSED CHANGES TO THE LAWS ON SEXUAL OFFENCES

The Criminal Law Revision Committee have produced a working paper on sexual offences following consultation with the Policy Advisory Committee on Sexual Offences. This was published last month and is available from H.M.S.O. stationers for £3.70. Here are some of the discussions and proposed changes.

Rape

The law should be changed so that men can be prosecuted for raping their wives, say the committee. There is some concern whether this will lead to unnecessary family arguments(!). It is expected that only very clear cases will come to court. Some of the committee are worried about possible waste of police time. The committee recognises that refusing to acknowledge that wives can be raped by their husbands is discrimination. This reform, if it goes through, breaks with the idea that a woman's body is her husband's property.

Boys under 14 years old should not be exempted from charges of rape, as they are frequently physically capable of of the offence.

There is some discussion about whether the charge of rape should also cover forced anal or oral penetration, or the penetration of the vagina by objects other than the penis. Most of the committee are against this.

The committee thinks that obtaining a woman's consent to intercourse through fraud or by threats which do not involve physical violence, e.g. loss of job, should be a serious offence, but should not be regarded as rape.

The committee want to make the rape laws more effective: so far they have had 3 ideas:—

(i) There should be 2 different types of rape charge. 1st degree rape would cover attacks involving marked physical violence and attacks by strangers which included threats of physical violence and would carry a maximum sentence of life imprisonment. 2nd degree rape would cover all the other forms of rape and would carry a maximum sentence of 3 years. The idea behind

111

it is that juries would be more willing to convict if they knew the sentence wasn't going to be over 3 years. The committee aren't particularly keen on this idea.

(ii) The corroboration rules should be changed, so that judges would no longer advise juries that it is unwise to convict solely on the woman's testimony, without corroboration. The committee reject this idea.

(iii) Making it possible to inform the jury of the defendant's previous convictions. Most of the committee do not like this as it does not happen with other offences.

We should be thinking of how the rape laws could be made more effective. How can you have a law against rape in marriage which works even moderately for example. I think the WLM ought to be able to improve on the Home Office's suggestions.

Non-consensual Buggery
The majority opinion of the Home Office is that this should remain a separate offence, and carry a maximum sentence of life imprisonment.

Indecent Assault
It is suggested that all cases of indecent assault should carry a maximum sentence of 5 years, whether they involve men, girls, or women. Maximum sentences at present are 10, 5, and 2 years respectively.

There was one suggestion about whether indecent assault ought to be split up into 2 categories; ordinary indecent assault which would carry a maximum sentence of 2 years, and aggravated indecent assault which would carry a maximum sentence of 5 years.

Another suggestion was that indecent assault should be renamed sexual assault.

One thing that the committee have not commented on, which should be, is that it is not indecent assault if the man asks the woman to touch him. One law book described this as an "invitation to touch the sexual parts"!

Sex with Young Girls
The committee thought that the age of consent should stay at 16 and agreed that the present maximum sentences should be kept. The committee noticed the extremely low rate of

prosecution for this offence and the fact that custodial sentences were rare and that the age of the girl and the difference in age between the girl and the defendant were taken into account.

But there are some extremely disturbing recommendations for changes in permissible defences for this crime. At present only men under 24 years old who have not faced a similar charge before can plead that they thought the girl in question was 16, and then only if they have reasonable cause for this belief. The committee thinks that *any man* should be able to plead that they thought the girl in question was 16 — *without being held to any standard of reasonableness*. The committee agree unanimously that men charged with intercourse with a girl under 13 years old should be allowed to plead that he thought the girl was 16.

This is extremely reminiscent of the notorious Morgan ruling in which it was decided that a man could not be convicted of rape if he honestly believed that the woman consented *no matter how unreasonable* that belief might be.

The committee are against the creation of "special relationship" clauses, whereby there are extra laws to protect young girls from sexual pressure from adults in a position of authority or advantage such as teachers or employers. The committee argue that, as we cannot have an exhaustive list of relationships of authority or advantage, we shouldn't bother specifying any at all.

(NOTE — there is a separate conference paper explaining why some feminists believe the age of consent should remain at 16, and not be lowered.)

Consensual Buggery
The committee provisionally recommend that buggery (anal intercourse) should not be a crime providing the woman consents, and has reached a specified age (either 18 or 21). They suggest a maximum sentence of 5 years for buggery with a "child" aged between 13 and 16, and a maximum sentence of life imprisonment if the child is under 13.

Indecency with the Young
The committee are concerned that all sexual activity with a boy or girl aged under 16 is illegal. As prosecutions for

indecent assault by a close acquaintance (petting with a boyfriend would fall in this category) are virtually unknown there seems little to worry about.

Incest
There are sharp disagreements as to whether incest should be decriminalised if the participants are both over a specified age (either 18 or 21). If incest is to remain a criminal offence, the committee recommends that daughters and grand-daughters under either 18 or 21, should be allowed to plead that they acted under coercion. They suggest that legally adopted daughters should be protected by the incest laws, but not step children, foster children, de facto adopted children, or children of the female partner of a common law marriage. The committee say they will give these problems further consideration if they receive convincing evidence that 16 and 17 year old girls are being abused.

They recommend that prosecutions for incest should continue to be left to the discretion of the DPP, and that the offence remains restricted to acts of sexual intercourse.

Sex with the Severely Subnormal
The committee have received a lot of different opinions about this. The NCCL and the sexual law reform society thinks that the present law restricts the freedom of severely subnormal women and men to sexual intercourse. (It is an offence to have intercourse with them.) There were 5 prosecutions under the present law in 1973. The committee is reluctant to support repeal unless some alternative law is passed to protect severely subnormal women from rape as many of them would be incapable of giving evidence at a rape trial; they are also worried that these women may acquiesce to sexual intercourse without being fully aware of what they were doing.

. . . . . .

Public comments on these suggested law changes are invited. If we want/don't want any of these to become law — e.g. if we want rape in marriage to be illegal — we must write saying so to: The Home Office, Queen Anne's Gate, London W1.

Valerie Sinclair, 21 November 1980

114

RAPE, SEXUALITY AND CRIMES OF VIOLENCE

Rape is a sex crime. There have been some arguments put forward for making it a crime of violence. First I will summarise them. Then argue against it.

Arguments for Rape as a Crime of Violence

- Women do not experience rape as a pleasurable sexual experience. In fighting rape cases, we have been trying to get this across to the public, no easy task. 'You can't shoot a guy for trying to give you a good time' said one of the jurors at Inez Garcia's first trial.
- Criminology texts frequently list rape next to victimless sex 'offences' like consensual homosexuality, giving the impression that rape is a trivial offence.
- Violence is one recognised way that any power group maintains its power over another group. Certain acts of violence then take on special significance and maintain the subjection of the dominated group, eg lynching of blacks by whites in Southern U.S.A. By likening rape to that, something generally recognised — as men do it to men — women can talk about rape as a form of social control of women by men, without mentioning sexual control, the form of control men only use against women.
- If rape were defined as a crime of violence there would be no justification for introducing the woman's sexual history.

Arguments for Keeping Rape as a Sex Crime

1. *Rape, where violence, in addition to the rape, is not used, would become even harder to prove than now.* I think that when violence is used, beatings, stabbings, chokings, etc. the man should be charged in addition with this. Currently such violence is used to prove that it was rape. And cases where extreme violence is used are the easiest to prove. Defining rape as a crime of violence would just formalise this status quo. In ordinary assault cases, you must produce

115

at least bruises to make a case. This is not yet quite so in the case of rape, as rape is a sex crime. But making it a crime of violence would mean *just* that.

'The introduction of past sexual history of the victim into the courtroom stems from the view that rape is just one form of sexual intercourse. It negates the fact that a distinguishing feature of rape is the use or threat of physical force and violence'[1]

So goes the argument for making rape a crime of violence. This ignores that rape — for men — is just one form of sexual intercourse. And many women 'give in' without the marks to prove 'violence'. In practice the man's size, age, fists, words, don't count as threats of force, only guns and knives do. Rape for women is intercourse against our will, whether violence is used or not.

2.   *Defining rape as a crime of violence will lead to the elimination, in law, of minor sex crimes.* Perhaps the dangers in the 'rape as violence' approach can be more clearly seen from looking at the Indecent Assault law. If indecent assault became the same as ordinary assault we would have to have the marks of physical harm to bring a case. Currently if a man molests us — touches us up, or grabs our breasts, or grabs hold of us and kisses us saying something like 'let's fuck' we can prosecute him for indecent assault.

While the law clearly does not prevent this crime, to change the law to being like ordinary assault would mean that men would be free to indulge in this behaviour with no fear of prosecution.

Other minor sex crimes, like indecent exposure would not count as crimes at all. 'Where', men would ask, 'is the violence in that?'

3.   *Women who object to 'purely' sexual assaults will be dismissed as prudes.* Already there is a tendency towards this (see paper on flashing)*

Lorenne Clark & Debra Lewis in their book, *Rape: the price of coercive sexuality*[2], spell this out.

According to their theory of rape, sex inequality began with private property held by individual families, in which

---

*   Indecent Exposure. Conference paper by Sheila Jeffreys.

the sole authority rested with the father. (How this system arose they do not say.) So to ensure he could pass on his property to his heir he had to be sure he was the only man to penetrate his wife. This led to women seeing their bodies as private property, *because* that is how the men saw them, *as property* (highly questionable). So women use their bodies as bargaining tools, a kiss for a date, virginity for a marriage, $50 for a fuck. And rape is the price (we pay) for this coercive sexuality. However they also see sex as something we have that men want. Rape results when we won't give 'it'.

They suggest that in a system of no private property, rape will cease to be a problem. What do they mean by that? If we 'have sex' and 'hoard this attractive commodity' men are still going to 'want it'. This still sounds to me like come across baby or I'll rape you.

No, rape will not cease in this 'ideal' system, but it will cease to be a problem. The problem of rape is women. Women who see their bodies as property, and in this new system we won't (HUH).

However in the transition to this wonderful system some unfortunate women will carry on seeing their bodies as property. Clark and Lewis recognise this. For such unfortunate women, who won't accept that rape is just an assault to the genitals like a punch might be an assault to the head, there would have to be compensation. But is that not a bit unfair on the guy who happens to rape one of these unfortunate women? Well yes, but precedents exist, for example the 'glass jaw rule' (see page 169), whereby if you hit someone who has a weak jaw and it breaks, that's your hard luck, you are done for jaw breaking.

So once rape is established as just a crime of violence like any other, if there's no physical damage, the woman will have to prove mental damage (i.e. that she is some 'unliberated' prude) to make a case.

If all this sounds like science fiction of no relevance . . . remember the views of those who do research on rape, affect the law. Backed by Clark and Lewis there is now a proposed amendment to the Canadian Law making rape a crime of violence.

4. *Splitting off rape from sexuality makes it appear that any form of sexuality that is not rape is ok.* Catherine

117

MacKinnon, in *Sexual Harassment of Working Women*[3] says that the approach to rape which says rape is violence not sex, and splitting it off from sexuality, has made it harder to fight cases of sexual harassment at work. If rape is seen as so different then normal heterosexuality is seen as 'natural' and wonderful and ok, whereas there is much wrong with it. On these grounds she criticises feminist books on rape such as Susan Brownmiller's[4] 'This literature shares a starting point with the system it criticises: both attempt to distinguish sexual abuse from sexuality which must be healthy eternal and natural . . . but is ordinary sexuality, under conditions of gender inequality, to be presumed healthy?'

In Conclusion
To separate rape off as a crime of violence would not lead to more successful prosecutions for rape. We would still need to prove by the marks, that we had fought for our lives.

To separate rape off as a crime of violence would leave all the other forms of sexual harassment 'up to' rape as what? Normal natural healthy sexuality?

Rape and threat of rape is integral to the system men have evolved for maintaining power over us, but not simply as violence. Does rape fit in to a classification of bodily violence like this: maiming, blinding, rape, black eye?

That is not how we experience rape. Male power over women is maintained by sexuality and rape is a part of this.

Sandra McNeill, 5 November 1980

1. Lewis (Debra) Address to the National Conference of Rape Crisis Centres, Victoria, B.C., Canada. Quoted by Justice Minister Ron Barisford, in proposing changing the rape law to a crime of violence. See Victimology. Vol. 4 No. 2 1980.
2. Clark (Lorenne) Lewis (Debra) Rape the price of coercive sexuality. The Women's Press, Toronto, Canada. 1977.
3. Mackinnon (Catherine A.), Sexual harassment of Working Women. Yale University Press, U.S.A. 1979.
4. Brownmiller (Susan), Against Our Will. Penguin U.K. 1977. (U.S.A. 1975.)

AGE OF CONSENT

Power Imbalance
There is a power imbalance between men and women in scoiety. This is built into society's structure by men, and all men benefit from it. One of the benefits is that their definitions are seen to be 'everyone's': for example equating 'having a sexuality' with desiring penetration by a man.

Also adults as a group have power, physical economic and psychological, over children and young people. Thus an individual adult has authority/power over a younger person. (We may wish this were not true, but the way to change it is NOT to pretend it does not exist.)

We think that a mutual non-oppressive relationship is the only base for sexual relations, otherwise the dominant person is exploiting the other, and reinforcing the power structures. We see no chance, in this society, for a sexual relationship between an adult male and a young woman/ child to be mutual and non-exploitative of the woman. We therefore oppose moves to abolish/lower the Age of Consent.

Supporting State Laws
We approached the question of Age of Consent, like any other sex law, by asking 'what is in women's interests?'. Laws against rape, indecent assault, indecent exposure do not mean that no men commit these offences. Nevertheless we feel that to abolish such laws would increase, not decrease their incidence.

Ask yourself, think back, think of your relations with men. Would abolishing the age of consent be in women's interest?

Abolishing The Age of Consent
One suggestion is that we abolish the age of consent, and the courts will decide case by case, if the young woman/child consented.

Already academic criminologists are dividing child victims of sexual assault into categories of 'precipatory' and 'non-precipatory'. 'Precipatory' children include those who showed affection towards an adult, accepted sweets from him etc. prior to the assault. If the court decides the child is capable of giving consent then every attempt will be made by the defense to prove she gave it.

If the age of consent were abolished child victims of rape and sexual assault would have all the difficulties adult women face at a rape trial. Plus the fact that the younger you are, the less likely you are to be believed.

To argue that men who sexually abuse children can easily be prosecuted under the rape/indecent assault laws, is tantamount to calling for an open season for the rape and sexual abuse of children, who are in a more vulnerable position than adult women.

Who are the Paedophiles?

Supporters of the Paedophile Information Exchange (PIE) berate feminists for 'using the concept of the child molester' in our arguments. It is not the concept that worries us, it is the reality. A recent edition of Magpie (the PIE journal) carried a centre page spread of a young boy lying face down in the sand, captioned 'a nice bit of bum' and an article on 'how to be a chicken hawk' (pick up children).

In fact 10 girls are assaulted for every boy, and the most common rapists of children are their fathers. What's more psychiatrists cannot find anything wrong with these men (in their terms), they appear to be normal males.

We think that to abolish the age of consent will mean an increase in the number of adult males who sexually abuse children.

What is Consent?

One argument is that young women and children should have the right to consent to sexual relations with adult men. Exceptions have been suggested — for example adults in a direct power relation over the woman/child, e.g. stepfather or teacher. One sister at the NAC workshop commented 'They would have to include all adult men in that special relationship, including the man next door. When I was young I did what an adult told me.'

In a letter to The Leveller, Zoe Fairbairns described 'consenting' to masturbate a man when she was 9 (and the effects this had on her). 'No coercion or threat was involved. But looking back and wondering why I didn't just run like hell, I realise I was already coerced. I had always been told not to talk to strangers, but the absence of any specific details of what the dangers were meant that fear of the consequencies of being rude or disobedient were uppermost. I knew a bit about sex, but only in the context of love and reproduction; the notion of sex as male aggression was quite unknown.' She concludes 'Not all sex acts are rape, but all take place in a social context of patriarchy and rapism. Until they have sorted that out, I think men should deny themselves the opportunity of even the gentlest and most loving sexual activity with children, just in case it might be misunderstood.'

Arbitrary Age

To avoid putting children through the trauma of having to prove non-consent, there must be an arbitrary age. If a man has sexual relations with a woman below that age he must be deemed guilty. The argument then focuses on what that age should be. Some people argue for its reduction to 14.

One argument put forward for reducing it to 14 is the numbers of young women 'taken into care' for 'promiscuity' — something which does not happen to boys. But lowering the age of consent will not stop that. Indeed the Sex Law Reform Society have argued that the age of consent be lowered to 14 but the age for taking women into care for promiscuity be raised to 18. So it would be legal for any man to have intercourse with women aged 14 to 18 but the women would be liable to be punished. Also lowering the age of consent to 14 will mean more pressure on women under that age, to engage in sexual intercourse. Just as sex with 14/15 year-olds is treated lightly by the police, courts, society, (I thought she was 16 your honour) so will sex with 12/13 year-olds be seen if the age is lowered to 14. More sexual pressure, more coercion, more women taken into care younger and younger. We never heard MEN bemoan the fate of young women being taken into care till they began to campaign for lowering the age of consent. The heinous practice of taking women into care for promiscuity must be fought as an issue in its own right. We would urge women to add their voices to the protests of such groups as Rights of Women, on this issue. And not accept the lie that lowering the age of consent will stop it.

Another argument is availability of contraception. We

think Family Planning Associations should publicise the fact that they are willing to prescribe contraceptives to women under 16. The DHSS has issued a circular advising doctors that they are committing no offence by doing this and recommending that these women have the same rights of confidentiality as women over 16. At the same time we would like it made clear that there is no contraceptive that is 100% safe for women and 100% reliable.

There is tremendous pressure on women to see penetration by the penis as the sexual act. One group of young women who did give evidence to the Home Office said they supported the retention of age of consent at 16, as if it were lowered their boyfriends 'would no longer hope for sex, they would expect it.'

Our arguments for retention at 16 are as follows:

1. 16 is when one can leave school, earn an independent income. Before then a woman is dependent on her parents. Incest is a crime for the woman as well as the man once she has reached age of consent. Under 16 she is at extreme disadvantage versus adult men, step-fathers, teachers, all men.

2. Effects on younger women. As we said above we see reduction to 14 as leading inevitably to pressures on women aged 12/13.

3. Marriage. It is unlikely sex will be allowed before marriage is. Thus the age of marriage will have to reduce to 14.

4. Prostitution. The age of consent was raised to 16 due to campaigns by feminists last century. Mainly they were concerned by the vast numbers of young women becoming prostitutes. 14 years for age of consent means making it legal for men to engage women of that age in sexual intercourse for money.

Sexual activity cannot be abstracted from the system of power relations in which it takes place. Since this is true for adult women, then it must apply even more so in the case of adult men and young women.

How the Law Works in Practice

Unlawful Sexual Intercourse, with women under 16, is the

only offence on the statute book with a higher rate for cautioning than prosecution.

It is simply not true that huge bodies of 16 year old males are being imprisoned for having sexual intercourse with their girl friends.

Prison sentences are reserved for cases where the woman is under 13, and cases where there is a very large age discrepancy.

Telling Young Women What To Do

In supporting retention of age of consent we have been accused of telling young women what to do. This accusation obscures the fact that a vast body of people, mostly adult men, are already telling young women what to do. They use all the pressure of advertising, pornography, literature, films, magazines, etc. to hammer home the message to women that we are there for man's pleasure. To support retention of an age of consent does involve telling young women what to do, but in view of the pressures in the other direction, we see this more as righting the balance (well trying to). Yes, having the age of consent at 16 does inconvenience many young women, but to lower or abolish it will more than inconvenience many more.

Sandra McNeill/Valerie Sinclair, 28 August 1980
Leeds Women's Liberation Age of Consent Working Group

This article was first printed in the National Abortion Campaign Special Newsletter on Sexuality, September 1980.
For further reference see previous articles by this group: WIRES 84; Revolutionary/Radical Feminist Newsletter No.3; The Leveller, March 1980.

STRATEGIES AND TACTICS –
South East London Women Against Rape

We started meeting in March this year after a woman who had been violently raped happened to ring the doorbell of a local feminist to ask for help. Each of us came to hear of the meeting which was arranged to discuss what we could do, either through friends or from our involvement with the local

Women's Centre. We were a pretty disparate group in that some of us were already very active in the Women's Movement, some were more active in mixed left wing organisations, others had had little experience of political action before, in fact we were hardly a group since as our weekly discussions got under way new women kept on coming. For the first few weeks we talked again and again about the woman who was raped, how we could support her, what we could do to the rapist and how we could publicise the awful way the police behaved. We kept covering the same ground because new women kept coming and because we couldn't decide what to do. We were very angry — none of us had really realised before just how easy it is for men to calmly inflict on us such dreadful suffering and how powerless we are to do anything about it. This woman had simply accepted a lift home from a waiter in a hamburger bar, having been told by a woman who worked there that it was O.K. Having been taken to his house, locked in a room and raped by the waiter and another man she was kept at the police station for twelve hours and treated like a criminal.

We all wanted to scream about it, we just couldn't believe that it could happen and that nobody cared. Every week we talked through it and talked about what we must do to the rapist and then how we couldn't do anything because the woman was scared to death of him and she thought he may have her address. Also there was a hope that the police would prosecute; whatever action we took had to be such that it would not jeopardize the possibility of the men being convicted.

Together with our anger was a feeling of desperation about the fact that in our experience with the woman, nobody cared for her — the police accused her of being a whore and kept her for hours without food and drink; her doctor refused to examine her and the casualty department at the hospital nearly sent her to the psychiatric unit for being hysterical (a feminist consultant saved her from this and joined us in the group).

So our first thoughts were torn between violent revengeful action and immediate support for victims to help them through the system which treats them like criminals. A woman came and talked to us about the vigilante group she is in about which we felt very enthusiastic, but there seemed to be so many problems with this — most important of all that we might actually make the victim more vulnerable. Another woman talked to us about Rape Crisis and we realised that there wasn't enough of us with enough time to be able to set up another centre and run it (there is another rape crisis centre in London).

Due mainly to these practical problems and also to our political differences we decided to organise a big local demonstration. Planning and preparing for this kept us together — we found out there are a huge number of rapes, attacks and even murders of women in the area every week and we used our anger to work for the demonstration.

We contacted all the London feminist groups and women's groups we thought might be interested in this form of protest. Local newspapers were sent details, and on the morning of the demonstration two women from the group were interviewed on local radio albeit at about 7.30 on a Saturday morning. The weekend before the demonstration itself members of the group leafleted in Lewisham and the surrounding areas — the leaflets consisting of details of the march itself and a short paper on the myths and facts of rape. The response to this was mixed but not entirely unencouraging.

The demonstration itself was very successful. It was a sunny day and a large number of women came from all over to give us their support. It was led by musicians which gave the procession an almost carnival-like atmosphere. The feeling was one of strength and determination. Our one regret was that there were very few black women amongst us, although this was partly our fault for not making a concerted effort to contact local black women.

It was successful in terms of local publicity and raising the issue in the Borough and also in that it brought new women to the group. At the same time working in this way enabled us to ignore our political differences or at least act as though they didn't exist.

When we came together after the demonstration to decide where we went from there, the question still remained of every woman's fear of walking the streets at night alone. We knew of many women who just did not go out after dark.

While demonstrating, letter writing and general politicising are effective to a certain extent many women wanted to be involved in more positive acts: self-defence groups were started at the women's centre and were attended by women of all ages.

The emphasis of these classes is to avoid physical confrontation but where this is not possible, to teach women how to get out of awkward situations where you are being grabbed, held or sat on by a man and also to inflict a great deal of pain with as little effort as possible. What is more the effectiveness of these skills is not dependent on a woman's physical strength or size.

Through a teacher at a local girls' school who had come to know of our group as a result of the demonstration we were invited to give a talk about rape and sexual violence against women to the lower sixth form of the school.

We found them very responsive having obviously given the subject some thought, however it was strange talking to young women about this subject who didn't already have a feminist framework. Hence some classically male lines on rape and male violence were heard. We concluded with a self defence demonstration which was very well received. The postscript to their letter of thanks ran "Our Headmistress unfortunately does not agree with our idea of changing the school motto to 'grab, twist and pull' "!

After the demonstration our direction was open again and we felt in danger of being divided by political differences. We did not know each other well enough to cope with these differences and relate them to what we were doing, and so for a while we just ignored them and tackled immediate practical matters. Several women who had been raped joined the group hoping to be involved in providing support for rape victims, but the atmosphere wasn't conducive to revealing traumatic personal experiences and some women left.

We regret that women left, but we feel that this wouldn't happen now because the group has become much more stable. We are still very action based, but we spend more time assessing what we are doing and gradually the difficult issues are creeping to the surface and we are beginning to talk about them. We know that some of us relate to men and some don't; that some of us want to take violent revenge on rapists and others don't; some of us believe it is worth putting energy into men and others don't and that we are conscious that we have done nothing about the fact that we are an all white women's group in an area with a large number of black men and women.

As regards future action we are preparing a large exhibition on rape for International Women's Day at a shopping centre in Lewisham. We feel it is very difficult to reach local women and we are hoping that by organising such an exhibition and by having a live self defence demonstration our purpose and message will make an immediate impact.

A number of women are involved in the Women's Rights Working Party and through working with local councillors are raising issues such as street lighting, housing, and sexism in public advertisements. The women on the committee are also monitoring press reports on rape. We hope to use these to expose the sensationalism of the media.

Due to our concern about police attitudes to rape victims we intend to draw up a code of conduct for the police to follow.

We want to be able to respond to any situation that arises and, following the recent rape and murder of Karen Davies in Brockley, South East London, there will be a Reclaim the Night March on Friday 28th November. Assemble New Cross Tube 6.30pm.

South East London Women Against Rape
November 1980

The group, which was formed about a year before the Sexual Violence Conference, originally called itself South East London Women Against Rape — but it never had any connection with Women Against Rape/Wages for Housework, and, after the conference, it changed its name to South East London Women Against Violence Against Women (SELWAVAW).

CAN WE USE THE MEDIA TO GET ACROSS OUR MESSAGE?

This paper sets out to look at how we spread feminist ideas about male sexual violence through theatre or film. There is a real need to expose male myths about rape etc. perpetuated and reinforced through visual material using that same media. The problem is how.

I begin with questions.

How do we feel about mixed audiences at feminist productions dealing with male sexual violence? How do we speak with men present when their reactions undercut or co-opt what we are trying to say?

The problem is less acute in literature as we have internal newsletters. Some men may read them admittedly, but as reading is done alone women have the space to consider and develop their ideas without being interrupted or confused or prevented from so doing by men. But in film or theatre there is a physical audience. Women go with boyfriends, brothers, husbands and they sit next to one another. It is more difficult, if not impossible for her to experience the ideas alone. He may make antagonistic or negative comments to try and control how *she* sees the play; to prevent her thinking that men do rape, batter, child molest. 'He wouldn't do a thing like that', despite what is being shown on screen or stage. Totally unpalatable bits he will criticise as 'unrealistic'. Threatening concepts will get turned about, wilfully misunderstood, changed to his advantage. Like: the woman asked to be raped, look how she was dressed, etc. Not all men are potential rapists.

Worse he may get off on seeing rape or lesbianism portrayed and make her feel uncomfortable/embarrassed to identify with the woman in the film or play. That means: he will alienate her from her sex, her body, her interests. So a feminist production that is politically convincing becomes unenjoyable. He ruins her pleasure, thwarts her understanding. She blames the production, not him, and his policing of her continues, for example, she does not recommend it to her women friends.

This argument would suggest that feminist productions dealing with male sexual violence towards women should be restricted to women only audiences. That however may limit the number of potential viewers to women already in the movement. It isn't easy to trundle off to see a play or film on a Saturday night without your particular man. Men don't like being excluded. She may learn something beyond his control. He'll make accusations of chauvinism; call her sexist. She may decide it's simpler not to go. Hence for outreach, there are difficulties in specifying women only.

Can we then speak to women about rape, about battering, about sexual coercion, about incest and child abuse, about prostitution, with men there?

Some feminists have tried, are trying.

The crux of the problem is: in order to reveal just how despicably men treat women, the play/film has to illustrate it. And in showing men being sexually violent towards women, there is an acute danger that the production reinforces the ideology that male supremacist behaviour is 'natural' rather than specifically designed to control, i.e. cultural.

To us, with our sophisticated feminist analysis, a rape scene in an X-movie is horrendous. (Please read 'rape' in the widest feminist definition of the term not the patriarchal stereotype.) We find it difficult to believe, as a woman is being violated on screen, that any woman will not identify with her terror. So why do we need to publicise sexual violence against women, when every woman lives in fear? And if a woman lives the contradiction that men rape women but not her because she conforms to male standards (read policing — doesn't go out at night alone, live by herself, has her own personal protector, never mind the danger he presents), then how can we convince her otherwise? Is one block to understanding, the knowledge that men (her man?) identify with the violators . . . that woman-hatred is so near the surface? And for her to continue living in heterosexual society, the realisation must be continually denied.

How can we stop women blaming women for what happens to them in the performance and show that men are at fault. For we are all taught that women are culpable.

Woman in this patriarchal society is seen in terms of her sex. She is Miss or Mrs. according to her availability to men — whether or not she is some man's personal property. She is virgin or whore — all in relation to whether she is available and willing to fuck or not. She is hated more if she is 'unattractive', if she is old. So, in a feminist play or film, how do we represent woman? A short-haired, dungaree clad, Doc Martin shod woman is somewhat removed from the image perpetuated by the media as a 'typical' woman. But if we dress her in high heels, pencil skirt and Silvikrin hairstyle, we are reaffirming male notions/constructions of femininity. How, basically, can we represent woman as a positive individual, not a sex-object, when men insist on seeing all women that way?

The media reconfirms man in his belief that the world belongs to him. Through film and theatre men learn that there is no come-back when he exercises sexual power over women. (Often he gets validation for his behaviour — gains esteem in the eyes of other men.) Great care must be taken that in trying to reach women we do not continue to bolster the male ego, to feed male myths. We must ensure that he cannot alter our meaning to suit his ends.

A depiction of male sexual violence by a feminist film-maker or playwright must be different from the 'normal' representation by men, otherwise the purpose of the feminist work is lost.

Annie Smith with help from friends
10 November 1980

P.S. I think it is essential that we do expose the fact and frequency of male sexual violence towards women through visual material. Just because it is incredibly difficult, there is no justification in giving up as that leaves the field clear for male myths and fantasies. Film, especially, is a potentially powerful weapon in the fight against male supremacy.

THREE YEARS ... FOR KILLING A MONSTER

3 Years Jail for Daughters Who Kill Brute of a Father :
Leeds Crown Court, 17/11/80

2 Years Probation for Husband Who Kills Nagging Wife :
Leeds Crown Court, 14/11/80

What justice for Women? What Protection for Women? What Message for Women?
'Don't protect yourself against the fists of a man.' This is the message Mr 'Justice' Smith gave to women at Leeds Crown Court on 17/11/80.

Thomas Maw had been a brute to his wife and daughters

for years. Banned from pubs for 2 miles round his home, he used to take drink home and take his violence out on his family. Many times the police had been called, many times neighbours had heard screams. One night after 13 pints of cider he was particularly 'demented and with wild eyes' (Mrs Maw's testimony). First he punched Charlene then he attacked Annette. He pursued her from bedroom to living room. As the blood poured down her face Annette shouted "Please God someone help me." Charlene did.

Driven beyond fear Maw's daughters fought back. Annette stabbed him with a knife given to her by Charlene. Both pleaded guilty to manslaughter — 'with mitigating circumstances and elements of self-defence'.

Mr Justice Smith chose to ignore these circumstances. *3 years in prison was his sentence on Annette and Charlene Maw.* Yet he did not have to jail them — the sentencing options open to him ranged from absolute discharge to life imprisonment.

The stabbing proved fatal — had she only wounded him, what would he have done next? Murdered her in 'self-defence'? Unless a woman is a karate expert her only defence against male brutality IS to take up a weapon. When will the law recognise this? The message from Leeds Crown Court is obvious: that we should passively endure such beatings

We support Charlene and Annette Maw and all women who actively fight back against male violence.

Annette and Charlene were sentenced last Monday. In the same court the previous Friday Douglas Coles pleaded guilty to the manslaughter of his wife, Ethel Coles. The mitigating circumstances in his case were not that she was attacking him or that she had beaten up and terrorised him, but that she nagged and was neurotic. He got 2 years probation.

Jail sentences are supposed to punish crimes and protect 'the public'. It is clear that there is one justice for men and another for women. Men are protected. But there is no protection for women from male violence. We condemn this parody of 'justice'. Free Annette and Charlene Maw.

Annette and Charlene are appealing against the sentence. We ask all women to join with us in supporting this appeal.

Protest: Outside Leeds Crown Court at 10.00 am Monday, November 24th.

Write: in support of Annette and Charlene c/o Women's Aid, P.O. Box 89, Wellington Street, Leeds 1.

Leeds Women's Liberation

Press reports of trial are in the coffee room. See notice-board for:
- Saturday workshop on support for women who take action against individual men.
- Sunday workshop on how we can best support Annette and Charlene Maw and Beryl Maw's fight to free her daughters.

THIS STATEMENT WAS PUT OUT FROM THE CONFERENCE AGAINST SEXUAL VIOLENCE TO WOMEN

500 women from all over the country met in Leeds last weekend at a Women's Liberation Conference to discuss all forms of sexual violence that women suffer at the hands of men.

Why does sexual violence happen? It is one of the ways men control women. As women gain greater independence so men use more sexual violence to maintain their position of power over women.

Sexual harassment at work undermines women's confidence. Rape and sexual assault which serves to keep women off the streets.

Sexual abuse in the family which cripples the lives of women and girls. Obscene telephone calls which make women feel unsafe in their homes. Pornography which incites men to hate and be violent to women. Rape in marriage which is not even recognised in law.

Gynaecological and obstetric practice which violates women's bodies. Prostitution which exploits women and shows how perverted men are.

The conference produced many plans for campaigns to combat male sexual violence against women. All over the country women are angry and determined to take action. We assert every woman's right to defend herself against male violence and the conference sent a telegram of support to Annette and Charlene Maw.

CONFERENCE
PAPERS

Male Power
and the
Sexual Abuse of Girls

JAN
82

NATIONAL WOMENS LIBERATION CONFERENCE
ON MALE POWER AND THE SEXUAL ABUSE
OF GIRLS
Manchester 30/31 January 1982

The usual idea of a child molestor is of a stranger, but far more common is assault by a man known to the girl, and in a position of authority over her. He could be her father, stepfather, mother's boyfriend, older brother or other man able to take advantage of his trusted position. Like rape, this abuse is much more widespread than the police statistics or the media indicate, and like rape, it is very traumatic and damaging to its victims.

It is overwhelmingly girls who are sexually abused and men who are the abusers. As feminists, how can we tackle this issue so central to women's oppression? How can we help women or girls who have suffered it or are suffering it? Before we can begin to answer these and many other questions, we need to bring the subject out into the open and talk about it . . .

A national conference is being held in Manchester on the 30/31 January 1982; it is for women only, there will be a creche run by women; accommodation will be provided, and there will be a bookstall, and conference papers.

The cost includes tea, coffee, creche, and papers. There will be a disco on Saturday which will be free to unwaged women who have been to the conference, there will be a small charge to other women.

We would like as many women as possible to register in advance as we have many costs to cover. After registration you will receive a conference pass, a map and advance copies of papers.

For further information please write to PO BOX 336, Manchester M60. Please send any papers and ideas for workshops to the same address. Papers should be typed on a multi headed stencil if possible.

Some suggested topics: Fathers' Power, Law, Establishment views, Child porn, Workshop for women who have been abused, and one for mothers of abused daughters, W.L.M. line on the sexual abuse of girls, Media, and any others.

THE SEXUAL ABUSE OF GIRLS —
Why a conference?

With much of the impetus coming from the opening of the London Rape Crisis Centre in 1976, the Women's Liberation Movement in this country has slowly and painfully faced the subject of rape and sexual assault, both their devastating effects on individual women and their political role in all women's oppression. A demand for an end to male violence and sexual coercion, together with the institutions which uphold it, has been adopted by the movement, though it came years later than our demands for equal pay, and access to abortion. Women's Aid groups have struggled to compel the public at large to recognise the horrifying nature and extent of many men's violence towards their wives and cohabitees, and Rape Crisis Lines are doing the same on the subject of sexual assault. And many, many more women and women's groups are also giving support and strength to each other to overcome the feelings of guilt, shame and powerlessness that we are trained to feel after being raped and beaten by men. We are beginning to see the connections between pornography and men's control of women and are increasingly refusing to tolerate the films, advertisements and magazines which invite men to treat women as things to be used.

Of course we still have a long way to go before we can put an end to men's violence against women — it is so crucial in maintaining their power over us in every sphere of our lives. Women are still being battered, raped, threatened and abused by men everywhere, every day, with the full back-up of our patriarchal society. Women who have been assaulted are frequently advised to "forget" it. We are all constantly bombarded with advice and rules on how to avoid men's aggression. We are encouraged to believe that by being 'sensible' we will be among the lucky ones who will not suffer the violence, pain and degradation of sexual attack. Violence *is* frightening, and the recognition of the extent of it is very hard to come to terms with, because it shows us how vulnerable we are. It's not surprising that we often try to avoid hearing exactly what men do to women under relatively innocuous terms like "rape" and "assault". Everything conspires to make women keep quiet about what's happened to them at the hands of men. This silence doesn't help anyone and, as Rape Crisis Centres have proved, women need to be able to share their experiences, name what has been done to them, realise they are not alone. We all need this to happen whether we have been raped or not; sexual assault has to be seen for what it is and not what the newspapers would have us believe it is. We can't start to fight back while we are still divided, while we still believe that rape only happens to certain sorts of women, or if we have been raped, that there was something we could and should have done to prevent it. We need to know that very large numbers of men do rape, and that they are not easily distinguishable psychopaths, but any man.

Now that we are starting to tackle rape as an issue, something that is concerning many women is the lack of action around, or even a real recognition of the sexual abuse of girls by trusted men. Sexual assault of girls by men in authority over them, particularly by fathers or father figures is extremely widespread and has terrible and long lasting effects. Susan Forward, speaking of the U.S.A., estimates that one out of ten women have been molested by a male relative or similar figure[1] and, like rape, the estimated figure could easily be much lower than the true one.

The taboo on speaking out about incestuous assault is enormous. All the reasons for keeping quiet about any sexual assault are there, with many more besides. The girl currently suffering such assault will probably be confused about what's happening and unable to know what is "normal" and what isn't. She will probably not want to risk telling another adult and being disbelieved — after all, *her* friends and relatives will also be *his*, and adult power is not easily challenged by a child. Her father, stepfather or whatever, will also very likely warn her against telling anyone, by use of lies, threats, promises and so on. And if a woman, years later, does dare to talk about assaults in her childhood, the response is very likely to be disbelief, based on her long silence up till now. Freud's influence is still felt too — faced with large numbers of women complaining of incestuous assault, the only explanation he could come up with was that it must be a very common female fantasy.

Women in rape crisis centres and other groups are now

raising the issue of girls being assaulted by men in authority over them and Angela Hamblin and Romi Bowen of London Rape Crisis Centre wrote an excellent article in a recent Spare Rib[2]. I don't want to duplicate that but would urge anyone who hasn't read it to get hold of a copy. A few brief points need to be made though:

1. **It's mostly men that do it and mostly girls they do it to.** London Rape Crisis Centre gives figures of 97% and 92% respectively. I don't mean that we should be unconcerned about boys who are abused — they suffer, as children, under adult power. Girls however are, in addition, being taught a lesson about male power and are being prepared in a brutal way for their future power based relationships with other men.

2. **Child sexuality is a red herring.**
Child molestors and groups such as Paedophile Information Exchange try to gain respectability and acceptability by pointing to the child's own sexuality and maintaining that relationships between men and young girls must be mutual, and mutually enjoyable. I am not denying the sexuality of children, nor saying they should not have the right to explore it. Being sexually approached as a young girl by one's father, stepfather, mother's boyfriend, house parent or whatever, is not how I would define exploring sexuality.

3. **Coercion is coercion, whether or not violence is used.**
Incestuous assault is rarely accompanied by violence and weapons. These are not necessary; the man already has power over the child. She is not in a position of choice as children do not have much choice, where the desires of adults are concerned. The child may submit to sexual activity because this is the way in which attention and affection are offered. She will be warned against telling anyone in direct or subtle ways. The fact that violence as such is unusual does of course contribute to feelings of guilt and confusion both at the time and for years to come. The threat of withdrawal of affection is a particularly nasty kind of coercion — a child should not have to provide sexual services to receive affection.

4. Mothers are not the ones to blame

Male offenders, "professionals" and the girl herself are all likely to blame the mother. The mother is frequently accused of "abdicating her role" of submissive wife and caring mother and consciously or unconsciously getting her husband off her back by steering him towards one or more daughters. A quote from Erin Pizzey and Michael Dunne writing about a "compliant mother" is a good example here:

> "I pointed out her part in renting out her daughter in return for neglecting to make any attempt to creating a warm and loving relationship for him or her family" (New Society 13.11.80)

No doubt a woman may frequently be aware on one level or another of what's happening to her daughter, but we need to think here of the powerless position of women in marriage, combined with the illusion of power which they are credited with. Women are expected to protect and nurture but are not usually allowed to have the financial independence or the emotional, practical and legal support to get out of a marriage where the man is violent towards her and/or her daughter.

If a man is having sex with a girl in his family or in his care then he is the one to blame, not his wife for failing to fuck enough or his daughter for being 'seductive'. He knows what he is doing and he knows the girl does not have an equal say in the relationship.

5. The effects of incestuous assault are profound and long lasting

All sexual assault has a lasting effect, both physical and mental, on girls and women. All aspects of our lives are affected both by the assault itself and by the reactions of blame and disbelief from other people and from society in general. Guilt, shame, and a feeling of being dirty are common reactions to rape, as well as difficulties in forming future sexual and emotional relationships. All these effects apply to girls who have been abused by trusted male adults. In addition there is their isolation and the frequent estrangement from other family members, the traditional givers of comfort in times of trauma. For incest to be one's first sexual experience and "relationship" will inevitably leave scars for life.

. . . . . .

The sexual abuse of girls is an upsetting subject but it is going on. Thousands of girls are affected by it — either because it is happening or it has happened to them in the past. Before we can do anything we need to name it the crime that it is and see it in the context of male power and male violence generally. Women who have suffered need to be able to say so, to express their feelings in an atmosphere of support, not one of disbelief and suspicions. Girls who are suffering *now* need a way out of the situation. Somehow men have to be stopped from feeling entitled to use any available female to gratify their desires for sex or power. These are all daunting tasks but many of us feel that we must start confronting them, inside and outside the Women's Movement. That is why we are holding a conference on Male Power and the Sexual Abuse of Girls.

We hope a lot of women will attend, write papers, help with the organisation. We've ignored this issue long enough, come along and talk about where we go from here.

Hilary Saltburn

1. Susan Forward and Craig Buck. "Betrayal of Innocence — Incest and its Devastations". Penguin 1981. £1.95.
2. Angela Hamblin and Romi Bowen. "Sexual Abuse of Children". Spare Rib No. 106, May 1981. 50p + 20p post & package from Spare Rib Back Copies, 27 Clerkenwell Close, London EC1.

Reprinted from Manchester Women's Liberation Newsletter, November 1981.

SEXUAL ABUSE OF BOYS

We have received this paper on the sexual abuse of boys and since this conference is specifically about the sexual abuse of girls, we have not included it in the main body of the papers.

We do however acknowledge that boys are sexually abused by men and are subject to male power, so we have made this paper available to women who wish to read it.

Conference planning group

THE SEXUAL ABUSE OF BOYS

In deciding the title for this conference, we began with 'Male Power and the Sexual Abuse of Children'. It was then decided that it should be 'Male Power and the Sexual Abuse of Girls'. Some of us were concerned that thereby we were ignoring male sexual abuse of boys, and I want to present my own thoughts on this issue — thoughts mainly, since I have not had time to go into much literature on the subject.

Susan Forward and Craig Buck, in 'Betrayal of Innocence', claim that among *reported* 'victims of incest' girls outnumber boys by seven to one (Hilary Saltburn quotes London Rape Crisis Centre as giving a slightly different ratio: 92%:8% or 11.5 to 1). Given that we believe there to be an enormous number of incestuous* assaults, it follows that a large number of boys are sexually abused, though far fewer than the number of girls.

It might be argued that girls are less likely to report a sexual assault, incestuous* or otherwise, than boys, so that the *actual*, as opposed to reported, number of assaults would show an even higher female to male ratio. This can only be guesswork, but personally I would imagine that a boy would be just as unlikely as a girl to tell anyone, either at the time or when he grows up. This would be because of the fear of being seen as — or seeing himself as — gay (assuming he had not already made this choice). In the male heterosexual world, to be gay is to be weak, 'womanly', the object of

141

scorn or abuse. In male prisons, homosexual assault is sometimes used to assert power and dominance over 'weaker' men in order to degrade them; and the degradation is blamed on the victim, as it is on the woman who has been raped. I have sometimes heard men talking about how they have been 'touched up' or propositioned by other men in lorries, pubs, etc. Behind the jokey way in which these stories are told there is a fended-off fear, and the jokiness is meant to impress on the listener that the teller is *not* gay. How likely is it then, that a boy or man would feel able to tell anyone about an actual assault by a man? Especially if he had 'participated' in it?

Male sexual abuse of boys could, then, affect quite a large number of boys. Why should we not be concerned about it? Is it a fear of being considered anti-gay (i.e. not wanting to align ourselves with the common prejudice that a gay male schoolteacher or youth worker is more likely to assault/seduce a child than is a heterosexual man in the same position)? Is it that we forget that trusted adults within a family, including fathers, may be gay? Or are we not making the connection with sexuality per se; seeing sexual abuse as having more to do with power than with sex, but forgetting that men have power, not only over women and girls, but also over younger/weaker males, and that this power can be used sexually over them as well? Forward and Buck state that where father-son incest is concerned, the 'motivation' of the father is rarely homosexual but has more to do with inadequacy and the need to prove power over someone. Do we feel that this power can be ignored when the 'victim' is a boy?

Perhaps if, to put it crudely, we identify men — and young men — as the enemy, we feel less inclined to care about the plight of boys, since it is in our interests to care about the power of patriarchy over women. Hilary Saltburn states that, although boys who are abused suffer, as children, under adult power, girls are, in addition, being taught a lesson about male power, and being prepared in a brutal way for their future power-based relationships with other men. She states the case where girls are concerned very cogently, but I think she is only partially right about boys. Men do have sexual power over women, in addition to economic power, both being backed up by capitalism, law and the state. Men do not on the whole exert sexual power over other men, but they do exert male power of different sorts over each other. I believe that, in their up-bringing, little boys are taught a lesson about *male* power, not just adult power, and are often prepared in quite a brutal way for *their* future power-based relationships — with women and with other men.

Is this lesson taught through sexual abuse? Forward and Buck state that, where father/son incest occurs, the son is likely to grow up shy, insecure, unable to communicate with others, and uncomfortable with his sexual identity. They state that 'a man in our society is raised to require confidence and self-respect, *to feel dominant*, and when these feelings are negated by his own father, he loses not only his dignity, but his identity'. One of my reactions to this is 'perhaps not a bad thing' (not to feel dominant). After all, dominant over whom? — women presumably. What is implied is that the 'normal' boy is brought up to feel dominant over women, to be a 'real man', to take his place in patriarchal society. From what Forward and Buck say, father-son incest causes the normal conditioning to go *wrong*, whereas it is easy to see the sexual abuse of girls as part of their 'normal' conditioning to feel inferior to/fearful of men.

Perhaps then, while we should be concerned about *any* abuse of sexual power over children (from the point of view that neither women nor men should grow up shy, insecure and shameful), the sexual abuse of male children may not act to strengthen patriarchy in the same way as sexual abuse of girl children; and may even weaken it. However, I do think that we should look at the other ways in which male power is perpetrated by men on boys, and perpetuated 'from father to son'. I think we should be concerned, whether or not we are or may in future be mothers of boys, whether we are lesbian or heterosexual, because until and unless *all* our children are brought up in a different way, patriarchy will continue.

It does seem that the boy learns about patriarchal power, not just from his own privileges and by witnessing adult men's power over women, but also through that power being used against him. The Oedipus myth, parodied, runs as follows: little boy desires mother; fears father will castrate him; hence renounces mother and identifies with father and his phallic power, in the belief that his 'birthright' (possession of women) will be his when he grows up like his father. You don't have to subscribe to Freud to notice that: boys who are close to their mothers begin to treat them more distantly and emulate their fathers; men are often more jealous of their sons than their daughters, expecting them to be tough, not cry, fight back, not be a softy or sissy. Men are often pretty cruel to their sons; they expect them to be able to achieve more, behave better, than they are capable of at a given age. They will make sure the son knows 'who is boss'. They will not tolerate weakness/fear/upset in their sons; these are 'female' emotions, and they train their sons to hide/repress them, teach them that other men will not tolerate them. Much of this is written into Marilyn French's novel 'The Bleeding Heart', and I have seen it in a man I know well and his young son, and in the families of the people I work with as a psychologist. It seems that boys are taught (as are girls) 'I have power over you' by their fathers. But boys are also taught 'you must not show your fear of me but fight me back; erect the same defences as I have; become like me'. By this analysis, boys acquire their psychological patriarchal power through fear of men as much as because of the rewards and privileges they thereby acquire. Other analyses focus more on the fear of *women* as causing men's hatred of women; but what Phyllis Chesler says, in her complex and fascinating book 'About Men', is that 'men are consumed by a silent fear of other men' — and 'sons transform their fear of fathers into a safer fear — a fear of or contempt for mothers'. In other words, the fear of men comes first, but can rarely be fully admitted by men. Instead, women are blamed — as usual.

Perhaps, then, the sexual abuse of boys is comparatively rare because the usual father-son 'lesson' has actually gone too far if sexual abuse occurs. The son has to survive his father's power in order to identify with it and grow up to wield it against women and his own children. If his father — or another adult male — sexually abuses him, perhaps he is too damaged by the experience to identify as a 'man'. Or perhaps he can't then see his father as someone to become like. I don't think we know enough about this, and perhaps this is not really the conference to discuss it. But while we are looking at what men do to female children, I think we should also look at men's habitual — if less dramatic — abuse of their power over boys. In the absence of any feminist theory of this, women will continue to be blamed by most people for the ways that boys grow up.

Hazel Seidel, Manchester 1982

*I am aware that many feminists do not like the word 'incest'. Here I am using it as shorthand for sexual abuse of children within the family. Most of what I am saying applies to abuse of boys by a trusted adult male or rather to any man seen as a 'pater' as in patriarchy, as opposed to a biological father. This could include other male relatives, teachers etc.

Chesler, Phyllis (1978). About Men. The Women's Press.
Forward, Susan and Buck, Craig. (1981). Betrayal of Innocence. Penguin.
Saltburn, Hilary (1981). The Sexual Abuse of Girls — Why a Conference? Manchester Women's Liberation Newsletter, November 1981.

SEXUAL ABUSE OF CHILDREN

I am not sure how old I was when it happened. I might have been younger than eight. My mother was out working in the evenings and I can remember my father coming down to my room and taking me back to their bedroom, into their big double bed, and my father rubbing his penis up and down my vagina. He'd talk to me and say things like "Does that feel nice?" I would not reply but lie there looking at the ceiling with the most terrified, confused nauseous feelings you can imagine. The light was always off and I never saw his penis or ever looked into his eyes. There was just this outline of the man, this big man, my father, doing this unknown, secretive act to me. I was told I wasn't to tell anyone that it was something between him and me. Then he would send me back to my bedroom.

Katherine, in Broadsheet, New Zealand feminist magazine

It is impossible to know the true incidence of child sexual abuse because, like rape, it is a grossly under-reported and hidden crime. When we read in the newspapers that a child has been sexually assaulted it is almost invariably an account of an assault committed by a stranger. What we do not read about is the vast number of children who are sexually abused within the confines of their own homes. It was seven years before Katherine was able to tell anyone what her father was doing to her. Now, as an adult woman, she has allowed her experiences to be published in a feminist magazine in the hope that it will help others.

The sexual abuse of children has become familiar to those of us who work at the London Rape Crisis Centre. This article is based on our work there. We draw on our collective's own experiences of sexual abuse and, whilst respecting confidentiality, also draw in a general way on the experience of the women who have contacted us.

As more and more women speak out about their own experiences of childhood sexual abuse; as more children try to tell (in whatever way they can — that they're afraid of Uncle, or Daddy, or the man next door); as more of us start to listen and really hear what it is we are telling each other we begin to see the emergence of a familiar pattern.

The adults who sexually abuse children are overwhelmingly male (97%). The children they abuse are overwhelmingly female (92%). We are talking about a crime which is committed (almost exclusively) by adult men against girl children. It is committed usually in circumstances where the man is in a position of trust and authority over the child, and where he has chosen to use the power this gives him to abuse her for his own gratification. As feminists, we recognise that what we are confronting is the same male power which allows men to rape and batter us, and that the fight against the sexual abuse of children has to be an integral part of our struggle.

How do we define the sexual abuse of children?
Sexual abuse of children covers a whole range of crimes. It may involve exhibitionism, touching/manipulating the child's genitals, getting her to touch his — through to oral rape, anal rape and vaginal rape. It may occur once or be repeated over a number of months or years.

In defining child sexual abuse we do not like to use the word 'incest'. This is because separating off incest from the sexual abuse of women and children blurs the fact that the location of power in men/fathers allows them to abuse women/children in all situations, whether in society or the family. It is also a term which implies mutuality and

146

participation by the girl being abused.

It also has a very specific meaning in law. It only covers sexual intercourse when many other forms of abuse are involved and it is an offence only with a woman whom the offender knows to be his granddaughter, daughter, sister or mother. It does not include assaults by stepfathers, adopted fathers, uncles or a whole range of trusted adults close to her family.

Sexual abuse or sexual liberation?

Over the last decade we have witnessed a growing and sinister trend, on both sides of the Atlantic, to make the sexual abuse of children by adult males socially acceptable. These campaigns appear in many guises but what they are all aimed at is the lifting of social taboos against adults having sex with children and the removal of any legal obstacles which would continue to stand in their way.

In the early seventies Judith Reisman, a media researcher from Ohio, began a six year study of the philosophy behind Playboy and Penthouse magazines to ascertain the effect that it had on influencing public attitudes.

By 1976 she was in no doubt that these magazines had embarked on a subtle propaganda campaign to prepare the ground for what she called 'media conditioning into paedophilia and incest'. This softening-up process, she says, began slowly with cartoons associating children with sex. It then progressed to the use of real life photographs of women, dressed up as children, in 'seductive poses'. By 1976 Playboy had become even more explicit when it featured a photo-story showing a nude adolescent girl and used a caption which said it all: "Yes, she's old enough to be your daughter!" These subtle and not-so-subtle messages that sex with young girls is now OK reached an estimated male readership of around ten million. In the US, TIME magazine reports on what it calls the 'pro-incest lobby' — well known researchers and academics who are conducting a propaganda campaign to not only break down the ban on incest, but to create a social climate in which incest would be regarded as positively beneficial. Those who object are simply dismissed as 'up-tight and repressed' or 'behind the times'.

In Britain the Paedophile Information Exchange (PIE) was set up in 1974 to enable those who are sexually attracted to children to get in touch with each other for mutual support and to campaign for the legal and social acceptance of paedophilia. Not surprisingly, its membership has been comprised almost entirely of adult males (97%).

In a skilful tactic towards the end of the seventies PIE changed direction, and instead of campaigning for the right of adult men to have sex with children, it now campaigned for the right of children to have sex with them. This was to prove a shrewd move because it enabled PIE to present its case under a banner of children's rights and accuse all those who opposed its aims of being anti-sex moralists out to control or crush childhood sexuality.

Much of the so-called 'radical' argument put forward in this country to legitimise adult males having sex with children is presented as though it sprang from a broad-based sexual politics movement encompassing the women's movement, the gay movement and the left. As feminists, we reject this claim and insist that these issues be discussed and understood within the framework of a society where men have power over women and children.

Who are the abusers?

They may be the father; step-father; adopted father; house-father of children in care; uncle; grandfather; mother's male lover; older brother; lodger; babysitter; man next door; family friend; teacher; school bus driver or a stranger. The list is endless. Almost any adult man is a potential sexual abuser of a child, but it is more likely to be someone whom the child knows and trusts. According to one study, in 75% of cases he will be known to her.

The stereotyped image of the child molester is that of a perverted, insecure, possibly alcoholic, over-sexed or under-sexed, emotionally deprived, possibly homosexual male with 'poor impulse control'. It is also suggested that sexual abuse occurs only in poor and over-crowded families. Research and our own experience at the London Rape Crisis Centre, however, have shown us that, on the contrary, most sexual abuse of children, whether on boys or girls, is committed by heterosexual males with 'normal' personalities who come from all races and classes.

The nature of male power in families means that there is always a possibility of sexual abuse on any child, because

148

men and society regard families as places in which men do
what they choose. Abusers see "their" women and children
as belonging to them — not primarily as individuals with
feelings and needs and rights but there to service/fulfil
their emotional, sexual and domestic needs. The girls it
happens to are not any different to those who are not abused
— rather some of us escape because the men who are our
fathers/guardians/friends choose not to abuse their power.

How does it happen?

Most of us have read, with horror, about children who have
been abducted on their way to school or coming home
from the sweet shop and then brutally assaulted and/or
murdered. These brutal attacks, in fact, represent the end
of a continuum of sexual child abuse — but they are often
presented as though they constituted the whole of it. What
happens to the children who are sexually abused by close
relatives or friends; that is, by people in their immediate
environment whom they know and trust?

In our experience men who sexually abuse children,
like most rapists, do not do so out of some sudden and
uncontrollable sexual desire. They plan in advance what they
are going to do and often carry this out step by step, over a
long period of months and years.

The trusted male adult may approach the child at a very
early age under the guise of play. He may admire her genitals
or indulge in chasing games where he 'catches' her then
fondles or masturbates her. These games can become part
of their relationship, teaching her at a very early age to
accept sexual advances from him and thereby preparing
her for the intercourse that often follows. Some fathers,
however, do not follow this pattern and may rape their
daughters at a much younger age. He may show affection
all the while he is getting his way but if she tries to end it
the affection changes and he then orders her to do what he
wants. If she refuses he may beat her or threaten her. She
may never dare refuse him again.

At this stage the girl realises he has led her throughout
her childhood into a trap from which there seems to be
no escape. If she has loved the man and has enjoyed his
affection and attention she may now feel implicated. The
man, of course, will encourage her to feel this; and will use

her feelings of guilt and shame because what better way is there to ensure her silence and therefore his own safety?

Children very often want attention and affection but what the child who is sexually abused by an adult learns is that attention and affection are not freely given; she must 'pay' for them with sex and later on in life she may become afraid to express affection, or her own sexuality, for fear of being abused.

Many of the 'pro-incest' advocates or campaigners for the acceptance of adult males having sex with children (whether inside or outside the family) argue that there are no harmful effects on the child and that the child should be given the freedom to consent to sexual relationships with an adult. We would like to deal with both these claims separately.

Some of the effects of sexual abuse on children

In our experience at LRCC we have found that women and girls are affected in many different ways by sexual abuse. Each one of us is different and we do not all have exactly the same reactions. However, it is very important for everyone to recognise just how harmful both the short-term and the long-term effects of sexual abuse can be, damaging as they do our very being and sapping our energy and sense of self worth.

The young child who is being sexually abused may experience recurrent states of acute anxiety and fear but she has not words with which to describe what is happening to her. She may cling desperately to her mother, without 'apparent' reason or wake up in the night crying with 'night terrors'. She may be withdrawn and uncommunicative or restless and unable to concentrate, particularly on her schoolwork. Additionally, she may be suffering from painful vaginal or anal injuries as a result of the assaults.

If we have been abused as a child our failure to ask for help comes not, as is claimed, from enjoyment of the sexual abuse, but from fear that we will not be believed, that we will be blamed, removed from home or the adult imprisoned. One of the major effects of sexual abuse is to silence us and isolate us. We have to keep an enormous secret. We may feel we are holding the family together. We cannot risk anyone knowing. We may cut ourselves off from other people. In many cases we are not free to hate or be angry with the man who is abusing us — we must comply with him or risk losing his 'love'.

When we become adult women feelings about the sexual abuse may come and go sweeping over us or in the form of vivid flashbacks leaving us numb, depressed or acutely anxious. There is no doubt that we will feel very deeply the betrayal of someone trusted who exploited our dependence and desire to please. At the same time we may blame ourselves, feeling that maybe there is something different and awful about us that made this man abuse us. These feelings of self blame and loathing carried alone can make us feel depressed to the point of breakdown or suicide, or make us want to punish ourselves or our bodies by drugs, alcohol or physical abuse. Many of us may have moments of feeling dead inside — sometimes feeling our body is no longer our own — that he still has a part of it. Memories of the abuse may return when we are having sex, whether our lover is a woman or a man, and this can lead to the most intense distress.

Being subjected to sexual abuse at an early age can make us wonder whether anyone will be able to love us now, or whether we will always be abused in relationships. We may also be left with feelings of not being able to trust anyone. Who can we share our pain with? We may fear the way others will react to the knowledge and this can be enough to silence us again. Cheated out of our childhood we may feel pain, humiliation and outrage. We may feel angry and upset that our mother did not protect us and this may permanently affect our relationship with her.

The effects of sexual abuse in childhood are lasting. It is a testimony to the strength and courage of so many female children that, despite this legacy of abuse and ill-treatment, we survive and often grow into strong and resourceful women.

Can children consent?
When considering the question of consent we as adult women cannot separate ourselves off from children and young women. As we grow older we may begin to know what it is we are consenting to but are we really free to truly consent to sex with men in a society where men and women do not

151

hold equal power? Married women, for example, do not have the legal right to say 'no' to sexual intercourse with their husbands. (Men cannot be charged with raping their wives.)

To consent, a person must know what it is she is consenting to and she must be free to say yes or no. We argue that a child does not have the power to say yes or no. Children do not have the knowledge or independence to make a decision about sex with an adult. They have been brought up to obey adults. They depend on adults for the resources to live. Many abusers especially in the sanctity of the family are able to define the child's entire reality — they tell her it's normal to have sex with daddy/adults, that it's sex-education, or he tells her it makes him happy. Girls, in particular, because of the way they have been taught to be female and 'good' want to please adults, especially men. They, like adult women, find it difficult to say no to male demands. If they do say no it does not always make any difference.

Young children do not necessarily know what adult sex is about. They may want to be held, to have love and affection. If this makes the adults feel sexual it is they who choose to act on those feelings not the child.

Along with the argument that children can consent goes the argument that they are seductive. Girls may behave in a way that men consider provocative — indeed they are rewarded for being flirtatious. They may do this to please adults, to get attention — they do not do it for sex. Men claiming they have been seduced by little girls sound all too familiar. It is the same excuse used by rapists that they were led on.

Men also use a variety of other more explicit ways to ensure girls' 'co-operation' and keep them quiet. The threats vary depending on her age. It may be enough to threaten to tell her mother of some separate inconsequential mis-behaviour, he may tell her that the family will be broken up, that he will be sent to prison, that it's all her fault. He may bribe her with presents or money and then chastise her for taking them. He may threaten to deny her food and clothes. He may use the threat of beatings or actual beatings to silence her.

Age of consent

Under the present law it is a crime for adult men to have sex with children and if it is proved that the man has actually committed the act and that the child is under the legal age of consent then his guilt is automatically proven. If, however, the law on incest and the age of consent were to be abolished as many paedophile and libertarian campaigners are urging, then the abused child would be placed in the same position as that of an adult woman who has been raped, namely that she would be required to prove that she did not consent. This would shift the legal responsibility for child sexual abuse away from the adult male abuser and onto the (usually) female child.

Disbelief and so-called mother-collusion

Writers and practitioners working on sexual abuse continue to elaborate a mythology which is extremely effective in perpetuating child sexual abuse. The most likely reaction a child will get if she is able to tell someone what is happening is disbelief. This disbelief protects men. Professionals — social workers, psychologists, psychiatrists — take the view that it is better to disbelieve (and allow the abuse to continue) than interfere, particularly in the family.

Psychoanalytic theory adds justification to this position. It originated in Freud's refusal to believe his 'hysterical' women patients had been sexually abused as children. Instead he explained it away in terms of fantasy.

Additionally the concept of 'family dysfunction' is now widely used to put the blame and responsibility for sexual abuse not on the man who commits the crime but on the mother and daughter. We have seen the way the girl is blamed. Mothers are held responsible in a number of ways. The main argument is that the couple have a bad sexual relationship creating tension in the fathers/abusers. The implication of this is that men have a right to have their sexual tension needs met by women, if necessary by their daughters. They do not.

The much used words 'mother collusion' suggest not only that mothers are involved in the sexual abuse but that they have an equal share of power within the family. In reality mothers have very little power. Professionals argue that they almost always know that the sexual abuse is going on (consciously or unconsciously — the mother can't win), and she, not the abuser, is held responsible for not protecting the child and stopping it.

If mothers are told/know about the sexual abuse they have to decide whether to intervene to stop it. They currently have to act alone, without support. They must face the prospect of bringing up children without a male wage and without the security of a man in a world where much social acceptance is attached to being in a heterosexual loyalty to her husband and her daughter. She may be afraid of his anger and violent abuse. There are many possible reasons for her inaction. The irony is that other family members and neighbours and professional workers may also know of the abuse and not act. We are not saying that it's all right for mothers to know and not act, but as feminists and mothers we must work out ways to help mothers and children act to end sexual abuse.

Whose fault is it?

It is not families who sexually abuse children. We must ask who is responsible for the real injustice. Our starting point must be that the person responsible for the crime of sexual abuse is the man who commits it — no one forces him to do it. When he does it, it is an expression of his power.

Florence Rush, in her study of sexual child abuse in the US has said that the female's early experiences of sexual abuse "prepare her to submit in later life to the adult forms of sexual abuse heaped on her by her boyfriend, her lover, and her husband. In short, the sexual abuse of female children is a process of education which prepares them to become the sweethearts and wives of America."

It is no accident that, at a time when more and more women are refusing to accept these 'adult' forms of sexual abuse, an increasing number of men are redirecting their sexual attentions towards little girls.

We would like to thank the women of the London Rape Crisis Centre for their help and support.

Angela Hamblin and Romi Bowen

First publication Spare Rib, Issue No. 106, May 1981.

RAPE IN THE FAMILY:
SEXUAL ABUSE OF CHILDREN

In the same way that rape of a wife is no crime, so incest is a social rather than a legal taboo, with much less severe penalties than for child rape (rarely more than ten years' imprisonment, while rape can be a life sentence). Similarly, sexual interference is very hard to prove, being only one end of a continuum of physical contact — when does a loving cuddle become sexual? (In our society, of course, touching children is seen as the right of adults — I always felt insulted by the interminable pats on the head from doting uncles, yet how many people would see that as assault? I am guilty of it myself, no doubt.) And, since the basis for sexual abuse of children within the family is the power relations and emotional commitment present in a family situation, it is exremely unlikely to be made public. If the child realises what is happening she/he is unlikely to have the power or knowledge to make it public. And if she/he were to do so, society's response is likely to be more harmful to her stability and personal relationships then letting the situation continue — so what can be done?

Some statistics — (from Brownmiller)*
Dr. Charles Hayman's Washington study revealed that 12% of rape victims brought to D.C. General Hospital were aged 12 or under. Brenda Brown's study of rapes reported to the Memphis police showed that 6% of all victims were aged 12 and under. Amir's study of reported rapes found that 8% were aged 10 and under, and 24% 14 and under. In 1969 the Children's division of the Humane Association, led by Vincent de Francis, investigated adult sex crimes against children in Brooklyn and the Bronx. Amongst their major findings were:—

1. The sexually abused child is statistically more prevalent than the physically abused, or battered child.
2. The median age for abuse is 11, but infants have not escaped molestation.

---

* Susan Brownmiller, Against Our Will, Penguin 1976, first published U.S.A. Martin Secker & Warburg 1975.

3. 10 girls are molested for every one boy.
4. 97% of the offenders are male.
5. In ¾ of the cases the offender was known to the child or her family.
6. In more than 40% of the cases the sexual abuse was not a single isolated event but occurred over a period of time that ranged from weeks to 7 years.
7. Force or the threat of force was used against 60% of the children. Another 15% were enticed by money or gifts. For the remaining ¼ the lure was more subtle and was based on the child's natural loyalty and affection for a relative or near-relative.

Cases frequently never reached court because of lack of corroboration of the victim's testimony or because a parent withdrew the complaint to avoid 'embarrassment' to the family. Brownmiller provides facts and figures from other surveys which support the findings of this one.

Reading about child abuse, one thing which constantly emerges is the similarity of attitudes towards children and women who are sexually abused. Police and court officials are reluctant to believe the testimony of women and even more so of children. (Brownmiller cites a particularly revolting case of a 3 year old girl — nobody would believe her word against that of a 'respectable' man, although such a young child could never have invented the details she described.)

On the surface, public morality is outraged by the sexual abuse of children — even amongst prison inmates child molesters are seen as 'the lowest of the low', and treated with contempt by their fellow prisoners. Closer investigation, however, reveals that child molesters are stereotyped (dirty old men in raincoats, or, more recently, nice, timid men who are unable to form satisfactory relationships and are therefore to be pitied). This is how, of course, all 'ordinary' rapists are typified (strangers in dark alleys, psychopaths, etc.), yet surveys of offenders (de Francis, Gebherd, etc., all cited in Brownmiller) reveal, as with all rapists, that there is little if anything to distinguish the 'typical' child molester from any average man. Again, stereotypes are invented to disguise the truth — any man is a potential rapist or child abuser, and the average child probably has more to fear from Uncle Fred than from the stranger who offers her a ride in his car.

We can see the arrogant male assertion that 'children enjoy it' (c.f. 'women enjoy it') in this quote from Kinsey ('Sexual Relations in the Human Female') when trying to explain to his own satisfaction that ¼ of the women he interviewed had reported an unwanted preadolescent sexual experience of some sort with an adult male. "It is difficult to understand why a child, except for its cultural conditioning, should be disturbed by having its genitalia touched, or disturbed by seeing the genitalia of another person . . . Some of the more experienced students of juvenile problems have come to believe that the emotional reactions of the parents, police and other adults . . . may disturb the child more seriously than the contacts themselves".

Whilst there is no doubt that children, like raped women, are put through a terrible ordeal by the authorities investigating a case of this kind, and indeed some parents may react against the sexual abuse from a totally different standpoint from that which most of us are likely to adopt, Kinsey's comment is typical of male advocates of the 'permissive society' — 'Well, don't we all accept nowadays that sex is fun and enjoyable, and women and children enjoy it as much as men, so what's all the fuss about?' No mention of choice, mutuality — women (or children) enjoying sex is once again taken to mean being all the more available for men whenever *they* feel like it. Kinsey goes on to say, 'The current hysteria over sex offenders may well have serious effects on the ability of many of these children to work out sexual adjustments some years later in their marriages' — could not this 'inability' be a very positive rejection of the unequal power relationships which exist at present in conventional heterosexual relationships?

As with women who are raped, blame is frequently attached to the victim. Just as it is a woman's 'fault' if she gets raped, Freudian psychoanalytic theory frequently pinpoints the child's 'seductive' behaviour. Freud himself declared that most disturbing reports of childhood assault were fantasies that the child contrived as a defence against her own genital pleasure and her guilty wish to sleep with her father. The similarities are clear; like women, children want to be raped, enjoy being raped, 'ask for it' — little wonder that both adults and children who are raped may be filled with guilt for years to come, like the little girl in Brownmiller who was so disturbed by the court case, imprisonment and subsequent release of her assailant that she did not speak for many years.

Probably the most difficult problem of all in analysing the sexual abuse of children is distinguishing between mutuality and coercion in adult/child relationships, as the debate around paedophilia has shown. To quote Brownmiller, "The unholy silence that surrounds the interfamily sexual abuse of children and prevents a realistic appraisal of its true incidence and meaning is rooted in the same patriarchal philosophy of sexual private property that shaped and determined historic male attitudes towards rape. For if a woman was man's original corporate property, then children were, and are, a wholly owned subsidiary."

Without a clear perspective and analysis, feminism can easily bear many apparent resemblances to Victorian morality. Just as we are easily associated with Mary Whitehouse in our campaigns against pornography, so we may be seen as sexually 'unliberated' if we oppose statements such as those of Kinsey which I quoted earlier. Thus it seems more and more essential that we work out our theories and make them explicit — that we oppose pornography because it degrades women, not because we dislike sex, that we oppose sex without consent in marriage because we are opposed to an institution which supports and maintains male power over women, that we want to bring incest into the open and fight it, not because we feel that the innocence of children must be protected from all knowledge and experience of sex, but because we gravely doubt the mutuality of most relations between adults and children, given the almost total powerlessness of children within the family and society at large.

The more I think and write about these issues, the more impossible it seems to deal with any of them in isolation. We will never get rid of rape in a society which retains male-dominated institutions like marriage, we will never stop the sexual abuse of children while children remain the most totally owned, possessed and dominated of all human beings. While male dominance continues, so will sexual coercion and violence — nothing short of feminist revolution can do more than patch up the cracks.

. . . . . .

This article originally came from notes written by Jill and a discussion in the Nottingham group.

Women from Nottingham Rape Crisis Group

BEST KEPT SECRET?

Recently, the sexual abuse of children, particularly within the family, has become recognised as a major area of sexual violence and coercion perpetrated at the very heart of our society. Work done in the USA and this country has exploded the myths about "incest" and created a situation where we can no longer ignore society's "best kept secret".

Two recent incidents stand out in my mind. Two men in a car pass a group of three girls playing in the street where I live. The men lean out, make obscene gestures and remarks. The girls are silent, disturbed, puzzled. The men in this incident were perhaps 30. The girls were 6 or 7.

A group of 14/15 year olds did a series of impromptu plays at the girls' night where I work. Of 4/5 plays every one focused on violence — usually in the home.

Over the past 2 years I have been reading and thinking about incestuous assault or more appropriately the sexual abuse of children. "Incest" is defined as sexual contact between blood related persons — incestuous assault describes more clearly what the "contact" is i.e. an assault by an adult male on a female child. 97% of reported offenders are adult males, 87% of child victims are female. Court cases involving incest offences reveal that 90% involve fathers and daughters, stepfathers and stepdaughters, grandfathers and grand-daughters. Of the remaining 10%, half were assaults by fathers on sons.

It seems appropriate to raise this issue in the context of working with girls. Why is it an issue for youth workers?

We are not expected to deal with it, and mostly we don't expect it. It's a specialised, isolated problem best dealt with by social workers and police. No young person we work with has even mentioned incest as a problem for them.

The reality is that the sexual abuse of children is our society's best kept secret. Figures gathered in 1969 in the USA estimate that, on the basis of ten million victims, one in every ten women is/has been sexually assaulted. If the category is widened to include sexual abuse by non blood relatives (marriage related adults, parents' friends, next door neighbours, teachers, etc.), the estimate is that one in four women are sexually abused by the age of 18; current American estimates are that there are *25 million* victims of incestuous assault in the USA today. As far as I know no one has even attempted to count the number of girls and young women who are sexually abused in a more general sense. Realistically, sexual abuse in one form or another is a common experience for all young women. "But it's never come up in my work." I am sure I am not alone in hearing throw-away comments from young women about so-and-so's father, not wanting to go to so-and-so's house, not baby-sitting for *him*, this or that teacher at school or this or that youth worker ... I'm definitely not alone in not taking these comments up, or in assuming it's not serious. Many factors prevent us from even thinking about, let alone taking up these issues.

Assumptions about what "incest" or sexual abuse is, and what sort of family/community it occurs in, are the biggest block. Most people who write about, and research this issue report having to re-adjust their assumptions about poor, overcrowded, deprived families and sexually provocative, enticing children in order to be able to recognise that sexual abuse is, as one writer puts it, "relentlessly democratic". It occurs in 'normal' families and communities, regardless of class, race, family size, attractiveness — even age. Children assaulted can be any age and the assault can go on for an average period of 7 years.

Perhaps what makes us most unwilling to recognise that sexual abuse not only exists but is widespread is that it forces us to see that "incest" is integral to "normal family life". It is the man's position in the family, 'as head of the household' and with unquestioned rights of access to his children and other family members, that produces the very situation where incestuous assault can occur and continue. A man's home is his castle, and God help you if you try to intervene. The family, rather than being a safe and protected place, is in fact one of the most dangerous places female children (and women) can be. And none of us want to admit that.

Partly because of this, "professionals", the police and the general public want to believe that the girl is responsible, that she led him on, that she enjoyed the relationship, and in today's social work view, that it is often more damaging to stop the relationship than to allow it to continue.

There is absolutely no evidence — nor indeed can there be — that sexual abuse is initiated by the girl, enjoyed by her or in any sense her responsibility. It is surely an indictment of our society's concern to protect the adult male regardless of the cost to girls and women, that girls as young as 5 or 6 have to defend themselves against the accusation of encouraging their father (or other adult males) to force them to engage in sex. Instigating and continuing a sexual relationship with a child who is absolutely powerless to do anything to prevent it, and who is not even able to understand what is happening to her, is the responsibility of the adult regardless of the situation. The defining characteristic of sexual abuse is that the adult male is known to her, trusted by her (75% of *all* reported sexual abuse). Estimates vary between 50% — 90% of cases not being reported — and the evidence suggests the higher figure. Even when discovered, adults are far more willing to report abuse by a stranger than a family member. How can a girl who is being abused by her father say no? She does not even know what she is saying no to. She is expected to obey her father, she needs love and attention from him, and she is often told by him this is a normal relationship for fathers and daughters. At the same time, she is told not to tell anyone, and therefore has to bear the burden of guilt and confusion — usually in silence. Abuse often begins with sexual touching at a very young age and then develops to intercourse (rape) as the girl matures. She is made to feel that she has somehow allowed it to continue and if she does tell, the most immediate reaction is — well, after all these years, she must have enjoyed it if she let it go on for so long.

What is clear is that the effects of being sexually abused

are devastating and long lasting. While many convicted aggressors do not express any awareness of having done anything wrong. The sexually abused girl bears the guilt of having been used, and not having been able to prevent this and then being subjected to cross examination, medical examinations, being removed from home into care, being classified as being in moral danger and ultimately feeling responsible and being blamed for putting her father behind bars and breaking up the family and its economic support. She feels she is being punished and her guilt is compounded.

Silence — and the fear of the consequences of breaking that silence — is perhaps the major weapon in maintaining the continued sexual abuse of children. Abuse only comes to light if the girl gains the courage to tell someone (or becomes pregnant or contracts VD). In this case she can be ridiculed as immoral before anyone discovers how she contracted VD or became pregnant. Young women can be forced to take the only way out — to run away, only to be returned to home and further abuse or find themselves in equally dangerous situations. The American "Runaway Newsletter" (1975) found sexual abuse to be one of three main reasons for all young people running away. Yet night shelters and other such provisions are usually mixed sex and rarely recognise sexual abuse as a possible reason why young women are there.

Women who have been sexually abused frequently remember being expected to do as adults told them, being unable to get angry with their fathers, and knowing that other people might blame them.

While the access of adult males to children in the family is unquestioned, girls are denied the right to refuse that access. To survive in the most powerless situation of all, they learn to subordinate their needs to others more powerful. Fathers in particular can rely on their daughters' respect and affection, and their dependence on them; consequently sexual abuse is rarely discovered. Saying no is not something we teach female children to do to adult men.

What can we do? Ultimately, recognising sexual abuse depends on your willingness to believe it exists, and on the value you put on girls and what they say. The most common reaction I have found in discussing male violence of any kind with other workers is that it's "a bee in my bonnet" and surely I'm not naive enough to believe what girls say? Well — if we are going to value girls, we must value what they say, and create a situation where they feel able to talk.

It is vital that young women who are being abused have access to an adult woman outside of the family who will listen and take them seriously. Moreover, it is our responsibility to make it known that abuse *is* widespread and that we will listen. Any discussion on violence should include sexual abuse — in most groups there will be a young woman who is being abused. If she breaks the secret then a crisis is inevitable, but we must be clear that we should give her every possible support. Preparation and discussion are vital — women working with girls need to support each other in both examining the issue and dealing with it; if we are taking sexual abuse seriously, we must have discussion on it before it comes up. Tactics need to be well worked out so as to allow the young woman herself to decide what she wants. This could be difficult in that the worker will be aware of criminal assault and may not report it, because in calling the police she can put the girl or her mother in a chain reaction she does not expect and cannot cope with. The consequences of acting must be fully explained — especially since they can be more serious for the abused girl and her family than for the aggressor. If she is over 16 — the age of consent — then the law is framed in such a way as to include criminal liability for her too. But if we do not break the silence we are perpetuating it as we are if we don't create the space for girls to challenge it.

Rape Crisis Centres, Women's Aid groups or other women's groups who have experience in this area can offer support and act as resources but women who have direct contact with girls and young women are perhaps in the best position to offer on-going help and support. Encouraging an abused girl to look for help in her family — mother, aunts, sisters — could be a way forward. If her mother is able to support her she will be the best support she can get. If she claims to "have already told her" check it out, for many girls this could be a vague comment — e.g. referring to "stomach pains" which she feels should be enough but of course isn't. She may need help to find ways of expressing to her mother what is happening. Helping to heal a mother/daughter relationship where the daughter feels betrayed and the mother confused or in danger herself is not our usual line of work — but for us, it could be that the girl's needs *are* more important, if necessary, than the needs of the family unit. What we must be committed to is discovering ways of raising the topic and dealing with sexual abuse. There *are* ways. We cannot go on saying it is too difficult an issue. Because we cannot go on ignoring it.

Anon

This paper was reprinted from Working with Girls Newsletter, No. 6, Nov/Dec 1981. Copies are available from National Association of Youth Clubs, Girls Unit, Keswick House, 30 Peacock Lane, Leicester LE1 59Y.

SEXUAL ABUSE OF CHILDREN

The sexual abuse of children is considered an abhorrent crime by our society — so abhorrent in fact that offenders are unlikely to be convicted for fear of besmirching a respectable man's name.

The sexual abuse of children is in the United Kingdom an offence under the Indecency with Children Act 1960 and also under the Sexual Offences Act 1956 Section 5 — unlawful intercourse with a girl under 13, and Section 6 — unlawful intercourse with a girl under 16. If offenders are convicted they are likely to receive even lighter sentences than in rape cases. If the word of a woman carries little weight and is doubted, that of a child is even more so. As the sexual abuse of children often does not involve penetration, there will only be physical evidence of abuse where the child has become infected by the offender from the close proximity of his genitals to the child's mouth, vagina or anus. Not only does the child have to undergo all the indignity, fear and pain of the attack, she also has to contract venereal disease to prove her case.

If the abuser is a relation of the child, the laws against incestuous sexual relations may also apply. Incest is dealt with also under the Sexual Offences Act 1956 (sections 10 and 11) which state that a man commits incest if he has "sexual intercourse with a woman whom he knows to be his granddaughter, daughter, sister or mother"; incest by a woman of 16 or over is defined as permitting "a man whom she knows to be her grandfather, father, brother or son to have sexual intercourse by her consent". Practically, this means that if a girl is 16 years old or over and complains of sexual abuse by her father, she lays herself open to prosecution, for if the father says that she was willing then she may be prosecuted for committing incest.

The law covering incestuous offences does not cover step-children, the mother's boyfriend, uncles, etc., even though in some cases marriage would be illegal, and such offenders might very likely be in a father role to the girl. Practically, the law in this country makes no provision for the extra trauma, breaking of trust and misuse of parental power which is involved in the incestuous sexual abuse of children, and does not differentiate between incestuous relations between adults and incestuous abuse of children by adults, except in that if a man is convicted of incest against a boy or girl under the age of 18, he may be divested of all authority over the child.

As with rape, the true nature of child abuse is clouded by myths. Offenders are stereotyped as psychotic, or mentally subnormal strangers who tempt children with offers of sweets and rides in cars. If they molest boys, they are stereotyped as homosexual, either unable to relate to adult males or recruiting young boys into homosexuality and probably as only abusing boys.

However, in the majority of reported offences the man is already known to the child (and as men have control over their children, no doubt many cases must go unreported) and the myth which makes children wary and scared of strangers puts them more into the control of the authority figures, giving men more opportunity to abuse them. It also makes mothers more afraid for their children and in particular their daughters (although also their sons) who are more subject to abuse so keeping them more dependent for their protection on the men who are known to them. The men who sexually abuse children may be teachers, friends of the family or relations. In incestuous child abuse (including uncles etc. not legally included) one study by Susan Forward found that father/daughter abuse made up

75% of all reported cases, and she states that her colleagues' estimates of the incidence of incestuous sexual abuse by fathers of girls of *all* families with daughters ranged from 7.5% to 40%.

The portrayal of men who sexually abuse children as insane, mentally sub-normal, or impaired by the use of drugs or alcohol is also unsubstantiated. In fact, according to case studies by Ann Burgess et al., less than 5% showed evidence of psychotic illness except in as far as the abuse itself is seen as symptomatic. But then to say that sexual abusers are psychotic because they sexually abuse says nothing. There is no evidence that I have encountered that shows that offenders are likely to be impaired by either drugs or alcohol.

Girls are much more likely to be molested than boys. According to Brownmiller they are 10 times more likely to be molested. Burgess et al. suggest the difference is smaller; nevertheless it is still large.

Whether the abuse is incestuous or not, age ranges of child abuse go from infancy on into adulthood, with a median age of 11 years. With incestuous sexual abuse in particular, it may continue for several years. There is some evidence that men who sexually abuse children are likely to be specific to the age range of child they molest.

As in rape offences, attempts are made to shift the blame from the offender to the child, by suggesting that children, especially girls, who are molested invite sexual approaches from men by flirting and acting seductively. This presupposes of course that it is normal and acceptable for an adult to react to childish precocity with the full force of adult emotional sexuality despite the fact that the child is unlikely to understand, or be able to cope with such desires. Similarly they also claim, especially in incestuous abuse, where it may have occurred over a period of years, that the child enjoyed the relationship even when it is evident she is profoundly disturbed by the relationship. Surely all of this is just another example of men trying to shift the blame from where it really lies. Even in the cases where the child does behave seductively, is it not likely that she has learnt that this is how she is expected to act, probably from the offender himself?

Molestation of children is generally believed to consist of a single, possibly violent, incident, but in 40% of reported cases, the abuse has been over a period of time, sometimes as long as several years, and as these are cases in which offenders are likely to have greater control of the children concerned, and so of their access to help and/or welfare agencies, the percentage is probably much higher.

Children are taught to obey those who are older than them and those who are placed in authority over them. The person who usually has ultimate authority in the family unit is usually the father; other authority figures are likely to be men. The child knows she is expected to do what others tell her to do, and that if she fails to, the result will be unpleasant. All her experience therefore both as a child and a female, tells her she should co-operate even if she does not wish to. Few children understand the nature of the approach which is being made to them nor the intentions which lie behind a sexual approach, so the natural tendency is to comply.

Children are often enticed into sexual activity not only by offers of sweets and money, etc. but also to the child deprived of love and affection, with the offer of attention and affection from the adult, or with the threat of loss of approval and love by an adult who may be important to the child.

Once the sexual abuse has begun, the man again is at a great psychological advantage to coerce the child to continue. Physical threats are perhaps even more potent to a child than a woman; the child knows that the threats are no empty threats, as she may have been physically abused in the past. The man will demand secrecy from the child, so that not only has the relationship between the child and offender been distorted, but the offender for his own protection initiates a network of secrecy and deceit which disrupts the relationships between the child and other adults and traps the child in a feeling of guilt.

The closer the relationship in emotional terms of the child to the offender the more likely the assault is to cause psychological damage to the child. Not only does she have to contend with the fear of a further attack but a breaking and misuse of trust and dependency by an adult on whom she has relied, as well as a disruption of relationships with other adults because of the secrecy and guilt with which she is forced to comply.

167

A child who has been subject to sexual abuse and especially incestuous sexual abuse is likely to lack self-confidence and consider herself worthless. Susan Forward found that there was a very high incidence of women who had been incestuously abused as children among women with drug problems or who had become prostitutes. Also she found that other men often reacted to a child who had been abused as an appropriate person to abuse themselves, she was seen as no longer a virgin, and therefore as "sexual" and a "slut".

The fact that men who molest boys may also molest girls and are likely to be heterosexual suggests that such a man is unlikely to be acting purely for sexual gratification of his sexual desires. It seems likely that he would be specific as to the sex of the child if this was so. It seems to me that he is trying to assert his authority over the child and demonstrate that the child is under his control. While a girl is most likely to be abused by also being a woman whom he feels he has the right to control, a boy is someone he also feels he has rights over. This is shown by the attitude of offenders who have molested boys. They often describe the child as sexually passive and are frequently horrified by the idea of adult homosexuality, or the idea that their behaviour could in any way be considered as such. Their intentions are the control and suppression of those weaker than themselves by coercion and physical violence if necessary.

Where the offender is living in the child's home or is a relative, she has no escape, nowhere to run to, and the very people whom she would normally turn to for help are either the perpetrator or related to him so that she is afraid to accuse him. So she is trapped in a web of continuing horror with no escape.

Where the offender is the child's father, he may consider her his sexual property, a view which is only an extension of the traditional view that a daughter's virginity was her father's property until he "gave her away" when she married and so any loss of virginity of hers was an offence against him. Presumably if he wishes to take her virginity himself by raping her, this is only an extension of his rights. He just may not be able to get such a good husband for her later.

The reaction of the authorities to a case of incestuous

abuse is that despite what has happened (if they are willing to recognise and admit that anything has happened) it is usually best for the child to return to the control of her father, despite the misuse that has already been made of such control, and that the family should be prevented from breaking up. The desire by society to keep going an institution which has proved detrimental to the children involved can only be to some degree a sanction of the father's actions. The child's behaviour is modelled by that of the adults in whose care she is placed far more than by any other agency. Returning her to the care of an adult who has misused such control can only lead to the further subjection of the child, if not physically then psychologically. Kemp and Kemp say that in the Santa Clara study 90% of marriages where incest had occurred were saved and 95% of children returned to their families but that they had been less successful and had come to feel that these children should not be reunited " . . . Rather the best interests of the child should be served . . . once they have broken the bond of incest, society must not condemn these victims to an additional sentence, but provide loving protection and the support of adults who are better models."

Despite the fact that one of the disrupting elements in incestuous abuse is the strain the child undergoes in having to maintain secrecy from other adults particularly her mother, about the abuse, social agencies insist that even though they have no evidence to prove it the mother must have been aware of it. Once again women get the blame; if she is not accused of abetting or concealing the offence, it is suggested that by not fulfilling the sexual needs of her partner, she is to blame for his having to turn elsewhere. If in future she toes the line and is more willing to fulfil her marital duties, the family will continue as it should do, with her doing his wishes, as and when he wants so that he isn't forced to demonstrate his sexual superiority over his children rather than his wife!

Jane Fitzsimmons

CHILD PORNOGRAPHY

"I do not think it is an accident that the ideal of femininity is fast becoming the infantilized woman", says Florence Rush, former social worker and author of a book on child sexual abuse. "Men are attracted to a woman who has the helplessness of a child. They prefer children, whether they are large size or little size. Today our society either makes the child look like a woman or the woman look like a child".

Child pornography is very big business. According to researchers and reporters, child models are not difficult to recruit: many magazine publishers and film producers use their own children; others advertise to parents. A recent advertisement in Al Goldstein's magazine SCREW offered $200 for young girl-child models. It brought dozens of responses from parents with female children. A writer who followed up the ad reports:

> Some parents appeared in the movie with their children; others merely allowed their children to have sex. One little girl, age 11, who ran crying from the bedroom after being told to have sex with a man of 40 protested, "Mommy, I can't do it". "You have to do it," her mother answered. "We need the money". And of course the little girl did.

The last two years have brought much attention to the growing problem of child pornography, and fairly quick action has been taken by legislatures in our country*. But while protecting our children is an important part of the feminist battle against pornography, educational and legal activity should not stop there. It is easier for us to become outraged by what is happening to young children than by what happens to grown women. We forget that young girls grow up to be women. About the time they reach the age of consent, what protection there is stops and the legalised exploitation starts again.

. . . . . .

* U.S.A.

We do not have a history of taboos against the sexual use of children. Until recently, children were a paternal property and could be legitimately exploited, sold, or even killed by their masters. And since minors were also a sexual property, sex between male adults and children has been sanctioned, or at the very least tolerated, in our institutions of marriage, concubinage, slavery, prostitution, and pornography.

Today we expect the adult world to protect the young from sexual exploitation, but because we have neglected simultaneously to deprive men of their sexual privileges, our prohibitions represent the same confusion as do all laws and attitudes which arise from a double standard. Recently I heard a woman protest the marriage between a man of twenty and a woman of thirty. The bride was a "cradle snatcher", she said. When the protester was reminded of a male friend of seventy who was living with a woman of thirty, she spontaneously approved with "Good for John. I'm glad the old boy still has it in him". This common approbation of sex between young females and older males is also reflected in the law. In 1962 the American Law Institute recommended that the legal age of consent to sex (now between sixteen and eighteen, depending upon the State) be uniformly dropped to age ten. And until recently, the legal age of consent in the State of Delaware was seven; if a man of forty had sex with a child of seven or over, he did so legally.

There is little doubt that men are sexually attracted to children and entrepreneurs and advertisers attempt to capture this market. A good huckster will associate his product with a longed-for desire. Image-makers assure a man that if he uses the right shaving cream, a sexy woman will appear and obligingly demand that he "take it all off". And for those attracted to females of smaller dimensions, our media transform the most nonsexual items into an erotic garden of childish delights. Bell Telephone at one time circulated a picture of a twelve-year-old girl standing on a phone book reaching for something unseen. The caption read, "Are you using your phone book properly?" The message ostensibly instructed that the phone book is for finding numbers rather than adding height, but by posing the little girl with provocatively exposed buttocks the picture made a direct appeal to male sexual interest in little girls. The message was so obvious that a group of women lawyers finally had the picture removed. Today underwear companies have tots and teens modelling "demure briefs" and "sensuous thongs". Caress soap pushes its product with a T-shirt on which the word "Caress" invitingly covers a preteen bosom. In popular periodicals one can find a full-page photograph of a child about eight made up to look like Marilyn Monroe, holding a Teddy Bear, with the captioned promise that Baby Soft Cosmetics will give you that "clean irresistible baby smell grown up enough to be sexy." In the sixties Romania Power (Tyrone's daughter) age fourteen, became the model of high fashion, and Twiggy, the British model, age seventeen, stood five feet six inches, but weighed no more than ninety pounds; small, infantile, and childish was beautiful. Women who shopped at Bloomingdale's and Lord and Taylor could not find clothes long enough to cover their private parts. In the seventies Harper's Bazaar stated: "Just look at the movies. The kids are taking over Hollywood . . . Tatum O'Neal and Jodie Foster are already femme fatales and Chastity Bono is sure to be the tiny terrific of TV land."

But if the little girl is to be a sexual commodity, the rift between common decency on the one hand and male desire and the profit motive on the other must somehow be reconciled. Many devices are used to mitigate this rift. One is the naughty but sophisticated dirty joke. William Burroughs in his book 'Naked Lunch' had one child molester say to another, "May all your troubles be little ones". Weather forecaster Tex Antoine, after hearing a report of the rape of an eight-year-old, quipped: "Confucius say if rape is inevitable, relax and enjoy it." The coast-to-coast show, 'Mary Hartman', made an exhibitionistic flasher grandfather (flashers usually expose themselves to children) both lovable and funny. Another strategy employed to make the sexual use of children more palatable is art — preferably rebellious art. In the late nineteenth and early twentieth centuries, western society was obsessed with the image of the pure, innocent, sexless little girl. Several men of letters and art, who had never before made a political statement, suddenly found a cause. In opposition to her idealistic representation, they portrayed the female child as carnal. Cinderella kept a clean house and Alice in Wonderland had excellent manners, but Lolita was preferred. The prominent photographer O.G.

Rejlander, the painters Jules Pascin and Balthus, and the currently popular photographer David Hamilton have portrayed the female child as either sexually aggressive, wantonly, exuding sex, or depraved and harlot-like.

In Dostoyevsky's 'The Possessed', the downtrodden twelve-year-old Matroysha, first frightened when seduced by Stavrogin, soon becomes an unpleasant aggressor:

> Finally, such a strange thing happened suddenly which I will never forget and which astonished me: the little girl grabbed me around my neck with her arms and suddenly began really kissing me herself. Her face expressed complete delight. I got up almost in indignation — this was all so unpleasant for me, in such a little creature.

And in 'Crime and Punishment', the fifty-year-old paedophile, Svidrigailov, dreamed of a lustful five-year-old:

> There was something shameless and provocative in the quiet childlike face: it was depravity, it was the face of a harlot . . . now both eyes opened wide . . . they laughed . . . there was something infinitely hideous and shocking in that laugh, in those eyes . . . "What, at five years old", muttered Svidrigailov in genuine horror. "What does it mean?" And now she turned to him her little face aglow, holding out her arms.

While Dostoyevsky may have been using the seduction and corruption of children as a symbol of absolute moral degeneracy, nonetheless the frequent use of child sexuality by nineteenth-century authors contributed to the real use, abuse, and sexual manipulations of children.

O. G. Rejlander posed his eleven-year-old model, Charlotte Baker in the nude and semi-nude so that her immature body communicated incongruous adult sexuality. Pascin painted his female children as seductive, cheap, and available. Later Balthus exhibited the immature female body to sharpen erotic reaction, and today the popular photographer David Hamilton has his pubescent and prepubescent models pose vacant-faced and trance-like as they are sexually involved with themselves or each other. The novelist Alain Robbe-Grillet, in admiration of Hamilton's work, describes one Hamilton girl (addressing another) as follows:

173

"She is an idiot. She understands nothing. She sleeps
like an overripe fruit." Then come back toward the
bed and whisper lowly into her ear, saying clearly:
"You are nothing but a little whore, a slut, a damp
meadow, a half-open shell".

In this last decade we've had films like 'Taxi Driver', in
which a twelve-year-old prostitute happily gratifies any male
whim in order to please her loathsome pimp. Jodie Foster,
who played the adolescent prostitute, was so well received
in the role that she soon starred in 'The Little Girl Who Lives
Down the Lane', in which she performed as a thirteen-year-old
bundle of budding sexuality.

And then, of course, there is 'Pretty Baby'. 'Pretty Baby'
is an invention of the French film director Louis Malle. It
tells the story of a twelve-year-old prostitute, Violette, who
was born and raised in a New Orleans brothel in the early
twentieth century. On her twelfth birthday, the child's virginity is auctioned off to the highest bidder. Unaware of any
other existence, Violette takes her initiation into "the life"
with pride and equanimity. When the brothel is closed by
irate citizens, she moves in with the bearded photographer
Bellocq, whom she seduces. Critic Vincent Canby saw the
film as a "parable about life and art" but despite his enthusiasm for "art", he did not seem to care about the skill of
Brooke Shields, the twelve-year-old actress who played the
leading role. "I have no idea whether Brooke Shields can act
in any real sense", he wrote. But to Canby, as well as to
Malle, her skill (or lack of it) was irrelevant. Shields was a sex
object and nothing more. "She has a face that transcends the
need to act," said Canby. Judith Crist, on the other hand,
found 'Pretty Baby' to be visually beautiful but "pointless"
— especially the gratuitous flashing of "the heroine's prepubescent nudity". For all its artistic trappings, I found the
film no more than a pandering to paedophilic interests.

'Pretty Baby' was patterned after an actual child prostitute who lived in an actual brothel. But in the face of hard
evidence that, of the prostitutes who worked in the brothel,
no less than one out of twelve suffered the ravages of
venereal disease, drugs, and bodily abuse, Malle preferred
fantasy to reality and insisted that in this brothel world
there was neither a victim nor a violator. And if a depiction
of a child prostitute can be accomplished without showing

174

a victim or a violator then the statement, however artistic, can be no more than a legitimisation of a man's right to purchase a child for sexual use. The poet Christina Rossetti said of the artist that he paints the female "not as she is but as she fills his dream". And if the artistic creator of the female child refuses to acknowledge the power of one sex over the other and of the mature over the immature, then whether the little girl is fashioned as an objet d'art or a slut by an artist or a hack pornographer, her representation can be nothing more than an insulting reflection of her creator's mind's eye.

And when in the name of humour, art, or the rebellious spirit, sex remains a metaphor for contempt and hostility, the step from humour, art, or the rebellious spirit to pornography is a short, easy one. The illustrator Aubrey Beardsley, Felix Salten, author of Bambi, and Guy de Maupassant all contributed to child pornography.

Aubrey Beardsley in 'Under the Hill' described an orgy in which children pleasured carefree guests. 'The Memoirs of Josephine Mutzenbacher' is attributed to Felix Salten. Josephine, a prepubescent prostitute, shares the details of her profession with her readers:

> I was so worked up by this time that I went off as soon as I felt the head of it entering my vagina. His face was still sober, but he must have gone also as I felt my pussy getting all wet. He remained quiet, always with that grave look. Putting his hands under my ass and pressing me tight to him, with one more shove ... I felt his whole cock entering me. It was a short thick one but ... it was all inside me.

Guy de Maupassant in 'The Colonel's Nieces' has a father assist his son in raping a child. "Give it to her," muttered the father, who was feeling the lad's balls ... "Ain't she a beauty, boy? What a tight little cunt she's got ..."

And if the progression from erotization of children in art and humour to pornography is short, the step from pornographic fantasy to acting out the fantasy as a real-life experience is negligible. Sex biographers such as Casanova, Frank Harris, and the anonymous author of 'My Secret Life' all boasted of seducing children. Casanova suggested that a child could be more easily seduced in the presence of someone she trusted — an older sister perhaps. Harris recommended India "as the happy hunting ground for little girls", and Walter (the main character in 'My Secret Life') found a plentiful supply of "young quims" among the hungry children who wandered the London slums.

The Marquis de Sade, currently resurrected as a philosopher and revolutionary, even in fantasy never inflicted his atrocities upon equals; he reserved his sexual torture for women, children, and members of the lower classes. But if de Sade's life did not match his imagination, it was not for lack of effort. He was finally arrested for sticking young girls with knives, feeding them aphrodisiacs, whipping them, and other such delights.

As our threshold for shock diminishes and we become more and more immune to the dangers of pornography, we conjure up all sorts of rationales to perpetuate this voracious industry. In England in 1966, Pamela Hansford Johnson, who covered the trials of the sex mutilator and murderer of children Ian Brady and his assistant Myra Hindley, was impressed by the fact that over fifty volumes of sadomasochistic material was found in Brady's room with the Marquis de Sade as his major hero. In Johnson's opinion, in mine, and in that of many others, the violence found in pornography is "suggested to us, even urged upon us." George Steiner commented:

"There may be deeper affinities than we as yet understand between the "total freedom" of the uncensored erotic imagination and the total freedom of the sadist. That these two freedoms have emerged in close historical proximity may not be coincidence."

Actual living examples of a connection between criminal sexual assaults against children and pornography are too frequent to ignore. Police records throughout the country carry accounts of adult men and of juvenile offenders who have been found with pornographic material either on their person, in their cars, or in their rooms. Social workers, district attorneys, and police officers are consistently making connections between sexual assaults against children and pornography. Here is a typical example from the San Antonio, Texas, police force:

A 15 year old boy grabbed a 9 year old girl, dragged her

into the brush and was ripping off her clothes. The girl screamed and the youth fled. The next day he was picked up by the police. He admitted that he had done the same thing in Houston, Galveston and now in San Antonio. He said his father kept pornographic pictures in his top dresser drawer and that each time he pored over them the urge would come over him.

And this from Jacksonville, Florida:

We have four felony charges pending in our criminal courts... wherein adults are charged with various sexual offences involving minor children. In each of these four cases... obscene literature and other pornographic materials were used to entice minor children...

. . . . . .

Statistics

The kiddy-porn industry is extremely clandestine. Most statistics therefore are a loose approximation. In my opinion the numbers offered here represent only the tip of the iceberg.

- Of the $2.5 billion porn industry, about $1 billion is from kiddy porn.
- In 1975 Houston police uncovered a warehouse filled with child porn, and among the collection were 15,000 colour slides of children, 1,000 magazines, and thousands of reels of film.
- At Crossroads Store in New York City, a group of investigators found, among the usual displays of Lolli-tots, Moppets, and other kiddy-porn magazines, nineteen films on kiddy porn, and an additional sixteen on incest alone.
- One and a half million children under sixteen are used annually in commercial sex (prostitution or pornography).
- Most runaways can survive only as prostitutes or by posing for pornography. Each year there are one million runaway children whose ages range from eight through eighteen.

- Covenant House in New York City shelters 5,000 runaways each year. Over 2,000 are involved in pornography and prostitution, and of this number 1,000 are under twelve.
- Los Angeles police have estimated that 30,000 children are sexually exploited in Los Angeles alone every year.

. . . . . .

Child pornography is a thriving business. The money is good, easy. As in any other profitable business, pumping out kiddy porn has become routine. Ron Sproat, a writer, who worked in a "porno factory" (until he quit), described the formula he was instructed to use for kiddy porn:

> I was given a guideline. It said: "Emphasis on the innocence of children and the lechery of adults. Boys from six to thirteen and girls from six to fifteen. Emphasize hairlessness, tiny privates, lack of tits."

Until recently, much child porn sold in America was smuggled from abroad, but now most of it originates here. Robin Lloyd, reporter and author of 'For Money or Love', a book on boy prostitution, collected 234 different child-porn magazines, each costing an average of seven dollars. 'Where the Young Ones Are', a sex guide for paedophiliacs, contains a listing of 378 places in fifty-nine cities where the young can be found, and has sold over 70,000 copies.

There are over one million runaways each year, and more often than not they survive by prostitution and posing for the pornography trade. Father Ritter, director of Covenant House, a shelter for runaways in New York City, said, "These children cannot go home, cannot find jobs nor take care of themselves. First they are approached to pose in the nude, and it is a quick progression to engage in sexual acts for movies or in strip joints along Eighth Avenue for $100 for four performances."

What about our anti-obscenity and anti-pornography laws, one might ask? The fact is that anti-obscenity and anti-pornography rulings have existed since the eighteenth-century, but have rarely been enforced, and if enforced at all it was usually for political rather than moral reasons. Actually it was not until the early twentieth century, when women began agitating for sexual equality and the right to control their own bodies and reproductive functions, that obscenity laws were seriously executed. Margaret Sanger and Annie Besant were imprisoned for writing and distributing "obscene" literature on birth control. But while women and some men were persecuted for advocating sexual equality, no one prevented the American and European markets from being flooded with hard-core pornography. Actually men like Henry Miller, Frank Harris, and D.H. Lawrence were innocent victims of censorship. They never favoured female emancipation, and when it became clear that both creative writers and hack pornographers never intended the "sexy" female to be a sexual equal, censorship relaxed.

By the mid-1950s, a series of Supreme Court decisions resulted in progressively lenient attitudes toward sexually explicit material, and in 1970 the Commission on Obscenity and Pornography published a report which concluded that pornography is not harmful, it is even educational, encourages frank discussions between parents and children, releases inhibitions, is not a factor in the causation of crime, and is therefore not a matter of public concern.

But nothing could better illustrate the commission's lack of moral interest than its refusal to deal with the exploitation and victimization of vulnerable children in pornography. The commission reported such gross inaccuracies as "Paedophilia is outside the interests of pornography", or, in referring to stag films, "the taboo against paedophilia remains inviolate", and "the use of prepubescent children is almost nonexistent." It really takes very little research to discover that as soon as the camera was invented, dirty postcards of breastless, hairless children and of pregnant, naked child prostitutes appeared. And from the liberated sixties until today, "avant-garde" publications advertise films entitled 'Infant Love', 'Children and Sex', 'Little Girls' etc., in which one can see spread shots of children from six to thirteen as they perform oral sex. I never even found it necessary to browse in Forty-second Street sex shops for my research. From San Francisco to New York, in every airport, train and bus station, the most respectable bookstores and news-stands carry such titles as 'Uncle Jake and Little Paula', 'The Child Psychiatrist', 'Lust for Little Girls', 'Adults Balling Children', ad nauseam. With little difficulty one can easily obtain 'Lollitots', which introduces Patti, "the most exotic ten-year-old you'll ever meet," or 'Little Girls', which offers pictures of ten- and twelve-year-olds in intercourse with adult males. For forty-five dollars one can purchase a film in living colour and see a nine-year-old getting fucked by two Arab boys, then by an adult.

The commission's ability to ignore child pornography could only stem from a conscious or unconscious determination to tolerate male sexual interest in children and not to interfere in the lucrative child pornography industry. The commission managed to rationalize this determination by assuming that legal restraints on pornography could be justified only by proving bad effects upon the consumers. Admittedly pornography does not harm its all-male consumer population. It harms the items consumed. Unlike hair dyes and cigarettes, the items consumed in pornography are not inanimate objects but live women and children who are degraded and abused in the process. By adopting a "consumer-beware" attitude, however, the commission satisfied itself with the fact that juveniles rarely purchase explicit materials. Therefore, once such materials are labelled "For Adults Only" or "Parental Guidance Recommended", the commission felt its obligation to the young was fulfilled.

Some members of the commission produced studies, testimony and authoritative evidence which proved that pornography was physically dangerous to the young, that it encouraged child molestation and rape, and that it destroyed both the public image and the self-image of children. The commission, however, paid little heed to these protests from a minority of its members, and recommended the repeal of laws restricting the sale of pornography.

By 1973 the Supreme Court abandoned a national standard definition of obscenity, and allowed individual states to establish their own guidelines.

In the name of freedom many jumped on this strange bandwagon, and currently our most progressive and radical elements prefer to defend pornographers rather than to organize against them. Others have argued that if "forbidden fruit" is available, prurient material would soon become boring and interest would wane. Nothing could disprove this more than our current avalanche of child pornography. In 1977 Dr. Judith Densen-Gerber unleashed a crusade against this overwhelming onslaught and quickly discovered that putting this industry out of business was not easy. The Supreme Court ruling which permits communities to determine what is obscene allows individual judges to translate the sexual use of children into a "liberating and educational" experience. The child pornography industry is today in excellent health.

It is estimated that 1.2 million children under sixteen are involved yearly in commercial sex — either prostitution, pornography, or both. Those who have been a part of the struggle for a woman's right to a legal abortion have said that if men could become pregnant abortion would be a sacrament. And if women and children were the prime consumers of pornography and men the objects to be degraded and endangered, would the Commission on Obscenity and Pornography not then have declared pornography to be a crime? I think it would have!

Florence Rush

Paper taken from the collection TAKE BACK THE NIGHT — Women on Pornography edited by Laura Lederer, published by William Morrow and Company, Inc. New York, 1980, with author's permission.

CLITORIDECTOMY

The word *castration* almost always refers to men, but anxious as men appear to be about it, females are much more widely subject to castration. We use the word to refer to clitoridectomy (the removal of the entire clitoris), excision (the removal of the clitoris and the adjacent parts of the labia minora or all the exterior genitalia except the labia majora), and infibulation (excision followed by the sewing of the genitals to obliterate the entrance to the vagina except for a tiny opening). In the testimony on medical crimes, the German women referred to the removal of a woman's uterus and ovaries as castration, but we feel it preferable to use the word for the destruction of our sexuality.

The following testimony from Guinea was not given

personally, but was brought by a group of French women who have been researching this topic for some time.

Witness: Guinea

There was a wall around the place where we lived, from which you could see the big baths where women and men came to wash. It was there that one day I saw myself the savage mutilation that is inflicted on the women of my country between the ages of 10 and 12, that is, a year before their puberty. F. was stretched out on the pebbles on the ground. There were six women surrounding her; the eldest, the woman who was to do the excision (the exciseuse), was of her own family. F. was being firmly held down by the women, who held her legs apart and made every effort to keep her still despite the desperate convulsions of her body.

The operation was done without any anaesthetic, with no regard for hygiene, or precautions of any sort. With the broken neck of a bottle, the woman banged down hard, cutting into the upper part of my friend's genitalia so as to make as wide a cut as possible, since "an incomplete excision does not constitute a sufficient guarantee against profligacy in girls."

The blunt glass of the bottle did not cut deeply enough into my friend's genitals and the exciseuse had to do it several more times. The blood gushed, my friend cried out, and the prayers being intoned could not drown her screams. When the clitoris had been ripped out, the women howled with joy, and forced my friend to get up despite a streaming haemorrhage, to parade her through the town. Dressed in a white loin cloth, her breats bare, (although prior to excision women never appear bare in public,) she walked with difficulty.

Behind her a dozen or so women, young and not so young, were singing to the accompaniment of an instrument made of rings of gourd. They were informing the village that my friend was ready for marriage. In Guinea, in fact, no man marries a woman who has not been excised and who is not a virgin, with rare exceptions.

The wound takes two or three weeks to heal, and is horribly painful. My friend screamed every time she urinated. To alleviate the pain she carried a little jug of water with her which she poured on herself as she urinated. She was lucky enough not to suffer complications; infection and painful side-effects due to the cutting of the urinary tract or the perineum frequently occur.

Among some of my friends a "nevrome" formed at the point where the nerve had been cut. The nevrome sets off flashing pains similar to those felt with amputated limbs.

In my country, Guinea, 85% of the women are *today* excised and my country is said to be progressive. Clitoridectomy is practised in the Yemen, Saudi Arabia, Ethiopia, Sudan, Egypt, Iraq, Jordan, Syria, the Ivory Coast, among the Dogons of the Niger, the Mendingos of Mali, the Toucouleu in the north of Senegal and the Peuls, and among many other African tribes.

I would like to add that in some other countries this savage mutilation is not enough; it is also necessary to sew the woman up in order to really dispossess her of her body. After having cut without the benefit of anaesthetic part of the large lips are brought together by piercing them with pins. This way they grow together except for a space for the passage of blood and urine.

The young wife, before her wedding night, must have it re-opened with a razor. Her husband can, moreover, insist on having his wife sewn up again if he is thinking of leaving her.

I appeal to the solidarity of women to make their dignity as human beings recognised. I appeal to the solidarity of women to end patriarchal oppression and violence founded on fear and hatred of our bodies. I appeal to the solidarity of women to end these barbaric mutilations.

Testimony given at the International Tribunal on Crimes Against Women, Brussels 1976.
F.A.S.T. (Feminists Against Sexual Terrorism) Issue 4, page 9.

THE THINGS THEY SAY —
AND UNFORTUNATELY BELIEVE

I am doing research into the long term effects of rape, incest and domestic violence on women's lives. I spent many months wading through all the literature and past research. Little was written on either domestic violence or rape until the late 60's and early 70's, and for both of these there is a feminist analysis and research informed by feminism.

Incest is very different. It is only recently that feminists have begun to talk and write about incest, and it is only in the last year that any actions have taken place. In psychology type journals there is a long history of articles about incest. Many of these use a few cases seen in private practice to develop a theory about why incest happens, what its effects are and how to 'treat' it. I thought women might be interested in having some quotes from this literature — and these are by no means the worst!

In the earlier writings (up to the 60's) girls were often blamed for being 'precocious' or 'seductive'. This theme is still around but is less blatant. The most common theme, and particularly since the 60's, is the blaming of mothers. They are 'the silent partner', 'colluding', and even in some writing seen as 'setting up' the incest. This is either because they want to 'abandon' their role or responsibilities, or in the more Freudian papers as a 'revenge' because they feel deprived by their own mothers. The fact that there has been no research to date which looks specifically at mothers' feelings/reactions to incest does not prevent 'the experts' making statements that appear to be based on facts.

Very little comment is made about the fathers/men who have assaulted the girls, other than to mention factors that make their behaviour 'understandable' e.g. unemployment, stress, alcohol, immaturity, their wife refusing sex or being 'unavailable' (because of illness, death or shift work). References are quite often made in passing to the fact that these men are seen as 'family tyrants' or even 'patriarchs' and that they are often violent to other family members, but this is seen as irrelevant to incest.

Most of the early research, despite being based on very few cases, has been accepted unquestioningly by later writers. Thus ideas and even whole phrases are passed down the years and come to appear as 'the truth' in relation to each new set of cases. Later writing is sometimes slightly more subtle but the basic message is still the same. I hope you find a good use for some of these!!!

Incest Generally

1966 — Lustig — 'Incest: a Family Group Survival Pattern' (based on 6 cases) — this article is referred to very often and the underlined sentence appears over and over again in later work:

"We view incest as one of many socially deviant behaviour patterns which may be employed by a dysfunctional family in the maintenance of its own integrity" (p.32). Note that the title of the paper calls incest a 'family survival pattern'.

"Despite the overt culpability of the fathers, we were impressed with their psychological passivity in the transactions leading to incest. The mother appeared to be the cornerstone in the pathological family system" (p.39).

These jokes appeared recently (1979) in a book by Justice and Justice, to show how incest is culturally accepted amongst certain groups:

- "Incest is fine — so long as it's kept in the family.
- Incest — it's relative.
- Incest — a game the whole family can play.
- A virgin is a five year old girl who can outrun her puppy or her brothers.
- A virgin — a 14 year old girl who doesn't have a brother."

1979 — Shelton — 'A Study of Incest' (based on 13 cases from private practice) "the uproar is usually so great after the crime comes to light that none of the parties seem to wish to repeat the performance".

1979 — R. Geiser — 'Hidden Victims' (no information on cases, mainly a review). This is meant (I assume!) to be a sarcastic comment — its tastelessness and offensiveness to women is obvious — written by a man of course.

"If you are contemplating rape (and the majority of rapes are planned) be sure to check the statutory penalties for this crime in your state. Usually the most severe penalties are reserved for raping your neighbour's wife (20 years to life). The punishment is less severe (up to 10 years) for raping your neighbour's child. The penalty is even less (up to 5 years) for raping your own child. If this offends you, try raping your wife, in most states this is not considered a criminal offence at all."

Daughters/Girls

1955 — Weiss — 'A Study of Girl Sex Victims' (73 cases of sexual assault). The phrase 'participant victim' is often used and it implies some active involvement by the women/girls who were assaulted. In this research 'participant' is defined as more than one sexual assault i.e. multiple incidents with the same man, and that the man is known to the girl. It has very little reference to the girl's behaviour or feelings, but it implies them. It reverses what we know to be true, that a known adult has greater access and authority/trust in relation to the girl, and he is therefore more able to assault her repeatedly. These same facts are instead used to imply that the girl was involved and that because it happened more than once she consented. This way of seeing sexual assault affects the research throughout.

"The typical participant victim, as was noted by Bender and Blau, is often very attractive and appealing. She establishes a superficial relationship with the psychiatrist almost immediately. She does not hesitate to enter the playroom and, once there, she is more interested in the psychiatrist than the playroom toys. She may behave with the male psychiatrist as if he is an exalted authority, she may be submissive or sexually seductive with him, or she may attempt to win him masochistically by humiliating herself in order to get pity" (p.4).

I could write a whole page about all the assumptions and biases in this one quote let alone all the rest of the article — in order not to complicate the research they did not do a similar analysis of the 'accidental victims' (one assault by a stranger) there were too few of them!

1967 — Raphling — 'Incest' (based on one family, three generations of incest).
"In other psychoanalytic studies it was found that the

daughter's oral search for the maternal object leads to an over-estimation of the value of the penis which she does not possess. The daughter then incorporates the father's penis as a substitute for the mother's breasts which she has been denied" (p.506).

What can you say?

1967 — Medlicott — 'Parent/Child Incest' (27 cases, 17 'proved', 10 'alleged'). This is a comment on the effects on girls/women of incest:

"With or without obvious homosexual problems, penis envy with either masculine identification or strong antagonism to men and castrating impulses was a feature in seven of these patients" (p.184).

Of course these are seen as negative over-reactions resulting from penis envy rather than the effects of incest itself, and psychiatry must help them overcome homosexuality or antagonism to men.

1977 — Gutheil and Avery — 'Multiple Overt Incest' (one case study).

"The daughters although appearing precocious and mature are in fact oral-dependent characters with marked confusion regarding their identity. They turn to father to compensate for their deficient mothering and in some cases in a spirit of revenge against withholding mothers. A common fantasy is that they have been rejected because they lack a penis" (p.114).

Penis envy comes up fairly often in these papers yet in all the case histories presented there is not one remark by a girl that has any reference to it. Of course the medical profession has always known what we think better than we do ourselves.

And last but not least our own friend — this is from BAPSCAN News (a society for those working on child abuse) in a report of a talk given by Erin Pizzey at a study day on sexual abuse in 1980.

"It was helpful to be reminded how sexually provocative children can be and how easily they can become sexually aroused — children who are the victims of sexual abuse may only feel themselves to be real people when sexually aroused".

Mothers

1962 — Cormier — 'Psychodynamics of Father/Daughter Incest' (27 men offenders). This is a much quoted paper.

"We found a certain number were not frigid, but hostile and unloving wives. Some never denied their husbands and were described by them as good wives, but the relationship was ungratifying because of the inability of the wives to respond. Others were passive submissive women to the point that they were unable to stand up against the husband, even in known incest situations" (p.207).

Needless to say this is all based on what the men say about their wives.

Time and again mothers are blamed for all sorts of reasons — they are too independent/too submissive, they don't meet the needs of their husband (usually described in sexual terms) or their daughter (usually seen in terms of time and affection). The man's 'need' for sex is never questioned, nor is the sexual relationship between husband and wife. The possibility that she may be refusing him because he has been coercive in the past is ignored. It is considered an automatic reaction to the mother's actions that father and daughter turn to one another, and equally automatic that this is a sexual involvement. The fact that the needs they refer to in relation to the daughter are obviously emotional and not sexual is conveniently ignored. The needs of mothers are NEVER mentioned — not surprising really when we don't have any and if we do then that means we are too demanding so it's our fault again.

1966 — Lustig (see above).
"particularly amongst the mothers, whose defensive operations were rigidly geared to protect them from confronting their inadequacy as women" (p.36).

1967 — Matchotka — 'Incest as a Family Affair' (13 cases). The title says it all!

"The liaison is made possible and later perpetuated by the collusion of several family members: father-daughter incest typically results from the mother pushing the daughter into adult responsibility; the mother is dependent and infantile and reverses the mother/daughter role with the daughter. Thus assuming with her daughter the relationship she would have wished to have with her own rejecting mother. The mother generally feels worthless as a mother and as a woman; sometimes she encourages intimacy between father and daughter directly; her collusion is made possible by her very strong denial of the incestuous relation; in effect she is the cornerstone of the pathological family system" (p.99-100). There's that phrase again, and . . .

"Refusal to have intercourse with one's husband . . . setting up one's daughter's bedroom next to the husband's . . . requiring the daughter to take over household duties . . . being absent from the house . . . all are covert but unambiguous messages to both the husband and to the daughter that the daughter is to assume some of the functions normally exercised by the wife" (p.110).

This type of remark is extremely common, in this case it was based on three families and the examples of the 'messages' were only present in one. It is assumed that these factors make men having sex with their daughters understandable. Little questions like how many families have houses where their daughter's bedroom will not be next to their father's, how many mothers can be in the house all the time, how many girls are not encouraged at some point in growing up to help with household chores and childcare are ignored. What in the literature on incest is seen as 'role reversal' would in the literature on the family be seen as socializing the daughter for her later role. Most elder daughters will be expected to take some form of responsibility in the household, it is part of the expectation that women are responsible for domestic servicing, this will be particularly so if the mother is ill, in hospital or working full time. It would seem that these writers assume that whoever does the housework will be seen by the man as available sexually.

1967 – Raphling (see above).
"she places her daughter in the most difficult position of assuming the role of wife and lover with her own father, thereby absolving herself of this unwanted role" (p.505).

1968 – Eist and Mandel – 'Family Treatment of Ongoing Incest' (1 case).

"Rather than stimulating her husband's violence and vituperativeness in an attempt to avoid closeness, she began to be more accepting of her wifely and maternal responsibilities. Her husband's rages diminished and she became increasingly involved with him, both socially and sexually" (p.227).

Note that this woman is also blamed for being beaten. I have a suspicion that much of the treatment in incest cases consists of making a woman change and accept more of her husband's demands i.e. his power is reasserted over her, and validated by professionals.

1975 — Sarles — 'Incest' (8 cases).

"The most striking finding concerning the wives of incestuous fathers is their knowledge of and collusion in the incestuous affair. A synthesis of data from the literature shows that in almost every case the wife promoted the incestuous relationship by abandoning their husbands sexually, or by actively altering the living arrangements to foster incest" (p.637).

Here we have the one case in Matchotka of moving bedrooms becoming a common occurrence and the assumption that appears over and over again, that by refusing sex women in some sense give permission for incest to happen. The message is clear that if women refuse sex then they will pay for it one way or another.

1979 — Justice and Justice — 'The Broken Taboo' (112 cases).

"He often has little to do with his wife, who has long ago retreated from him sexually and emotionally and has tacitly moved the daughter into the role of wife . . . She (the mother) keeps herself tired and worn out . . . she feels both economically and emotionally dependent and is therefore frightened to assert herself".

This last remark is one of the few attempts to look at the actual position of mothers in the family. In the context it is written, however, it becomes almost meaningless. Women's right to refuse sex, their right to autonomy, their need for affection and emotional support are never referred to. And finally from the same book . . .

"Other mothers go into hospital setting up the final conditions for incest to occur . . . some mothers set up the opportunity by starting to work at night, others go to play cards or visit friends".

How dare they go into hospital, work, have friends of their own — they ought to know that men cannot be trusted to ignore these opportunities. Basically anything a woman does can be used against her and seen as contributing to incest.

Mothers and Daughters

1975 — Desen-Gerber — 'Incest as a Causative Factor in Antisocial Behaviour' (118 girls in a rehabilitation project for drug addicts).

"the absence of a strong female figure who can protest, may ultimately be more damaging than violation by a man".

If a man had not assaulted her then she would not have needed protecting.

1977 — Gutheil — (see above).

"Rather than face the issue of the mother's failure in the nurturant role, the women resorted to a 'sexist' defence of deploring the father's failure to provide care. Even though the mother could briefly acknowledge that her husband turned to her daughters for what she had refused him, the daughters could not pursue this theme; all their anger was instead focused on the father. The women thus denied the previously established consensus that incest was a family phenomenon involving all the members in their common repugnance of separation. Father was made to appear the only entitled one, who had hurt everyone. Having made the father the culprit, mother angrily revenged herself on both him and the male therapist by summarily deciding to take the children and flee after the 22nd session. We felt this flight represented an acting out of long deferred anger against her own mother's failure to nurture and subsequently separate from her own growing daughters" (p.112).
daughters" (p.112).

What they mean to say is that it had nothing to do with the fact that they wouldn't listen to what these three women had to say — their method and theory are fine, it's just these crazy women who think they know better and cannot understand what incest is really about.

191

1967 — Medlicott — (see above). This paper includes 3 cases of father/son incest with 24 father/daughter cases.

"It is extremely doubtful if any of the fathers of these three patients had proper appreciation of what they were doing to their sons, and one suspects that their seduction of their wives' cherished sons was part of a battle going on between themselves and their wives" (p.185).

No such concern was voiced for the girls and this clearly reflects the relative value of men and women, and also that father/daughter incest does not in its practice (although it may in its effects on women later) threaten heterosexuality.

1972 — Oliven — 'Sexual Deviance' (a review).

"the fathers tended to be passive, immature individuals, sometimes highly susceptible to seduction" (p.94).

1978 — Summit and Kryso — 'Sexual Abuse of Children — a Clinical Spectrum' (based on a variety of sources and private practice).

"A father should be harmless to flirt with. He should be approving, admiring and responsive to her growing sexual attraction and he should provide a controlled, self-limiting prototype of the sexual experiences she will develop with other men as an adult ... Through inheritance and conditioning she has become an uncanny likeness of the girl who once spurred him to greater accomplishments, who made him feel strong and loved, who excited him in unquestioned potency and virility" (p.243).

What little there is written on men attempts like the above to explain why they did it, so that we can understand and feel sorry for them. In contrast the attitude to mothers is usually that of making them responsible, and sometimes this responsibility extends to the daughter too. There are no doubt complex issues surrounding father/daughter incest between mothers and daughters, but the idea that mothers always know and in many cases consciously permit it to happen are myths created by researchers and based on very few cases. These ideas have been repeated in later articles and have become 'the truth' about mothers. In a sense it's not surprising since most of the early research was based on psychoanalytic concepts and written by therapists, psychologists etc., and we know what the majority of them thought, and still think, about women.

I can only describe the majority of the research/writing on incest as misogynist and the last quote sums it up.

1975 — Walters — 'Physical and Sexual Abuse of Children' — (mainly a review).

"some wives were very unattractive as women, homemakers and human beings" (p.123).

Liz Kelly, July 1982
(slightly revised version)

REFERENCES

B. Cormier et al (1962) 'Psychodynamics of father-daughter incest', Canadian Psychiatric Journal Vol. 7(5) 203-217

J. Denson-Gerber and J. Benward (1975) 'Incest as a Causative Factor in Antisocial Behaviour: an exploratory study', New York, Oddessey Institute.

H. Eist and A. Mandel (1966) 'Family Treatment of Ongoing Incest', Family Process Vol. 7, 216-232.

R. Geiser (1979) 'Hidden Victims: the Sexual Abuse of Children', Boston, Beacon Press.

T. Gutheil and N. Avery (1977) 'Multiple Overt Incest as a Family Defence Against Loss', Family Process, Vol. 16(1), 105-116.

B. and R. Justice (1979) 'The Broken Taboo: Sex in the Family', New York, Human Sciences Press.

N. Lustig et al (1966) 'Incest: a Family Group Survival Pattern', Archives of General Psychiatry, Vol.14, 31-40.

P. Matchotka et al (1967) 'Incest as a Family Affair', Family Process, Vol. 6(1) 98-116.

R. Medlicott (1967) 'Parent/Child Incest', Australia and New Zealand Journal of Psychiatry, Vol. 1, 180-187.

D. Raphling et al (1967) 'Incest', Archives of General Psychiatry, Vol. 16, 505-511.

R. Sarles (1975) 'Incest', Pediatrics Clinics of North America, Vol. 22, 633-642.

W. Shelton (1975) 'A Study of Incest', International Journal of Offender Therapy, Vol. 19, 153-193.

R. Summitt and J. Kryso (1978) 'Sexual Abuse of Children: A Clinical Spectrum', American Journal of Orthopsychiatry, Vol. 48(2) 237-251.

D. Walters (1975) 'The Physical and Sexual Abuse of Children', Bloomington, Indiana University Press.

J. Weiss et al (1955) 'A Study of Girl Sex Victims', Psychiatric Quarterly, Vol. 29(1), 1-27.

INCEST AS AN EVERYDAY EVENT IN THE
NORMAL FAMILY

This paper is about incestuous relationships in the 'average' family. We wrote it after talking about our own experiences of sex as children in our group. We are not saying that every girl gets raped by her father or other male relative: none of us in the group recalled being orally, vaginally or anally penetrated by a penis, but *nearly all of us* could remember several incidents with relatives (male) which freaked us out in one way or another (whether we enjoyed them or not). We see this as the subtle sexual abuse of girls.

We don't want to argue that we are in the same position as women who have been severely abused as children, as this would gloss over the specific problems that these women are up against — such as being isolated, stigmatised, and terrorised into silence — not only by men, but also by women who have accepted the view about incest propagated by men and male controlled media and institutions. Let alone the abuse itself.

But on the other hand we don't accept that there are two opposite groups of women: one group who are reared in families where there is absolutely no adult male — young girl sexuality and another minority group who have been grossly sexually abused by male relatives. Apologists for incest frequently argue that it is just normal family affection that has gone a bit too far. Whereas we think that some sort of line should be drawn between a father cuddling his daughter and him sticking his dick in her (quite where one would draw the line is not clear) . . . we do think there is a connection between 'normal' and deviant male behaviour to female children. But incest apologists imply that incest isn't really so bad as it's got a lot in common with 'normal' behaviour. We're saying that 'normal' behaviour isn't really so acceptable.

Here are some of our experiences which came out in consciousness raising sessions . . .

"My grandfather became a dirty old man. No doubt senility played a part, but his actions then caused me to rethink the entire relationship, and recall earlier things. He ruined my

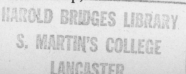

happy childhood memories for ever.

He was at the time badly crippled from arthritis. His hip had never recovered from being broken. His leg was bandaged to the hip.

The district nurse came to change the bandage. I visited him every Sunday. These visits became more and more of a trial. He kept begging me to change the bandage and massage him. 'I dreamed my little girl would do it'. The oil and new bandage would be out waiting. I started insisting that Dad accompany me on these visits. But Dad always managed to leave me alone with Grandad, poor man, at some time during the visit.

Then one day he exposed himself. I rushed out into the garden and sent Dad in. Dad was full of excuses for him. 'Probably it was accidental. I've told him to keep himself covered.' etc. etc. But after then he did stay in the room with me.

After I moved to London Grandad got worse and had to go into hospital. I visited him there with Dad and Uncle John. I specifically told Dad not to leave me alone with him. Right at the end of the visit he did just that. Deliberately leaving me 'to say goodbye to Grandad' on my own, going out with Uncle John. I leaned forward to give Grandad a goodbye peck on the cheek as usual. He grabbed me. What strong arms — from his crutches I suppose — he forced my mouth onto his and stuck his tongue in my mouth. He held me for sometime struggling. He let go and as I reeled back shocked he jeered 'Scared, scared, you're scared' and laughed.

That was the last visit he got. In spite of his subsequent pleading with Dad and Uncle John.

Mum backed my decision. I told her as soon as I got back from the hospital. I also told her of the flashing incident. See, she had broken off with him years before. She never visited him after Gran died. She hated him, so she backed me up when Dad suggested further visits, 'He's only a poor old man,' etc. etc. And I didn't go to the funeral either.

Why should I go and let him mock me? Let him see my fear and need of male protectors. Let him prove that he was still a man (i.e. sexual threat). I hope the old bugger died miserable.

As a little girl I always went for walks with Grandad, and played with Grandad, while Mum and Gran talked. One game I can remember is him tickling me, tickling my legs. I liked that. Mum put a stop to it when I was 9? 10? saying I was "too old" for that now. No explanation was given. Another game I recalled was him and me taking a pee together in the woods. As a child this to me was 'just another of our secrets' . . . things we did that Mum and Gran not approve of. Like stealing turnips from a field, him peeling them and cutting off chunks with his knife. (Eating raw turnip gives you worms, was the theory we were defying.) And him letting me climb trees, even in my Sunday clothes, and playing on stepping stones, covering up for me if I got wet.

I simply would not have remembered things like the 'taking a pee' had it not been for later incidents. Then I did remember one occasion I had looked round at him, and he actually had his trousers down. I remember seeing the white lining men's trousers always used to have, and looking very quickly away. Now I recall other things. Grandad was known for liking all children except boys (to quote Lewis Carroll). And he only liked small girls 'before they became cheeky'. Except for me: me he always loved. But my companions on walks changed over the years; from cousin Ann, to cousin Mary, to cousin Sue, as each one grew too old or 'cheeky' for Grandad. I now recognise a classic paedophile complex.

Another thing, he was an amateur photographer and had the AP interest in porn. Or Art, as he called it. One of his triumphs was to get women who just wanted a portrait picture to end up in an 'art' pose. He took one such of me, aged about 7, semi-draped in a lace curtain and not much else and with a vase on my shoulder (like the biblical Rebecca at the well, in a picture he had). I thought this 'dressing up' was fun. I recall that Mum and Gran did not approve much. But then they approved of so little that that didn't mean anything to me at the time.

I am only glad that his inclinations were held in check till I was in my twenties and he was in his eighties. The pleading for massage, the flashing, and the penetrating kiss sexualised the relationship, or rather showed up the sexual components. Now I can't think of the past, eg. the Rebecca incident, without wondering 'Surely I must have known. Surely I must have encouraged it?' And also, though outsiders could be forgiven for seeing an idyllic Grandad/Grand-daughter picture, 'Surely Mum and Gran must have known. But let it go on, as it got him, and me, out of their hair three times a week.'

Can you see how my happy childhood memories of fun times with my Grandad were totally sullied by his *later* acts?

I can recall no incidents at all with my father. Apart, of course, from his leaving me vulnerable — to cheer up a poor old man."

· · · · · ·

"My father wanted a daughter, after my mother had produced two sons; and it was counted extremely fortunate all round that I was the next child. My father was happy, and my mother didn't have to have any more children.

All through my childhood, a 'special' relationship was built up between my father and myself. This was applauded by the rest of the family. My father was always very loving with me, and very stern with my brothers. I got cuddles and the special privilege of sitting on his knee at the end of a meal; my brothers got disciplined, horse-whipped across the legs. Looking back, I can see that the 'special' status I had was useful to my mother and brothers. My father's foul temper was always likely to explode at any moment, it seemed: so often I would be pushed in his direction to keep him sweet, so we wouldn't have yet another family row at the mealtable (prevention being easier than cure).

When my mother bought me clothes, I had to dress up in them and show them to my father. I always thought that this was so he would be able to OK my mother's use of money, a neat move by her. I still think this was true from her point of view; but it was also a parade, a showing off of the 'potential' female he had produced. Later on, his friends congratulated him on this achievement, and he gained some kind of satisfaction from it, and from his possession of it.

From my present point of view, the physical relationship with my father makes me feel quite queasy — it was really quite different from the other family relationships which never included physical contact. The most powerful male in the family singled me out for his favour by touching and handling me. The 'special' bit cut me off from my mother, in fact it turned me against her. Even now she asks me to talk to my father as a favour to her. I understand why now, but it still feels as though I'm a gift to him. It was such a good introduction to the heterosexual world where I was flattered if a man took special notice of me, but also aware of the incredible *force* that *could* be let loose if I stepped out of line."

. . . . . .

"As a child I used to spend a considerable amount of time with my paternal grandparents. I hated my Grandmother and adored my Grandfather. At the age of 14 I stopped loving my Grandfather because I realised that he didn't see me as a person, merely as a sexual broodmare. Much later, I've thought how the hatred (which still exists) between my Grandmother and me, was caused by him.

When I went to visit my Grandparents, I was always dressed up in exceptionally feminine and frilly clothes. This was to please my Grandfather who would praise the way I looked endlessly. He used to prance me up and down the room, so that he could really 'admire my finery'. I'd gladly dance about and show off and flirt with him and caress his cheeks since this brought rewards — he would call me a 'real little lady' and supposedly treat me like a grown-up (i.e. like a woman). He would behave like a 'gentleman', giving me wine with dinner, discussing the food, serving the liqueur with the coffee, all the while flirting away. No wonder that my Grandmother and I didn't get on. Here was yet another female falling for my Grandfather's 'seductive charm'. He was getting me to behave as a sexual object for him through making me feel grown-up, and hence more powerful. It reminded her of the times he'd left her for other women, leaving her alone with two small children to feed and clothe on no money.

When I was 14 my grandparents came to visit after I hadn't seen them for a while. My Grandfather summoned me to stand in front of him. He told me to turn on the spot so he could see me 'properly'. While feeling a bit peculiar about it, I still complied. "Very nice" he muttered, "Come here and let me look at you" ... I reluctantly moved closer, "Open your mouth and let me see your teeth" ... I just stood there, frozen with fear for a few moments, trying to figure out what it was that seemed so wrong. Then the thought rushed to my mind — "He's treating me just like a horse, they always look at horses' teeth to see if they're good breeding stock." I never talked to him again, unless forced to, and luckily he's now dead.

If my Grandfather hadn't acted in such a blatant way, I think I would have continued to flirt with him and play 'lady' to his 'gentleman'. After all, being placed on a pedestal as a sexual object made me feel powerful. But, I only felt more powerful, because in a society like ours, where men are the ones with actual power, I was a male creation bathing in the glory of my creator."

. . . . . .

"When I was really young I tried to stick my tongue in my father's mouth when he kissed me goodnight: not because I was a juvenile sex cutie — it was just something I had seen on telly — maybe I was trying to act grown up. I knew I'd done something awful when he more or less threw me across the room. Still, imagine what *could* have happened if my father had been more of a child molester. After all, he'd have had every excuse in the world, wouldn't he? (?).

When I was thirteen, I went to stay at my Uncle's for a week, he was my favourite relative, in fact my favourite adult, so I was really pleased that he was even more attentive to me than normal. He started taking me on trips to cafes, dancehalls, and seats in the park that he used to go to when he was a teenager. He would ply me with cigarettes and put his arms round me and tell me not to tell anyone (something I'd got no desire to do — My God would I have got a rocket). I found it all a great adventure, but felt very guilty as I realised I was seeing my uncle almost as a boyfriend. I thought everyone, especially my uncle, would be horrified if they guessed!"

. . . . . .

"When I was about 8 my father, a professional man, often gave me a bath. He told me exciting stories about his life, and afterwards I would sit on his knee while he tickled my back. This I always loved, and still do. Sometimes I can orgasm from it, without any direct genital contact. I did then too, 'tho my memory has blotted out the details. Did he touch more than my back and bottom? How long did it go on? I don't know. At the time I encouraged it, but it was definitely a guilty tho' unspoken secret — my mother mustn't know. She'd smacked me for masturbating when I was younger so I knew it was wrong, more proof of my dirtiness and unworthiness compared to her purity and goodness.

A year or so later we moved house, I went to a new school and completely stopped touching my father. In fact I developed quite a physical horror of him which lasted till his death. Almost blind, crippled with serious illness, he reached out to hold my hand, I stood it for a minute, made some excuse, and withdrew. Guilt, triple guilt. I was very fond of him — so why?

Did more happen? It was the classic situation for incest, I read recently — a girl about 8, middleaged father away a lot, mother and father in separate rooms, and in the bathroom, "the most dangerous place in the house", says Erin Pizzey.

14, out alone with my father, he'd treat me as a grown-up, give me cigarettes to splutter over, take me into all-male "rough" company. My mother would have been shocked and furious. It was exciting, scarey, and a bit creepy.

16 and 17, I had boyfriends, he was huffy, refused to meet them. "It's natural" said my mother. "All fathers are jealous like this."

20, my mother dead, my father and I alone in a hotel on holiday. At the hotel disco the staff asked if that was my husband. *Horror* — how *could* they think it. Cold shivers down my back . . . I didn't tell him.

22, living with a man now, my father says he is "very ugly". Strange remark. My visits home, presented to men in pubs, like an offering up, a sacrifice.

Hitching abroad, I visited a man whose address my father had given me. He made a pass; it was heavy. Indignantly I reported it on return, my father laughed indulgently; "Oh old Bill, he always was like that — I'm not surprised".

Do all fathers turn to alternatively guarding their

daughter's honour, and pimping them out? Cementing male bonding with the female flesh-of-their-flesh?

I certainly think that he fancied me. He admitted that he would have been jealous of any man he thought good enough to be my husband. He never wanted to know of my lesbianism, but I think he was pleased, no more competition — Daddie's girl, forever.

Shortly before he died, I met a woman who was studying incest. How *could* she I wondered. I shuddered at her books, hid them under cushions, left the room when it came up. I mysteriously got a migraine and stayed at home when my Women's Liberation group discussed it and avoided workshops on incest like the plague. After a year, I became able to think why. Slowly, with a lot of help from my lover and other lesbian feminists. I still can't say it easily to friends or at all to strangers. I fight against feeling dirty and disgusting, fear that others will think me so. That I'm covered in filth and creeping slime.

And I remember some years ago, when I was mixing with sexual libertarians. One night I told a few men about the bathroom incident. "Ah" . . . Nods of approval, "he was getting you ready — preparing you — wasn't he? That's really good." *They* knew. Men usually do, whereas women excuse, belittle and hide. Men like this are now involved in looking after young girls."

. . . . . .

We were all surprised at the number of incidents that we remembered. (Only some of them are written down here.) We found ourselves remembering more and more as we talked. But just because we forgot these things doesn't mean that they had no effect on us. Quite the contrary.

We'd all been disturbed by it, whether we'd 'enjoyed' it or not. It wasn't something you talked about — you just suffered in silence and felt guilty: especially if you had enjoyed it or if you felt your own behaviour had contributed to the situation — or maybe it was all in your head baby. We now see this as our training as sex objects for men starting in infancy, before we're old enough to know what's going on, or do anything if we do realise. It's made a lot worse as we're almost completely dependent on our family at that age.

As well as learning to be sex objects for men, we turned against our mothers. We blamed *them* for failure to protect us from these men: at the same time we felt superior to them, as Daddy or whoever *important man* had chosen *us*. Two of us who grew up with educational and middle class privileges, when our mothers didn't, felt this especially strongly.

Some of us also felt reduced to the status of a thing: as our mothers were forced to use us to sweeten up our fathers, as our fathers used us to get at our mothers, as we were presented from one male relative to another like a gift.

This is how girls grow up. Boys do not grow up in the same way. (Studies of child abuse estimate that *10 times* as many girls are abused as boys.) Besides, boys who are abused learn a double message: that they can be abused, but also that they too can abuse, as they too are male. Girls learn a single message — that they are there to be abused because they are female.

Most women grow up in average families such as ours; being isolated, weakened, trained as sex objects for men from an early age, turning against our mothers. The men in these families gain; some of us remember seeing how much our fathers' or uncles' egos were boosted as strangers mistook us for their mistresses. But the effects of these sexy relationships between us and the men in our families are not restricted to the family.

ALL MEN gain from incest, whether it is subtle or grotesquely obvious, whether men live in family type situations or not, whether they themselves have sexual type relationships with girls. As women are made weaker through sexual control and set against each other men become proportionally more powerful.

Some Revolutionary Feminists from Leeds

INCEST AND SILENCE

We are a London-based campaign with nationwide contacts dedicated to breaking the silence that surrounds incest in our society, from its public aspect to its most private. In our paper we want to show how this silence stifles the woman who goes through incest, at every stage of her life, both as an abused child and as an adult survivor. To break free we need to restore that lost communication, since our experiences of male domination and possession are not the exception but the rule: they lie at the heart of all women's oppression. But most of all, we survivors need to speak out to each other. Just talking is for us a political act, as well as a method of personal survival.

1. Taboo

This is the first "Silence" that springs to mind — "a religious horror", the source of many myths and artistic creations which have sidetracked scholars and anthropologists ever since. The works of Levi-Strauss, Freud et al. are a tribute to such moral woolgathering. (Needless to say, the priests, writers and scientists concerned are all men, and the obsession is with the supposed seduction of sons by mothers.) On a more trivial level we have all observed the awkward pauses or paltry witticisms offered by outsiders when the subject is brought up in casual conversation. Pornography, as we know, feeds on taboo and converts it to titillation. . . . To avoid misunderstanding of these kinds we give this definition of our experience:

> ". . . the sexual molestation of a child by any person perceived as a figure of trust or authority — parents, relatives (whether natural or adoptive), family friends, youth leaders and teachers, etc. We see the questions of blood-relationship and taboo as red herrings which obscure the central issue: the irresponsible exploitation of children's ignorance, trust and obedience. Incest is the abuse of power."

The presence of a taboo not only protects the perpetrators, but also allows "Experts" to imagine that incest has been a norm in some societies (Ancient Egyptian Elite, children of Inca chiefs, unspecified "native" tribes). This idea protects them from the truth, *that the norm in ours is Child-Abuse.* We must re-educate our society — make incest an acceptable topic for discussion, much as baby-battering emerged in the late 60's, so that more cases can come to light and be dealt with. Our campaign has made a lot of progress on this score: for details of our media activities see latest newsletter. The most important project we have undertaken so far is a film on Sexual Violence to be distributed to schools by an associate of the Cinema of Women.

2.   Incest as a crime

The greatest public Silence in our society is demonstrated by the weird gaps in British law (see our first report). The inconsistencies here have been well summed up in a recent long article written by the London Rape Crisis Centre, for "Feminists Against Sexual Terrorism" Newsletter. They frequently depend on sexual double standards: in a case we heard of recently a girl of 17 was persuaded by social workers to testify against her father (who had once raped her) in order to strengthen the evidence of her little sister, who was still being abused. The older girl was subsequently prosecuted, for at the age of 16 we are no longer "victims", but "participants".

These injustices and the way they are further distorted by sentences actually given (for disparities between possible and actual terms of imprisonment see elsewhere — not enough room here) seem muddled and various in origin, but they all hinge on the fact that our Incest laws are laws of *property*. The family as it stands is still a safe, legal refuge for petty tyrants who in turn create their own arbitrary "legislation".

The police and social services are the two legal channels through which an abused girl can seek protection: for a discussion of their inadequacy see again the FAST Newsletter. We have ourselves heard from many social workers who are even now perpetuating the Silence; they pass the buck on children in their care rather than face their own powerlessness and fear. One of us had a social worker who, obliged by law to report the incest, preferred to make the girl herself deny the abuse. As for the police, very few of our contacts even got that far, only to meet the usual disbelief dealt out to lying whores and brats like us:

"They gave me bloody hell, laying the guilt on me.
Eight hours of hell."

3. "Treatment"

Prosecutions and police reports represent the tip of the
iceberg: for many more of us incestuous abuse is seen as a
"personal problem", to be dealt with in private therapy. To
date there is only one centre in Britain working specifically
with children who have been sexually abused, and this
involves Family Therapy ... Arrgggghhhhh. The deafness
of the medical profession is profound. Even today, doctors
pass over countless childhood complaints, such as "stomach-
aches" and "bedwetting", without a second thought. Adult
psychiatry still clings desperately to the old Freudian
doctrines, that incest is the product of our own lurid, morbid
fantasy. Even if the therapist can overcome his own terror
and discuss the abuse as a real event, he treats it as a
"relationship" in which we "participated". One of us was
told at the age of 17 that she must be "inviting" her father
to beat her up in some way, if he did it so often. After
some experiment she discovered that the "behaviour pattern"
she had "set up" involved screaming and running away when
he initiated the attack. If she kept quiet and still, his violence
disappeared. The Silence she learnt in this way was hailed
by the therapist as a great step towards the patient's psychological recovery. Another argument therapists may use to
dismiss incest (and their own utter ignorance of it) is the
"past is past" line. This is an insult to our present consciousness of the huge continuum of sexual abuse which surrounds
us, reflecting and repeating our first suffering over and over
again. Even if they silence our social criticisms they cannot
deny our "symptoms": migraines, stomach aches, insomnia,
anorexia, self-destructive neuroses, chronic suicidal depression, above all the nightmares. The constant threatening
presence of the incestuous aggressor is totally internalised
by the child. He poisons us from within, extending his
influence far into our adult lives. Perhaps the nightmares
are the worst of all.

4. Turning to other adults

If a child turns to other adults for help or protection she

may meet the saddest Silence of all. Other men may take further advantage of her, on the "buttered bun" principle common with men who use prostitutes and gang rapists — that responsibility once shared is absolved. Too often the "Experts" attribute this spreading characteristic of "incestuous families" to the child's supposed charms.

The ignorance or disbelief of adults close to the child is enough to set off massive guilt/secrecy complexes which cause her to doubt her own mind and senses. For many isolated incest survivors the greatest grieved loss is that of a mother's trust and support. This is a recurring topic of discussion in our Campaign too, and deserves more space than we can afford here. One principle we are definitely agreed on is that if eternal Motherhood is scapegoated yet again, we are only succumbing to the male divisive tactics which separated women in the first place. As might be expected, Eve is very popular with Incest Experts and appears frequently on their pages in the guise of the famous *Silent Partner* — a theory beloved of such authorities as Susan Forward, Craig Buck, Jean Renvoize, Erin Pizzey, etc. etc. The mother is seen as a direct participant in the abuse, egging her husband on against her daughter because she is frigid and wants to avoid her responsibilities. ... The only answer to this pitiful piece of misogyny is a feminist analysis showing how women throughout history have been bound and gagged by those poor helpless henpecked hubbies.

As for the argument that the survivor herself perpetuates the abuse by becoming in her turn a Silent Partner: we do not deny that incest survivors (along with thousands of other women) often "suffer" from revulsion to men in later life. But the fact that the disappointed husband has to turn to a child for his satisfaction, and not to another adult or even to himself, is a clue one might have thought to *his* immature sexuality, and not his wife's. From another angle: the sexual abuse a child receives may be the only form of communication she is taught, and some incest survivors suffer greatly from fear of the violence they might pass on to their own children, as if it were a curse or disease.

5. Self help — turning to each other
We can break these chains, both those of the generations and those of the individual, only by talking with each other.

Women's Refuges are already saving thousands from the violence of their husbands, giving them space to define their own lives. Soon we hope to see the same avenues of escape open to the 9-year-old girls we remember so well. Our own dream would be to set up an Incest Crisis Refuge.

Meanwhile, the correspondence we maintain with self help groups and single survivors throughout the country, the questionnaires (ask for one at this conference) and opinions we are collecting, are all immensely strengthening. We have a book in the pipeline, written and designed by survivors only. The setbacks our support groups suffer, such as frequent absences (= lack of trust, non-communication, depression) are minor compared to the deep relief of meeting others who share our experience, and talking openly of them, perhaps for the first time. With the help of other survivors we are beginning to recover whole periods of memory wiped out by the trauma, to reclaim our identity, redefine our experience and piece together our lives. A lot has yet to be discovered, but for us the Silence is finally broken.

Rider

The Incest Survivors' Campaign wrote this paper for the Manchester SAOG conference in January 1982. We have developed both in scope and in our politics since then. We recognise that our earlier analysis of incest relies too heavily on age differences between the abuser and the woman abused in its definition of power. If, as family therapists tell us, the older person is always more powerful, then a grandmother raped by a teenage boy would be defined as the offender. This is evidently wrong. For that reason our paper did not pay enough attention to the sexual abuse of sisters by brothers.

Incest Survivors' Campaign, January 1981

Incest Survivors' Campaign can be contacted
c/o A Woman's Place, Hungerford House, Victoria Embankment, London WC2.

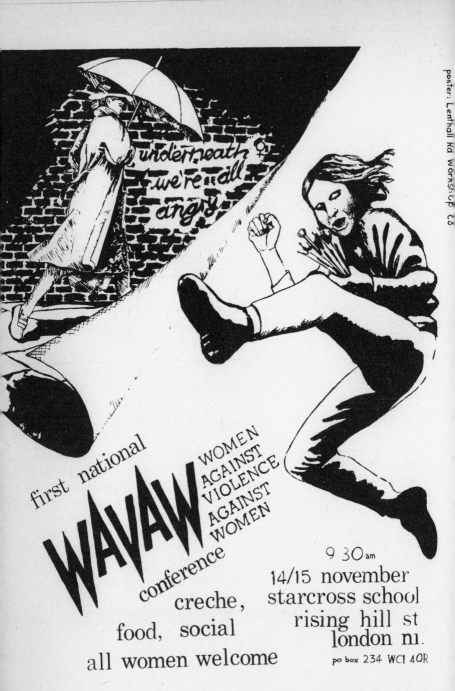

poster: Lenthall Rd workshop c8

underneath we're all angry

first national WAVAW conference

WOMEN
AGAINST
VIOLENCE
AGAINST
WOMEN

creche,
food, social
all women welcome

9 30 am
14/15 november
starcross school
rising hill st
london n1.

po box 234 WC1 4QR

FIRST NATIONAL CONFERENCE
Women Against Violence Against Women

Central London WAVAW are organising a conference to be held in London on the 14th/15th November, 1981 at Starcross School, London.

This conference, we hope, will provide a chance for women all over the country to meet to exchange information and ideas and to plan legal actions and campaigns. Women will be able to discuss setting up a network of communication across the country. It will also provide the chance for all women to discuss the issues (the WAVAW conference has *not* been organised only for women already in WAVAW groups but for *all* women).

WAVAW First National Planning Group

LONDON — 1,000 women came to the first National Women Against Violence Against Women Conference, which was held in a London school on November 14 and 15, 1981. Most of the two days were spent in workshops with a two hour plenary at the end.

Workshops included: Women's Aid; Rape in Marriage; Feminist Erotica and Sexual Pleasure; Pornography (2); Contraception as Violence against Women; Young Women's Workshop; Sexual Violence Against Black Women (Black Women only); Sex Therapy; Pressures to be Heterosexual; Women in Armagh Jail (Ireland); Language as Violence against Women; Sexology; Prudes and Puritans — the Attack on WAVAW (Women Against Violence Against Women); Community Study of Violence Against Women; Political Lesbianism; Rape Action Group; Age of Consent; Prostitution; Sexual Abuse of Girls; Women and Medical Practice; Fashion as Violence against Women; Obscuring Men's Power; Sex Shops and Strategies; Sexual Harassment at Work; and regional workshops.

One of the highlights of the weekend was a women's bop with three women's bands: Jam Today, Bright Girls, and P.M.T. At the end of the bop as 400 or so women came out onto the street we were treated to a spontaneous entertainment by 3 women juggling with sticks of fire. Dancing in the road — with beer cans stuck on the soles of their shoes, and extinguishing the fire sticks in their mouths — they held the traffic up for 15 minutes and we dispersed before the police arrived.

The creche was run by women who wanted to spend time with children. The cost of the conference was £5 for high waged; £3.50 for the medium waged; £2 for the low/unwaged, and there was a fares pool for travel funds.

With so many workshops to go to, we obviously couldn't be at them all, so this report is selective. It is selective in another way. Even the notes we took reflected what we considered more important, so this is a biased account and makes no claims to objective reporting.

Report taken from 'Off Our Backs'

PRUDES & PURITANS
Sexual Pleasure Politics and the Attack on WAVAW

'The women's movement has become a moralistic force' p.30 *Heresies*. 'The women's movement has become increasingly pro romantic love in the last decade. Lesbians are especially prone to the sentimental trend' p.33 (Ibid). 'Is there a single controversial sexual issue that the women's movement has not reacted to with a conservative, feminine horror of the outrageous and rebellious?' p.34 (Ibid).

'It seems feminism is the last rock of conservatism. It will not be sexualised. It is prudish in that way' p.62.

'at worst the feminist vision would bar some forms of sexual expression.!' *Talking Sex*, English, Hollibaugh & Rubin in Socialist Review no. 58, Vol.II No.4 July-August 1981.

The above quotes are representative of the view of the American feminist pro sexual pleasure lobby.

Sexual freedom versus women's liberation
According to these feminists we live in a sexually repressive society and our main task is to free ourselves from guilt and inhibition and experiment with our sexuality. This is the main theme of the 'Sex Issue' of Heresies. We must begin to strive towards a self defined sexuality rather than continuing to organise around what Paula Webster refers to as our 'otherness' and 'victimisation' (see her article on Pornography and Pleasure). She believes that we do the latter when we focus exclusively on the effects of male violence and sexuality upon women. We embrace our 'deprived condition' instead of creating alternatives. But the 'alternatives' which are posed in Heresies look remarkably conformist and reactionary when considered in terms of how little they further the liberation of women.

Essentially these women are sexual libertarians who believe in the absolute validity of any sexual variation. Their priorities are liberal not feminist, which therefore leads them to support all sexual minorities. Their emphasis on the rights of individual 'people' to choose and exercise their sexuality often conflicts with the demands of women's liberation; permitting the liberalisation of the sexual climate under male power can only restrict women's freedom and define women sexually in accordance with male needs. The Sexual Revolution proved this when the tide of previously invisible woman hatred was released in the form of pornography.

Lesbian sado-masochism

An important part of the sexual progressives' politics is their promotion and justification of lesbian sado-masochism. Pat Califia argues in favour of S & M in *Sapphistry* (her book), Heresies and Off Our Backs. Her lover Gayle Rubin (the bottom or masochist of the relationship) argues the case for pleasure politics in an article in Socialist Review (Feminism & Sexuality). There is also a lesbian S & M support group based in Berkeley.

Pat Califia and her supporters justify S & M in different ways:

1. It is negotiated and consensual. The bottom sets limits on the top's activities and therefore has as much power and neither partner is forced or coerced into it.

2. It is rebellious and innovative — it undermines the present capitalist society because it does not link sex to the family and reproduction. It shakes up convention and challenges the 'vanilla' sexuality of most lesbians (vanillas are presumably tame, unadventurous and insipid).

3. It is a game, a theatre, a fantasy — it should not be confused with a social reality. Sado masochists can act out cravings for power and powerlessness in sexual exchanges and the authority/subordinate roles are flexible and interchangeable, unlike real relations of inequality which exists outside the bedroom i.e. sex, class and race.

I don't find any of the arguments convincing. The endless images of fist fucking, flagellation, bondage and 'leather' sex which come flooding into my mind when I read about lesbian S & M are irrevocably associated with male power and female powerlessness. It is impossible to divorce the concepts of domination and submission from the sexual relationships between men and women. That is where they come from. What of all those women who *are* forced into humiliating and painful sex with men — women who have no 'choice'.

It seems that these lesbians are parodying the reality of this oppression and diffusing its significance. They play games while other women suffer. I think sado-masochism takes the heterosexual model and mimics and exaggerates all its horrors and inequalities. It comes from the system and it feeds back into it. It both reflects and re-inforces men's power over women. How can we hope to fight male power when we are practising male defined sexuality amongst ourselves?

The attack on WAVAW

The same women in the States who are promoting the pursuit of pleasure as *the* feminist sexual politics are attacking the anti porn and male violence groups. They consider WAVAW type groups to be aligning themselves with the right wing (particularly the Moral Majority) paving the way for increased censorship and sexual repression. But by supporting the increase in pornography, men's legal right of access to paid sex, the right of male paedophiles to have sex with girl children they are contributing to women's oppression.

They naturally have a lot of support from the male status quo, given that they pose no threat but even positively endorse male sexuality. The pimps and clients of prostitutes, the creators and consumers of pornography, the child molesters have nothing to fear from these women. The fact that some of the women practise S & M in their relationships means men can point to them as evidence that our sexuality is just the same as theirs.

These women are helping to tighten up and increase men's sexual control over us. Although this is primarily an American phenomenon at the moment we must anticipate the possibility of similar opposition to WAVAW occuring over here. Some of the arguments they use could have come out of the mouths of the sexologists and sex reformers at the beginning of the century — men who were instrumental in destroying the first wave of feminism by calling feminists frigid and unwomanly and encouraging women to actively engage in our own humiliation. Accusations of prudery could silence us once again.

Lesbian feminist sexuality and male violence

It has been said that anti male violence feminists have been silent about female sexuality, that we neglect our own sexuality and the struggle to re-define it. And when we do discuss it we promote a frigid and conservative sexual orthodoxy (see opening quotes), based on monogamous and romantic love. Personally, I don't feel the fight against male power and violence and the development of our sexuality as mutually exclusive tasks. I think as a lesbian I can strive for both in my life. But I do agree that some of us have remained silent about the latter and that has left us wide open to the accusation of being anti sex per se rather than anti the form male sexuality has taken. I think these women caricature their opposition when they say that if we are not into their alienated and male defined kind of sexuality, we must necessarily favour romantic love. There is no straight choice between skulking around bushes and lavatories and building racks in the basement for our lovers (to quote Pat Califia) and sending roses, perfume and soppy poetry to our ONE woman lover. I don't consider either of these choices to be an alternative to patriarchal relationships. As lesbians we are not immune to the messages and influence of the male system. As the S & M Lesbians demonstrate, being a lesbian is not enough in itself if all we can do is repeat and exaggerate present heterosexual patterns.

Jayne Egerton

With thanks and love to Trish, Hazel and Tina for discussions on personal politics.

About 70 women came to the workshop, and there was a general underlying assumption that we were talking about relationships between women. The following are extracts from the discussion:

— Do we mind being called prudes and puritans?

— It's the kind of thing men have always said about us, like attacking 'spinsters'.

— Do we mind more when it comes from other feminists?

— One woman said she was fed up having to be a wonderful example of smiling womanhood, let them call her what they wanted.

— But as long as we can be dismissed as prudes, our fight, our arguments against male defined sexuality, will not be heard.

— We should do both simultaneously — try to develop an authentic female sexuality at the time as fighting male power.

— What we do in private has political implications.

— But if we talk of lesbian sexuality it seems to objectify it, so there is a reluctance to talk about sexuality.

— One problem is that it is very complex and while others make statements we are left to clear up the complexities.

— There is a big TRAP. Men have created a thing that they call 'sexuality' quite separate from relationships between people. First they create a sexuality, then they go out and find someone to practise it on. Feminists who are into creating a female sexuality have fallen into the trap of doing the same — so they promote feminist erotica; fantasy; S&M; and use all the fetishistic tools of the trade. To prove to them we are not anti sex we are expected to produce the evidence of a 'sexuality' as men have. In fact we are in the process of developing a feminist sexual practice in our relationships and in our discussions as part and parcel of our politics.

— One woman said that WAVAW was perpetuating the idea that male sexuality inevitably takes the forms it does, and that all relations between men and women were as portrayed in porn. Another woman disagreed, saying that most women in WAVAW see the form male sexuality takes and hence all sexuality in a male dominated culture as NOT inevitable and biological and natural but deliberately constructed by men in men's interest to maintain their power position over women and justify it.

— People don't look at pleasure in a critical way. We're affected by the outside world. So there's no free expression.

— It's not just porn which affects our fantasies.

— Why do we have certain fantasies by the age of 5 or 6? Where is it coming from?

— Patriarchal power relations in the family?

— Punishment of girls for showing any sexuality?

— Abuse we have already suffered from males including boys?

— Heterosexual power relations are already established between children.

— We are the only oppressed group which has been taught to get turned on by our oppression.

— Some of us have fantasies we want to hang on to.

— Some women asked if there was a way of examining them — instead of just being told to stamp them out.

No one had any answers. But some of us thought we should not be examining our fantasies in isolation from where they come from, and the realities of male power, and without hope of change.

We talked about relationships between women as for us our sexuality is bound up with relationships, communicating ... the difficulties we face ... the notion of romantic love.

Then one woman said she wanted to talk about something she was not sure was relevant. When she came into the Women's Liberation Movement in 1974 there was much talk and writing about orgasms. She had joined a pre-orgasmic group. She was not anti-orgasm (much laughter) but felt we had become too orgasm oriented. There was more to sex, sexuality and relationships than orgasms. Another woman said this was very relevant as she too had gone to a pre-orgasmic group and been told to use fantasy, told to read Nancy Friday's book. Before then she never had any fantasies. Now she could not get rid of them.

Then we talked about feelings and 'instincts'. Like feeling turned on at a disco, or even in this workshop (laughter and some disapproval) by women we did not know.

— What is that about, are our feelings quite outside our control so there's no point trying to analyse them?

— Was being attracted to a woman on sight wrong — because of connotations of romantic love?

— We may not be in control of our feelings but we are in control of how we act on them. This was generally agreed upon, and one of the high spots of the workshop. Though interpretations varied from 'not having sex till we are really sorted out' to 'just making sure we are not having romantic illusions.'

One woman objected to the light hearted manner some women were discussing fancying women — it makes women sexual objects. Other women thought it was HOW women reacted to such feelings that mattered. Between women mutual attraction doesn't have the same power imbalance built in as between a man and a woman.

Probably because of the workshop paper no woman was arguing in favour of lesbian S&M or heterosexuality. Some women came wanting, looking for anwers to questions. Instead we went away with a new set of questions. Probably because we were listening intently to each other, not arguing from different positions. And that was true for the conference workshops on the whole.

Sandra McNeill with help from Rosie Snowdon

(The papers and the conference were clearly for women only. Permission to quote from a paper in a publication open to men readers was given by Jayne Egerton. Permission to report the discussions, with one exception — respected — was given by women at the workshop.)

Report taken from 'Off Our Backs'

SEXUAL PLEASURE and WOMEN'S LIBERATION

'A Woman's Right to Sexual Pleasure'?

The concept of sexual pleasure — and the whole cluster of related concepts such as sexual drive, sexual desire, sexual repression etc. — has for too long been taken for granted, not only outside, but also inside the WLM. There seems to be a widespread assumption that sexual pleasure is something every woman has a 'right' to, whether with herself, with other women, or with men. Indeed, some feminists seem to regard a woman's right to sexual pleasure as almost synonymous with women's liberation. How and with whom we experience sexual pleasure, and what it actually consists of, are also held to be matters of individual choice. Women who question or challenge, for instance, the use of pornography or sado-masochistic practices by feminists or gay men, are often accused by feminists (and, of course, gay men) of being interfering, moralistic and judgemental. Some feminists have argued that any form of sexual practice is valid, as long as it is an expression of genuine lust and entered into on the basis of mutual consent, and that to criticize some forms of sexual 'preference', such as paedophilia and S/M, is oppressive to sexual 'minorities'.[1]

I suggest that this is basically an 'anything goes' philosophy, which is hostile to any attempt to develop an analysis of how male power is exercised through sexuality. More importantly, it threatens to undermine women's resistance to male sexual demands and to sexual practices which they find not only unpleasurable but controlling. I do not see how we can ever assume consent under male supremacy, and it is difficult to see how a philosophy of 'anything goes' can help us to work out a feminist sexual practice. Feminism is a *political* movement, which means that we are working to change the position of *all* women — *for the better*. This means that we cannot avoid making value-judgements and facing moral issues, including in matters of sex. I shall return to these problems at the end of the paper. The main point I want to make here is that notions of sexual pleasure, desire etc., should not be accepted as givens, but examined as social constructs, in the same way as all other aspects of our lives. What follows is intended as a contribution to a feminist analysis of how 'sexual pleasure' has been constructed.

Sexology and Sexual Pleasure

Our notions of sexual pleasure have been shaped by many factors, but one of the most important 20th century influences has been sexology — the 'science' of sex. Its importance lies in the fact that, as a science, it enjoys tremendous status and legitimacy — science being the 20th century god. The findings of the 'sexperts' have found their way into sex education, marriage manuals, sex counselling and sex therapy. Most liberals, socialists and many feminists have viewed the influence of sexology as progressive, in promoting healthier attitudes to sex and thus contributing to both sexual liberation and women's liberation (often, wrongly, seen as the same). The work of the early sexologists, and of Havelock Ellis in particular, has been acclaimed as leading us all out of the darkness of Victorian prudery and sexual repression into the light of 20th century sexual liberation. Ellis has been especially applauded as one of the first men to champion a woman's right to sexual pleasure.

Sexual Pleasure and Power

Even a superficial reading of Ellis's books reveals a concept of sexual pleasure which seems so ideally suited to the maintenance of male power that one might be forgiven for thinking it had been constructed with exactly that aim in mind. Briefly, Ellis claimed that normal heterosexual sex is based on power i.e. male aggression/domination and female submission. This power relation is natural (= biologically determined), and therefore not only inevitable but essential to sexual pleasure. Feminine reluctance and inhibition are made to be overcome, and every sexual act is the re-enactment of the pursuit and conquest of the female animal by the male. Female resistance is not real, but merely the manifestation of her sexual desire — to be conquered. It is not difficult to see how this effectively undermines any objection a woman might have to the act of sexual intercourse.

Sexual Pleasure and Pain

Ellis also produced scientific 'evidence' to show that the sex drive in men and women is to a great extent spontaneous, i.e. we can't help it, and that its satisfaction frequently involves the use of force and the infliction of pain. He argued that there is inevitably a close connection between pain and sexual pleasure, especially in women, and that "the normal manifestations of a woman's sexual pleasure are exceedingly like pain". As an example, he cited the case of the 'nymphomaniac' who had an orgasm when the knife passed through her clitoris. In other words, women are masochists. (At about the same time, Freud was coming to similar conclusions.)

Frigidity: women's resistance

One of the most baffling problems for the sexpert has always been that many women do not seem to enjoy sexual intercourse. Ellis's 'cure' for frigidity was the 'art of love', a sexual technique by means of which to arouse in the woman an emotional condition which leads her to surrender. He considered it vital that the woman should actively participate in her own surrender, rather than lie back and think of England, though the orchestration of her pleasure was to be left in male hands: "she is inevitably the instrument in love; it is his hand and his bow which should evoke the music".

Judging by the popular and scientific books on sex published during and after the 1920's — the first stage of the 'sexual revolution' — frigidity rose to epidemic proportions, and was — correctly — diagnosed, not as an aversion to sex per se, but as a form of resistance, specifically to fucking, and more generally to the exercise of male power through sexual 'pleasure'. Women, it appeared, were not too keen on actively participating in their own conquest and domination. Both the 'frigide' and her sexually anaesthetic sister, the spinster, became the targets of attack by sexologists and sex reformers, male and female, from the 1920's right up to the present day. If sexual intercourse is such a naturally pleasurable experience, why have such strenuous efforts been made in order to *make* women enjoy it?

Female Sexuality: from passive to active?

The latest techniques for overcoming women's resistance to the joys of sex stem from the work of William Masters and Virginia Johnson. These sexperts have been credited with 'discovery' of the clitoral orgasm and transforming female sexuality from passive to active. In fact, their 'finding' that clitoral orgasms could be produced by penile thrusting in the vagina (indirectly stimulating the clitoris via the labia) only confirms the importance of fucking in the time-honoured way. Masters and Johnson are not only researchers but run a sex therapy business, teaching heterosexual couples the joys of sex. If a man hasn't a wife or girlfriend they kindly provide a female substitute. As well as teaching women to enjoy being fucked they teach them how to cure male impotence and premature ejaculation. Having orgasms is evidently not enough; some of them at least must be got by fucking. Masters and Johnson do not allow women to be passive during sex; not only do they literally put the woman on top (the 'female superior' position), they also make her take virtually total responsibility for the whole process — for her own arousal, for his erection, for being fucked, for fulfilling her multi-orgasmic potential. With Masters and Johnson, the sexualization of woman is almost complete; and she is now apparently in total control of her own sexual pleasure.

Sexual 'Variations' — (they used to be called perversions)
The idea that a degree of pain is normal in sex has been used by the sexperts as a springboard for promoting the normalization of S/M, bondage, flagellation and all forms of sexual variation involving force and pain. Ellis argued that the difference between fucking and the most extreme variations is merely one of degree, and this has become one of the basic assumptions of sexology. Research into sexual variations and sexual offences is an important aspect of the work of, for example, the Kinsey Institute, and is essentially an elaboration of Ellis's work. 'Progressives' have welcomed this research as promoting tolerance of sexual 'minorities'. What they fail to see is that underlying the tolerance is a thinly veiled threat: it is dangerous to repress the (male) sex drive.[2] If it is denied legitimate outlets it will seek illegitimate ones. In other words it's women's fault if the male sex drive goes out of control — we're not letting them do it enough. Anyone who looks at the changes in sex manuals over the years cannot fail to be struck by the way in which bondage, flagellation, S/M and other 'sauces and pickles' have been promoted to the point where they have

become 'acceptable' and 'normal'. Countless women (myself included) have experienced pressure from husbands and boyfriends to try out the 'sex games' promoted by trendy sex manuals, pornographic magazines and videos. Many have complied in order not to seem prudish — a fear that has always been used to whip women into line. S/M is not, of course, new. What *is* new is that it is fast becoming accepted as harmless and natural, as the barriers of resistance are pushed back.[3]

Violence Against Women as Sexual Pleasure
We must be clear what the sex games are about. Women are being encouraged and coerced into active participation in their own humiliation and brutalization. They are being trained to enjoy surrender and violation, and, occasionally, to practice a bit of role reversal and take turns at being dominant, just to prove that women can be as aggressive, violent, sadistic and powerful as men, if they really want to. Men are encouraged to use women as the targets of their violence, and to believe that the sexual pleasure they gain through this is legitimate. How can it possibly be argued that women consent to the violation of their own bodies?

Sexual Liberation v. Women's Liberation
Sexologists and sex reformers (mainly men, including gay men) have been the spearhead of the movement for sexual liberation, which began in the 1920's and was renewed in the late 1960's. Initially, this movement was not, as is usually thought, a natural reaction to Victorian sexual repression, but a consciously planned and well organized attempt to change sexual morality. Like most social movements, it contained many diverse and contradictory elements, including some strands of feminism. Although it was formally committed to equality of the sexes, women's liberation was confused with sexual liberation, and sexual liberation was conceived simply as the separation of sex from reproduction. Contraception was seen as enabling women to lead freer sex lives, thus abolishing the double standard.

Male Sexuality and the Control of Women
Many feminists, however, would have nothing to do with sex reform. These were mainly women who, in the late 19th

and early 20th centuries had been involved in political campaigns around rape, prostitution, V.D., sexual abuse of girls, male violence and all forms of female sexual slavery, which they saw as crucial to male control of women. Many of these women chose to be celibate because they refused to subject themselves to male sexual control, and advocated sexual withdrawal from men as a political strategy. A glance at the feminist journals of the period leading up to World War I shows quite clearly that the Votes for Women campaign included not only demands for political and economic independence, but a direct challenge to male sexuality, which they saw as based on the urge to conquer, dominate and control. They did *not* see this urge as uncontrollable, or biologically determined; on the contrary, the aim of their campaigns was to force men to change.[3]

The Backlash

I suggest that the whole ideology of sexual liberation can to a large extent to be seen as a backlash against women's resistance and the feminist challenge to the form taken by male sexuality. Most of the early sex reformers completely accepted Ellis's theory that male sexuality is biologically based on the urge to dominate, and female sexuality on the urge to resist in order to be conquered; that the sex drive in women and men is spontaneous (= uncontrollable); and that the link between sexual pleasure, pain and violence is harmless and inevitable. The effect was not only to justify male sexuality as the control of women, but to undermine women's resistance and the feminist challenge by conscripting women into heterosexuality and training them to enjoy being fucked, and to experience their sexual colonization as 'sexual pleasure'. This process has been continuing over the years in different ways; and this form of male sexuality has been transformed into a sort of unisexuality, so that concepts like sex drive, lust, sexual desire etc. are taken to be things which exist in all of us, women and men, lesbian, gay or straight, and which need to be satisfied — like hunger and thirst.

I feel, and I fear, that some of the feminists who are currently reasserting a woman's right to sexual pleasure are still stuck in this ideology of sexual liberation — some of them certainly seem to be basing their arguments on the same assumptions. This does not mean, of course, that I think that women should not concern themselves with 'sexual pleasure' — except that I don't want to use that term any more. Nor do I think that male sexuality cannot be changed. What I do think is that we must not confuse sexual liberation with women's liberation; and we should be aware that there is much that is in sexual liberation that is directly anti-feminist. We cannot base a political movement on a philosophy of 'anything goes', and we cannot separate our sexual practices from our politics, or seek individualistic solutions to the most private and personal problems in our lives. Nor can we wash our hands of the moral issues that are inevitably raised by questions of sexual 'desire' and 'pleasure'. Anyway, "Thou shalt not commit a moral judgement" is itself a moral commandment.

Margaret Jackson, November 1981

NOTES
1 See, for example, the article by Deirdre English, Gayle Rubin & Amber Hollibaugh called 'Talking Sex', in Socialist Review, no. 58, 1981.
2 The sexperts admit that sexual perversions are practised almost entirely by men.
3 These points are discussed in more detail in various articles in Scarlet Women, no. 13, part 2.

FANTASY AND MASOCHISM

This is one of the most subtle areas of women's enslavement by men.

- What relation is there between fantasy and reality?
- What function does fantasy fulfil?
- Is the function of fantasy different in men and in women?
- Can we direct and control our fantasies?
- Why do women have 'masochistic' fantasies?

A fantasy is an imaginative daydream, often with a 'story' to it. Fantasy is different in men and women. For women, non-sexual fantasies are usually escapist because reality is grim. For men, fantasy is the blueprint for future real-life exploits. Fantasies are based on reality. But they are often 'fed' and pushed in a particular direction by other fantasy material supplied for people to consume. Men control the media and men control the direction of fantasy created in the media. Fantasy gives women a 'breather' from real life ('true love tales'). For men, however, fantasy reinforces and raises their expectations of what real life should be offering them (astronauts, spies, super-detectives).

The same is true of sexual fantasies — for men. James Bond is the 'soft-core' version of the 'hard-core' uncontrollable rapist/sadist fantasy.

But what about women's sexual fantasies? — 'masochism'?

WOMEN DO NOT LIKE BEING ENSLAVED. WE DO NOT ENJOY RAPE, HUMILIATION, TORTURE, MURDER. MEN KNOW THAT WOMEN DO NOT LIKE TO SUFFER PAIN/DEGRADATION NOR TO BE ENSLAVED.

Men want women to be under their control and at their disposal. Men's sadistic fantasies teach them how to perpetrate unpleasant heterosexual practices and rape. These fantasies teach them to believe that women enjoy being brutalised and violated. Men like to believe that women *enjoy* assault and rape (etc) because that would free them from responsibility for hurting us, give them some vindication for their behaviour: if women want/need beating and raping, men cannot be guilty . . .

Men pretend that they believe that women like to be sexually abused, forced and subjugated.

Men produce all sorts of propaganda to support this convenient 'belief' about us.

FIRST they show we deserve such treatment:

- Women are inferior, without brains or souls or human feeling. We deserve worse treatment than animals.
- Women are wild and uncivilised. We need the direction and control of men. If women study medicine/get the vote/gain positions of power over men, the world will fall apart.
- Women are bad. We need to be punished — all the time, to remind us of our sin in being women.

SECOND they show we even enjoy their cruelty: by

producing all sorts of 'evidence' (Havelock Ellis) and in direct, crude propaganda — pornographic material. Pornographic material shows women being sexually aroused at the same time as being sexually abused.

PORNOGRAPHY EXPRESSES THE MALE IDEOLOGY OF WOMAN-HATRED. It shows men woman-hating in action, and how to do it. It also shows women what men want — how we are supposed to please men. We learn from pornography and media-produced sexual fantasy what men want and expect of us. For our survival, we have learned

1. to see the world through men's eyes
2. to try and anticipate what men want of us, and be ready to do it.

Having learned (all our lives) to look at the world through men's eyes and to look at ourselves through men's eyes, we view pornography of all kinds as if we were men. I include within 'pornography' all sorts of erotic material too.

There is a problem inherent in this, however: double-vision. We identify with men, but we cannot help also identifying with the women portrayed and described in pornography. We are women — and it is women who are being violated, harmed and killed in pornography.

And inside our fantasy world we desperately try to 'learn' to live with the contradiction of men's pleasure simultaneous with our pain — men's pleasure IN our pain.

WOMEN ARE NOT MASOCHISTS IN REAL LIFE. In real life, no woman seeks to be brutalised or murdered. No woman wants to be sexually abused.

In our masochistic fantasies, many women strive to reconcile the impossible: to feel pleasure (men's) and pain (women's) at the same time: that is, sexual pleasure (men's) and bodily pain (women's). In our fantasies, many of us become sexually aroused and enjoy rape, torture. We strive to enjoy what men enjoy — believing that thereby we shall survive.

It is ironic that in fact women are punished FOR BEING WOMEN. There is no way to escape this as long as men hold power over us, for even in doing what we think will please and placate men we are accepting punishment.

And when pleasing men and seeing the world through men's eyes involves going along with the injury and murder of women, we must begin to question what sort of 'survival' we are bargaining for by pleasing men.

Instead of rebelling, most of us most of the time have learned to accommodate ourselves to men's violence against us.

Masochistic fantasies in women are one way we try and deal with the pain we experience at the same time as knowing that men want and enjoy our pain AND WANT US TO WANT IT TOO.

We cannot deny that we are women. We cannot deny that as long as men have the power our survival is in their hands. The only way to ensure our survival is to wrest power back from men.

THE MORE WE FIGHT
THE LESS WE SHALL FANTASISE

danu

REPORT OF WORKSHOP ON MALE VIOLENCE AND THE PRESSURE TO BE HETEROSEXUAL

The workshop on Male Violence and the Pressure to be Heterosexual was called by 2 women, who wrote a paper. The 2 stories were true of many of our lives, and about 100 women came to the workshop which we split into two groups. Discussion in my half was often intensely personal; one woman asked why should she feel so *guilty* when refusing her boyfriend sex? Why did she do it when she didn't want to? We wondered how to bring lesbianism/sexuality up when we speak of WAVAW with women, without freaking them out; we spoke of how lesbianism threatened men. One woman wasn't sure: her father wasn't bothered. But it was because he was happy not to be in sexual competition with a man for her, she could be Daddy's Own Girl forever.

Heterosexual pressure is especially strong in women's and girls' magazines. Most, by now, have cleverly incorporated a lot of the feminist message — women are now pushier, more independent, may have jobs important to them — *but* they always land up safely *with a man*. Like some 'feminist' magazines, come to that, someone murmured.

Pressures work on women of different classes differently. Working-class women may see through the heterosexual promise, but it's much harder, practically, for them to get out, men having allowed them fewer resources (money, knowledge of where to go, etc.) and being more tied to their family and community. Middle-class women may have fewer practical barriers, so men make efforts in different ways to co-opt and brainwash them. Carrots are offered in the form of careers, shared childcare, marital therapy and male approval for the financially independent woman who dislikes and competes with other women.

This area wasn't deeply gone into and this report ties up the discussion more neatly than it actually was. Also the pressures to be heterosexual on Asian and Black women growing up/living in this country were not even mentioned — a reflection of the almost entirely white conference. Women with disabilities didn't get a mention either, and one woman made the assumption "we're all young and single here" — she was hotly disagreed with, but it's still true that the white, able-bodied, middle-class woman of 20-40 without children was the life experience taken as standard.

Generally at the conference and in this workshop there was an assumption that pressures to be heterosexual were bad (if not heterosexuality itself) and lesbian relationships better for women.

Al Garthwaite

MALE VIOLENCE AND THE PRESSURE
TO BE HETEROSEXUAL

This paper was written by two women with very different life experiences who have arrived at similar conclusions. Much of it is personal rather than analytical as we are both heartily sick of lines and slogans and want to re-establish the centrality of personal experience in feminist political debate.

We both feel the pressure to be heterosexual is one of the main ways men control us and divide us from each other. The pressure exists in a variety of ways, ranging from the threat of male violence to social ostracism and feelings of personal failure.

I want to talk particularly about the violence I have experienced from men in two ways and the extent to which I was both driven towards and finally away from men because of it. When I was in my early teens I naively believed myself to be the inheritor of enlightened and liberating attitudes to sex. We had the pill and as far as I could see, the double standard was diminishing, making it easier for women to be sexually active and assertive. Unlike my mother who was told never to say yes it was unpopular amongst girls I knew then to ever say no. We were controlled by men's demands as much as my mother's generation, only the form of control had changed. Throughout my teens I variously had sex with men in the backs of cars, at the fairground, under the pier and in lavatories a few times. Frequently I was either uncomfortable or in actual pain but I did not know how to protest or refuse. I had non-voluntary sex quite a few times particularly when I was drunk and the men were reckless as to whether or not I had willed it in the first place. Quite often I suffered from thrush and cystitis, but I would never tell men to stop because I was in pain. During that time I often felt sick with guilt and confusion but I still confused my constant sexual availability with liberation and freedom of choice. A couple of times I allowed men to bugger me and one of these times I bled so much I thought I had haemorrhaged.

Violence was implicit in many of these sexual encounters. I remember my arms being locked above my head so I could not move; I remember being bruised and bitten and scratched. I remember moments of rising panic when I thought the man was actually going to hurt me badly.

The brutality and coldness of these experiences were largely instrumental in pursuading me to have steady and secure relationships with men. I did not feel safe with lots of different ones. The threat of men's violence drove me into couple relationships. I feel ambivalent about these men. They were not unmitigated bastards and they did afford me 'protection'. My mother would often mutter ominously about the world not being a safe place for women and my experience could only confirm this. Being alone I felt, at times, besieged and up for grabs. Being with one man sheltered unwelcome attention from men in the streets, at parties etc.

I never considered lesbianism, although I had had a few one-off sexual experiences with women from the age of fifteen onwards. Women were my best friends and men were my lovers. I did associate lesbianism with being left unloved and undesired on the shelf. Most of my self-esteem came from men wanting me sexually (although mostly it wasn't *me* they wanted) and to give that up was to give up the most crucial prop and confidence builder in my life. It was only through my involvement in women's liberation that I was able to stop relating to men. It was a long time before I recognised the violence I had experienced as a single 'heterosexual' woman. Oppressed women were women 'out there' not me, or so I thought. The threat of violence which drove me to seek out individual male protectors was eventually to be one of the major factors involved in my giving up relating to men sexually.

This is a very condensed and partial overview of the last eight years and at points I've oversimplified for the sake of brevity. It is worth pointing out that I emphasise the positive aspects of being with women much more now than when I first came out. At that time the rejection of men seemed more significant both personally and politically than my lesbianism.

· · · · · ·

Oxford dictionary *hetero* 'preface meaning another, abormal, different, unequal'. It was a pity that I only found that definition recently and not while I was at school. However, this dictionary did not have all the other words I looked up, but it's refreshing to find an interpretation I agree with.

Throughout my teens I began to feel increasingly that I ought to have a boyfriend. I did; a boy who was away at boarding school most of the time. We got on well and the only sexual demands he made on me was to hold my hand and to have a long kiss goodnight. He completely enveloped me, opened his mouth as widely as possible and shoved his tongue right into my mouth, pushing it around. He seemed to get a lot of pleasure from this action, all I could think was 'I can't breathe'. Our relationship was treated with warmth and knowing looks from our mothers. I felt endorsed and proud when we were seen together, but I found it irritating that whenever we were spoken to — to give directions etc. — men and women always spoke to him.

I got involved in a very close friendship with a girl my age (14) and soon it became 'sexual'. I quote it because neither we nor anyone else recognised it as such, though we slept together, made love and had all girl parties where we all had sexual experiences together. This led to an interesting paradox, we did not feel jealous, possessive and 'involved'; it was from Niall that these concepts began to be of significance. He always asked about my other boyfriends — it was my father who began to ask about Desi. Desi and I spent a great deal of time together and had a lot of fun talking about all our friends and who we fancied. There was however a strong sense that it was wrong and that what Niall and I had was right.

We lived in an Army Garrison and though the threat of violence did not appear to be an issue it was the threat of ostracism that was. Parents began to not allow their daughters to come to our parties and we were banned from several houses. I thought it was a class thing at the time and no one was prepared to say out loud 'lesbian'. But I began to become very shy, ashamed and afraid of my sexual desires because they were never aimed in the right direction. Meanwhile my relationship with Niall became possessive. He spoke and thought of me as *his*, I accepted this as it seemed to be generally the correct way to view girlfriends and boyfriends. When he was away other boys also acted in the same way. My relationships (or should I say gropes in the cinema) with boys became shorter, averaging 2 to 3 days. My father and stepmother (mum had died by this time) talked about my cousins and other girls who had 'boys queuing up at the door' for them. I was supposed to and did feel inadequate, but I couldn't think of any boys I wanted at the door. Desi moved from the garrison, I began to put on weight, also to dream of being a boy myself so that I could go out with (as opposed to come out) with girls. The only world where sexual relationships took place was between men and women and nowhere else. Masturbation and orgasms were a completely separate aspect of my sexual needs and I never related it to making love. The only way I could get any pleasure from boys touching me was to disassociate them from the physical feeling. I imagine this was nothing new for them. The only alternative for me was I thought, to have a sex change. I fantasized that I was one of the boys at school. The fantasy took more and more of my time so that occasionally I really believed I was him, but every time I looked in the mirror I saw the reflection of a fatter and fatter, miserable girl.

I found that as my confidence began to flag more men began to find me attractive. This undermining process was a central part of my upbringing, but it had the most noticeable results as regards my sexuality and sexual feelings. I was in a milieu that wanted sexual passivity and since I had no desire for these men I was passive sexually with them, preferring not to kiss them or touch them. They in turn expected nothing else. I suffered trying to feel about them as I felt about women. I am sure that the pain I felt must have registered but they persisted and seemed genuinely surprised that I refused, as politely as possible, to allow them to shove their penises into me.

It was through my sexual and emotional desire and fulfilment from and for some of my friends that I came across the women's movement. The suffering I experienced at the hands of men and boys was always seen from the position of knowing there was something better.

Jayne Egerton and Louise Richey

EVERYWOMAN'S EXPERIENCE
OF MARRIAGE

This paper is one part of what was intended to be three different papers, reflecting the different experiences of marriage, as recalled and remembered by each of us.

We had a few discussions, and felt that there were some situations which were unique to our own individual marriages (reasons for marrying — reasons for leaving) and others which were common to us all.

In our discussions we began to understand that we had "individualised" the problems and feelings that we had within marriage — and there was a good deal of relief and laughter in recognising that we had in fact had similar reactions to the position we were in as "wives".

What follows is just one of the three parts — my own experience — although perhaps the feelings described are those that "everywoman" experiences at some time in her life.

. . . . . .

I only lived with my husband for approximately 6 months — which made 9 — 10 months of knowing him altogether. I don't find it difficult to come to certain theoretical conclusions based on my experiences — but I still feel as if I'm standing apart and outside the experience — no amount of theorising or analysing can describe the complexities of emotional feelings I experienced during my marriage (or after). When I analyse or theorise, it's almost as if I am talking and thinking about another person — not myself. So let me try and list these feelings and explain them:

FEAR		ISOLATION
CONFUSION	SELF-HATRED	IDENTITY LOSS
MISERY		LOSS OF CONFIDENCE

They are an interesting collection — THE EMOTIONAL STATE OF THE VICTIM. I can't remember anything except six months of negative feelings. I was afraid I would go mad — and I definitely considered murder, planning the act in great and careful detail — but I left while I could — while I was able to walk, physically and emotionally.

Fear
(a) My husband was physically violent three times. It was violent, but not brutal, although I was physically marked and couldn't work as a result. I only ever understood why

the second time, when unable to cope with his silence, I deliberately provoked(?) a reaction. After I left, we had the "let's try again" act, he and I in a crowded restaurant where we were both well-known, me listening to him demolishing my character, that of my parents and friends, and when I resisted and insisted on leaving, he threatened to kill me. And I believed him, I sat there, I smiled, I said the food was wonderful, and I was terrified. Would he have done in reality, could he have done, why didn't I ask for help from the others? Because, with my victim identity, I believed him.

(b) Fear of my sanity — I felt myself fragmenting — much like in descriptions of schizophrenia. Bits of me seemed to be breaking off and floating away, and it was always more of a problem to catch them and get them back, like catching soap bubbles.

(c) ... of course — fear of what others would think or say. Fear of shame and failure. I was married. My marriage had to work. It was my responsibility.

Confusion

Why had he married me? What did he want? He stayed out drinking, didn't come home; came home drunk; didn't like me; I wasn't exciting, dressed like a teacher; he wanted a mother, someone to be at home to look after him.

Who had he married? It wasn't me. Who had I married? Was it him?

Isolation — Identity Loss / Loss of Confidence = Misery

All these go together. They merge and feed one upon the other. I had never felt so lonely and alone. I was married — but it wasn't like the books or films!!

There was no companionship — no love and for four of the six months — no sex. Was the withdrawal of sex another means of control?

I was constantly criticised — overweight, unattractive, not behaving as I should, making too many demands; — my past life was seen as a succession of "loose affairs" — Ooh! EVERYTHING was wrong — with me.

I cried, I stormed, I took on his description of me, I wilted under the pressure of how to correct these so obviously irritating characteristics. But, was he, himself at fault. No, for I tried to be understanding. The problem was, he was under pressure at work, under financial stress, had problems adapting to the responsibilities(!) of marriage, a new home, the restrictions married life had put on him.

It never occurred to me to realise that he had no problems adapting to marriage; he wasn't adapting!

YET, I SURVIVED! I rationalised it — in the end I thought OTHERS MIGHT LIKE MARRIAGE — I DIDN'T — IT DESTROYED ME.

It's a long time after now — ten years. I can now understand some of the whys. With an understanding of feminism came a way of absolving myself of failure, of eccentricity, of non-conformity. Yet, I remain bruised — I keep my guard up, because despite sisterhood, support, friendship, I'm afraid at times that the next punch will splinter me forever.

If this reads a trifle negative and sad — it is, because I cannot yet extract those experiences and turn them into positive feelings. But I do still feel very, very angry, for all the women whose selves have been brutalised by men.

Sally, October 1981

RAPE IN MARRIAGE

This is a personal account of my experience of rape in marriage. As a way of presenting my story I think that there are connections between mine and other women's experience of marriage.

I got married in 1970, I was 19 and so was he. I found marriage a great strain at first adjusting myself to fit in with his personality, character, needs and wishes. Somehow I seemed to know this is what I had to do, I suppose it was all those years of brainwashing. But mainly it was losing my name and 'gaining' his. I didn't at that time realise I had a choice. Anyway I worked seriously at being a wife. I remember in the first year we did it every night — no orgasm for me, just a numb boredom. When during that first year, I went for a cervical smear I asked the doctor how often married people 'ought' to do it. Sex often made me sore and I wasn't getting a lot out of it. The doctor answered that it would get better and less frequent over time. Well in one sense he was right. I'm not sure whether it got better because it became less frequent or whether it qualitatively changed. I guess the latter since I started learning to have orgasms. But also sexual fantasies. From that point up till the birth of my first child we did it about four times a week. And in the main I was enthusiastic about sex, the physical pain seemed to stop, or perhaps I got used to it. Even then, though, I remember not always wanting to do it when he did, maybe I was tired, or just not in the mood but I wouldn't say no because he might be hurt or upset. I didn't at the time feel particularly resentful about this, generally I felt reasonably independent. I could have left him if I'd wanted to, and I didn't particularly want to — not often anyway.

It was only after my first child was born in 1974, that sex began to be a problem. In the first place my son was an accident, that is I didn't plan to get pregnant. Anyway I began to resent the sexual demands my husband made; sometimes I genuinely wanted sex when he did, so that was no problem. It was the other times, like those two years after my son was born when I was breastfeeding, or had to get up to comfort him. As well as this I was working full-time so I felt generally harassed. But I had been advised by all the good ante-natal and post-natal literature not to neglect my husband. So I didn't. I sexually serviced him, and it began to feel just like that. If I said no, as I sometimes did, there would be either a row, well into the night, or silence which might last for days. Either way my tension and strain increased so I learned to be available, even if I didn't want to. It was quicker in the long run, so I could get some sleep.

I remember feeling all kinds of hostile feelings against him when he invaded my body, sometimes during the night whilst I slept — I'd awake to find him fucking me. But I couldn't really articulate it, I felt trapped, in a way I hadn't been before the children were born. After the birth of my second child — a girl — things got worse — so bad that I made myself change. I had to for my daughter's sake. I was like some kind of automaton. I worked full-time (paid employment), breastfeeding the baby at night, took the children to baby-minders on buses. Did a full day's work and then came home to clear the breakfast things from the table to begin tea.

On and on it went with me totally drained of energy, but still I was expected to 'have sex'. In fact I did, without enthusiasm, just as another chore, like doing the ironing or bathing the kids.

About this time he began to complain that I was sexually unexciting and he was beginning to be bored. I couldn't cope with all the demands being made on me, something had to go if my marriage wasn't to fall apart. So I gave up my job. Not to my surprise, my husband 'managed' to find a job after being unemployed for a year. Anyway I decided to go to university, I also decided that I had better become more sexually exciting so I agreed to all his suggestions — kinky underwear, unusual positions etc., I didn't like most of the things he did to me, but I felt a little that I was supposed to. I faked liking what he did, including buggery which I found painful, but still he kept doing it.

I could catalogue all the separate incidences of rape — that is doing it against my will — but it's too painful for me to recall it all. In fact my experience is fairly commonplace. No major brutal acts, just a generalized abuse of my integrity. I don't want to give the impression that I was completely passive and unwilling all the time. Sometimes I wanted to 'do it', but more often than not I was too tired. After starting my university course I began to become more confident, getting away from the house helped me; and still thinking in terms of maintaining my marriage I went on the sexual initiative. I started making demands on him for what I wanted. His response was impotence. He went to the doctors who gave him pills and advice. Neither did much for me, since I had begun to find my life a mess, torn between roles, student, mother, wife etc. I decided that one solution to my problems with him was to get out of 'the bedroom', and have a room of my own, which I did without too much complaint from him.

In fact separate bedrooms didn't help a great deal, because although I had a greater chance to say no, I felt guilt tripped that I was neglecting him. So I often made trips upstairs at the appointed hour. I hated it, but I could get up immediately and carry on writing essays, duty done. My salvation came however, several months after; I met a woman. I left home immediately and defined myself as a lesbian.

It's well over a year since I left, and I think I'm beginning to recover. It's hard whilst it's happening to you to realize that you are being exploited, fucked-over and constantly raped. Because the effect of it all is to reduce your ability to fight back, or even to see what it's about. My confidence was constantly undermined and eroded, perhaps this is the reason women feel unable to work outside the home, after their children have left home. It's all those years of rape — perhaps subtle rather than brutal, but rape nevertheless. I was lucky I got out after ten years of marriage. It's only now that I can see what effect it had on me. It was rape and I couldn't name it. Had I known I'm sure I would have got out sooner. Rape in marriage is an issue, naming it is the first step in a campaign which could stop the misery of millions of women's lives.

L., October 1981

I have used only an initial because I'm in the middle of a dirty divorce case.

RAPE IN MARRIAGE CAMPAIGN

The Law on Sexual Offences is being examined by the Criminal Law Revision Committee (CLRC). They have made proposals for 'reform' and asked for comments on them. Lots of Women's Liberation Movement (WLM) groups have responded — this is likely to be the only time during our lifetime that we have a chance of affecting what the law on sexual offences is. A national WLM meeting was held in the summer to discuss sex laws and what we wanted to do about them. The laws and proposals for their reform are inadequate in giving protection to women or deterring men, and no-one at the meeting believed that the answer to sexual violence is changes in the law. But the law shapes public opinion as well as being influenced by it, so we must concentrate on changing the attitudes to sexual violence, and women, that the law causes and reflects. Rape in marriage is not the only issue to campaign about, but is one area where we can effect change and thus strengthen women's position. A lot of people are not aware that men can't be prosecuted for raping their wives. Historically women were our husband's property under the law. The rape law has its origins in this belief. A man cannot be charged with damaging his own property. The Church has always upheld marriage as a sacred institution no matter the cost to women. Funny how God has always operated in men's interests!

The CLRC is making a very limited proposal that would make rape in marriage a crime for the first time, so the media will pick up on it — and we can get a lot of publicity for what we are saying and any actions we do. We can use the campaign to destroy many of the myths about which men rape, why they do, and how little protection women get from the law, as well as revealing the extent of sexual violence, once again.

The Law and Proposed Changes

'Marriage — a license to rape'. Rape is defined as sexual intercourse (penetration of the vagina by the penis) without the woman's consent, where the man knows or does not care that she is not consenting. A husband can only be charged with raping his wife if they are divorced or legally separated and she has a non-molestation/interference injunction in force against him, or if he has VD. If a husband rapes and injures his wife, she can (now) bring less serious assault charges against him, so his punishment will be far less.

The CLRC proposes that women should be able to make complaints to the police that their husband raped them, but the decision to prosecute will not rest with the police as it does in other rape cases, but that the Director of Public Prosecutions (DPP) will decide. The job of the DPP is to carry out Government policy, so he decides whether the prosecution is 'in the public interest' rather than simply deciding if there is sufficient evidence to prosecute. The CLRC is saying the DPP will protect public interest because it is so important to protect 'the preservation of the family unit'. The legal arguments that the CLRC give are a sham:

1. 'The difficulties that already exist in obtaining sufficient evidence in cases of rape would be greater with a co-habiting husband and wife . . . the police would have to make distasteful enquiries into details of family life'. When a couple are co-habiting but not married, the man can be charged with rape by the police, similarly buggery and indecent assault are offences even in marriage, and it's just as hard for the police to get evidence for prosecuting then as in rape of a wife by her husband, so it is the marriage vows which make the difference.

2. 'These matters should be left where possible to the Family Courts'. *'Nearly all breakdowns of marriage cause problems. A breakdown brought about by a wife who sought protection of the criminal law of rape would be particularly painful'.* WHAT!

The same objections were raised about changing the law so women who were being battered could apply for injunctions and other remedies from the courts. We would live in a world of happy marriages if women did not complain about being battered and raped, is the message, not that men shouldn't batter and rape their wives.

The whole legal system is weighted against women so that it is relatively easy for a man to be acquitted because the prosecution must prove beyond any reasonable doubt that the woman did not consent. (Naturally we are trying to get this changed too.) If a man has a previous history of sexual violence the prosecution cannot use that as evidence, also his defence can be he believed she was consenting however unreasonable that belief was. In cases of a husband raping his wife this system makes it doubly hard for the prosecution to convince the jury, and the DPP would not risk his reputation in trials that he wasn't sure of winning.

So we are fighting for other changes in the law on rape as well as saying the DPP should not be involved.

All the myths about rape: that it is easy for a woman to call rape, that she must have asked for it/agreed to it, can be used against rape in marriage being a crime.

Making rape in marriage a crime will go some way towards challenging the idea that saying 'yes' once means for ever and any time he wants.

There are other areas of the law on sexual offences such as incest, age of consent, definition of rape, police and legal procedures, which are being reviewed. Many women are discussing these at the moment in order to take action.

Rape in marriage is a relatively straightforward issue, however we need to be careful that the campaign can't be taken to be saying that marriage and the protection women get from the law would be ok if the law were reformed to make rape in marriage a crime.

'I will . . . when *I* want to'

Questions

We need to think through very carefully what we are objecting to and what we are calling for in this campaign. These are some of the points that have come up in discussion.

1. What do we mean by rape, how does it differ from the legal definition and what the media says about it?
2. How can anyone justify the law saying that because a woman made marriage vows she must always be available sexually to her husband, no matter what he wants her to do?
3. Does our conditioning and position in society make us accept sexual pressure from men, which means we don't have a real choice about when and how we have 'sexual relations'?
4. Can we ever expect the law to give any protection to women?
5. Is the whole system of male/female relations so full of problems that we will never be able to eradicate rape?

Action

The following ideas for action came up at the national WLM meeting on campaigning against rape in marriage:

- Occupy churches and arrest clergymen for aiding and abetting rape.
- Flyposting registry offices and churches with posters of slogans against rape.
- Occupy shops that sell bridal wear.
- Confidential questionnaire, in streets and in women's magazines.

- Arrest Archbishop of Canterbury!
- Citizen's arrest of husbands who rape their wives (not legal).

Other Slogan Ideas
- 'I thought rape was a criminal offence until I discovered marriage'.
- 'Marriage is a bed of roses . . . beware of pricks!'

. . . . . .

Bring your ideas to the workshop on Rape in Marriage Campaign.

Rape in Marriage Campaign

WOMEN'S AID AND THE FIGHT AGAINST MALE VIOLENCE

The aim of this paper is to explain what Women's Aid is and does, and how I see our activities as *a part of* the fight against male violence. It is also to highlight some criticisms which are made of the way Women's Aid operates, to give some response to the criticisms, but hopefully to open it all up to discussion. I also want to make clear it is the result of talks with women in Women's Aid groups in London and elsewhere but it is finally the opinion of one woman.

Women's Aid groups were set up all over England, Scotland, Wales and N.Ireland to give practical help and support to women who experience violence from a man in their own home, or a man who made it impossible for a woman and her children to remain in her own home by harassing her.

Women who come to refuges have often lived with the threat and/or reality of being regularly beaten up by the men they live with for years, many women have permanent physical injuries, bad hearing, broken ribs, for example, from these beatings. Women have also lived with men who sexually intimidated them and their daughters, sexually ridiculed them calling them "frigid", or raped them. Violence does not just mean physical attacks. Many women have never been allowed out alone or have been timed whilst they go out shopping, have been threatened if they see friends or relatives, have had clothes and possessions destroyed, or have been told they were "mad" to the point where they believed it themselves. All these limits on a woman's freedom, some of which are experienced by all women, are *violence against us*. I am explicitly describing this violence to show the reality by comparison with the empty euphemisms used by agencies and police like "domestic violence" or "violent situation". I will also not use a label such as violent man/men to distinguish men who attack women as if they were a special category of man. All men benefit and many aid each other in inflicting violence on women. We all know of male taxi drivers who reveal the address of the refuge to men. We all know social workers and doctors who ignore women's black eyes and bruises. We've all heard "jokes" from men about "battered women" when we've been collecting money "that's my contribution, now I can go home and hit her, Ha Ha!"

Finally the men who get off on hearing women talk about violence they have experienced or who get credit for being "good men" because they're not obviously physically violent to women or even "protect" us from violence of other men.

How Women's Aid Gives Practical Help to
Women Leaving Men

First and foremost Women's Aid groups run REFUGES; safe houses for women and their children to come to where they can stay and make plans for their next move. There are very basic ties a woman must break from the man she has lived with if she wants to stay away e.g. divorce proceedings, custody, getting supplementary benefit, getting on housing lists, etc. Women in the house, workers, support groups can all give advice and support for women to do this.

Women's Aid also keeps contact with women who have left the refuge either to go back to the men they left or to be rehoused and women who are not ready to leave their homes but just want to come and talk can also come to the refuge for support. In supporting women who go back we are supporting women *not* men and making it clear we are there when the woman wants to leave again.

The Federation and local groups on their own or in their regions also take part in campaigns for individual women who have fought back and been prosecuted e.g. Joan Greig in Scotland and the Maw Sisters.

We also try to respond to and initiate discussions on male violence in the media and in particular to counter the 'violence prone women' (women like it really) arguments of Chiswick Family Rescue.

A lot of our time and energy is also spent in negotiating and generally dealing with agencies and official bodies; DHSS, Housing, Social Services both on a local level and nationally. I think this often leads other groups to see us as 'copping out' or being 'reformist'.

I want to give some response to this allegation with the hope that it will be opened up for further discussion. Because Women's Aid is concerned with women experiencing violence in their homes we are immediately involved in an area where social workers, police and doctors are already involved and an important role for all groups is to get their agencies to acknowledge that women are being attacked and take this seriously and not just put it down to an individual family or woman's problem.

When we try to find a 'safe place' for women to go away from their homes (and not all women do leave their homes — many get injunctions and Women's Aid often stay in women's homes to help enforce the injunction), we are up against the fact that the Council owns the type of large houses we need for the number of women who need space. This means we must negotiate for houses and the administration of a house means we need funds for refuge workers childworkers, vans to collect women, etc. Some groups do in fact squat in houses but these may not be secure enough for women who may be very shaken and in need of rest and security. Once women are in the house the practical processes of getting divorced, getting money, etc. involves Women's Aid with agencies and because of the number of women who need refuge space, we need to have an ongoing relationship with these bodies rather than fight the same old battles with them each time round.

When it comes to rehousing, the local councils have a

virtual monopoly. There is not enough alternative accommodation although local groups do have links with Housing Co-ops. So official channels such as 'social priority' have to be used to get women rehoused. A further way in which Women's Aid is drawn into contact with Agencies is because we not only take in women, but their children too. This involves schools, health visitors, social workers, etc. and means we need to have childworkers and playschemes which also need funding. However, funding is a doubled edged weapon, as hard as it is fought for, it can twice as easily be taken away. It is important to say that for many groups the DHSS, the council, etc., only grudgingly, if at all, accept Women's Aid experience and knowledge as valid; often they reject the collective way in which we work, wanting to speak to "someone in charge"; they accuse us of being uncompromising, aggressive, difficult to liaise with. If we're reformist, someone had better tell the councils of this fact.

Furthermore, though the Federation has to appear "efficient" and "credible" in the terms agencies use, many local groups are engaged in direct action against male violence. Many Women's Aid Groups took part in the Day of Action in December, local groups are often getting children back, passing women on to safer towns, picketing judges who don't give injunctions and daily confronting men who appear on refuge doorsteps "wanting to see their wife" or men who appear at court to harass women or use access as an opportunity to harass and abuse women physically and verbally.

A further criticism I want to highlight is that Women's Aid groups don't take their politics into the refuge, or that saying "we do not place enough emphasis on the choice to live without men".

Many women involved in Women's Aid have lived in refuges and others have made choices about how as women they wish to live their lives. Many of us live alone with our children, many of us are lesbians. This doesn't change as soon as we enter the refuge.

Women go back for many reasons; often because they can't live without the financial benefits of being back with the man, because rehousing takes months or in some cases years, because the children want to see their father, or because women still feel emotionally involved with the man they have left. We can and do try to explode the myth that only men provide security in financial and emotional terms. If, by drawing on our own experience, men appear to do this, the price will often involve abuse, threats and/or violence. Women can also see from living in a refuge that we can, as women, give each other support. In the end however, women can only decide for themselves what to do and we will continue to give support when they have made that decision.

I feel that Women's Aid is only part of the fight against male violence. Our special contribution is that we highlight the reality that male violence, or the threat of it, is not just inflicted on women as an extreme method of control, but that for many women it is an everyday occurrence in their own home.

Jo (Lewisham Women's Aid), November 1981

COMMUNITY STUDY OF VIOLENCE TO WOMEN

Violence to women has recently become a focus for militant action within the women's liberation movement. Women's Aid has spent many years organising to combat 'domestic' violence (e.g. violence in the home) but has only recently started to encompass the all pervasive nature of violence to women, wherever the crime is perpetrated.

Whilst consciousness on violence is being raised to the level of action, the full extent of violence to women remains unknown. We have sharpened up our theoretical line, and even our practice, in terms of defensive militant action, we have still yet to determine the incidence of violence to women. Which means that we do not know how much violence is directed at women. How much violence do women endure and never report to the police or any other agency, or even to a friend? It is clear that groups such as Women's Aid and Rape Crisis bridge some of these gaps, but only as a last resort, when women have reached breaking point and run for the nearest door.

Women do not generally report crimes against them. Women suffer violence of varying degrees with a cynical acceptance. Violence against women is the famous 'dark' figure of unreported crime. The term violence has legalistic implications so it is essential to recognise the difference between man's law and woman's perception and experience. We decided that the only way to find out about violence to women was to ask women. We did just that.

We received a small grant from the Ella Lyman Cabot Trust in America which enabled us to begin work. We decided to conduct a pilot study in the community where we live. The ideas behind this approach were that we wanted to conduct a study which would be more than an academic exercise and would result in a weapon for action and change. Our struggle needs as many weapons as we can muster and we felt that talking to women would uncover the 'dark' figure which writes us out of criminal statistics, police action and public concern. When we draw attention to violence to women we are silenced and put down because we are radical feminists, man haters, dykes or any other label that may or may not fit. We may be some or all of these things but like all women we face violence every day. Women do not report these incidents and nobody really knows how great the problem is.

We chose an area of Leeds in which to interview women using well established and recognised community action research methods in a feminist way. It was our intention that once the information had been gathered we would hold a public meeting for women in the area and report back our findings, perhaps helping to organise some effective collective action based on the results. We are hoping to write up the results and share with other women our methods of work. We also hope to be able to publish a pamphlet which will be a kind of 'do-it-ourselves' research book. This pamphlet will be aimed at women's groups all over the country in the hope of encouraging similar projects in other areas.*

As we talked with women's groups and individual women in Leeds about our ideas we gradually understood what we wanted from the project and how it would be useful to all women. We chose to work in Leeds because of the heightened consciousness of Leeds' women due to the 'Ripper' terror. Leeds was also important because of the fight-

*This has now been published: Hanmer & Saunders, *Well Founded Fear: a community study of violence to women*, Hutchinsons, 1984.

246

back that had taken place. We chose an area which gave us the broadest social strata and which housed many single women. 171 houses were called on in seven streets in the Leeds 6 area. We devised a questionnaire which we passed around many groups of women for comments. Once the questionnaire was agreed upon we began knocking on doors. 6 feminists were involved in the interviewing of 129 women. Out of the 129 women that we interviewed 84 of them reported incidents of violence in the last year. These 84 women reported a total of 211 incidents which had either happened to them personally or were witnessed by them. 65% of the sample group reported one or more incidents. There were 141 incidents that had been personally experienced by 76 women — this was 59% of the sample.

We asked women about threats, physical assault and sexual harassment that they had experienced over the past year from men. 24% of the women interviewed experienced threatening behaviour from men. 16% experienced physical assault. 45% experienced sexual harassment. These crimes took place at work, at home, in the streets — everywhere that men are allowed. Only 10% of violence that was witnessed by the women interviewed was reported to the police and 13% of violence experienced by the women themselves.

The sample is small, the findings are not, they speak for themselves. It is important to point out that we did not define violence for the women, they defined it for themselves. There has never been a national incidence study done in Britain on violence to women. It is not in the interests of the state to sponsor research which will prove that the analysis made by radical feminists is correct.

Jalna Hanmer & Sheila Saunders

Abstract for workshop: W.A.V.A.W. Conference, London, November 1981

We would like to acknowledge and thank all the women who contributed to this study, with special thanks to Ruth Bundey, Jenny Wardleworth, Sandra McNeill, Marianne Hester, Leslie Kay, Al Garthwaite and the South Headingley Community Association.

SEXUAL HARASSMENT AT WORK

A woman was offered the opportunity to assist one of the directors on a marketing project in Australia. She accepted on the condition that he made no attempt to touch her or approach her sexually. She had worked for him in the past and was familiar with his wheedling physical aggression. He reacted very angry and went about self-righteously informing other members of his department of her response putting the onus on her of raising the sexual issue between them — as if to say if she had expected sexual advances from him, she must want them.

Every night during the project he touched, coerced, aggressed and attempted to force her to have sex with him. When she showed him that he was not going to succeed he made her work more difficult by ignoring her plans during the day. At the end of the trip he told her she would lose her job if she told anyone in the company about it.

. . . . . .

The only room at work to have a number on it instead of the people's name was the typing pool. The women put up a large women's symbol beneath the number in retaliation. When they came back from lunch the fist in the middle had been replaced by a prick with a woman's hand doing a hand job on it.

. . . . . .

The married marketing manager and his unmarried secretary had a sexual relationship. The man decided to end it. The secretary created scenes in the marketing department. The head of the department put pressure on her to resign which she did. The man suffered no loss of status.

. . . . . .

A woman worked as a waitress in a pizza restaurant. She became suspicious of the attention shown to her by all the men who worked there. She discovered that they had all laid bets as to which would be the first to have sex with her.

She couldn't complain to the manager as he was in on the bet too.

. . . . . .

A lesbian and a gay man worked together as designers on the same books. They were friendly and the woman enjoyed hugging and kissing with the man but objected when he sexually humiliated her by slapping her bottom, making unflattering remarks about the size of her breasts, the smell of her vagina, attempting to take her trousers off when she was talking to a printer. She began refusing to let him touch her at all and hit him on two or three occasions. In the pub with a group of friends she elbowed him in the ribs when he would not stop harassing her. He slapped her round the face 'to teach her a lesson'.

. . . . . .

A black word-processor worked on a certain machine. Male colleagues pinned up the photograph of that machine with a half-naked black model on it next to her desk.

. . . . . .

A woman taxi driver picked up a mother and her 5-year-old son. The boy asked 'Is that a man or a women?' 'I'm a woman' she replied. 'You can't be. Only men drive taxis'. He repeated this throughout the journey.

. . . . . .

A temp secretary complained to her female agency manager that a client had thrust his hand down her T-shirt. The manager was sympathetic, but the temp had worn 'provocative clothing' and got no more work for three weeks.

. . . . . .

A 'plain woman' is very efficient at her job. She is constantly referred to by men as sexually frustrated, a spinster only able to find satisfaction in her job.

. . . . . .

Women in any situation with men are subject to sexual violence and abuse. Sexually harassing women, men show women and each other that they have the power to oppress women in whatever way they choose because and only because they are women. The sexual aspect of the harassment is an excuse: it is cover for hate. Women are told to feel appreciated and flattered by this behaviour. The fact that men harass women is seen as a result of women's 'attractiveness' and is excused by the belief that men are sexually 'uncontrollable'. Sexual harassment has nothing to do with men's sex drive — it serves to demonstrate and re-inforce the power that men have over women.

Sexual harassment at work takes the form of touching, chasing, staring, making comments about women's appearance, men's accounts of their sexual conquests, the display of pornography, repetitive songs and sayings that degrade women, standing unnecessarily for women, tripping women up, denial of women's ability to do men's work, insistence that women conform in dress and behaviour to male norms at peril of losing the job, men talking about the women's movement in order to placate or provoke further anger, humiliation of women for 'faults' which are seen as 'qualitites' in men, forced embraces, violent assault, rape and finally murder.

Most of these forms of S.H. are common practice in all situations.
What are the implications of S.H. of women by men at work?

For a woman work may be the one place where she asserts herself — financial independence from men and her own family — escape from trap of unpaid domestic labour — tasks performed on a conditional basis — trade union involvement — self-definition — exercise of skill.

S.H. serves to remind her that she is female: inferior, and that these aspirations deserve no recognition.

What does sexual harassment at work do to women?
- persistent harassment destroys self-confidence and belief in right to say NO
- anger at what is happening is continually trivialised and treated as a joke

- makes woman conscious of physical existence/vulner-ability as she bends over filing, stands on chair to reach up, runs up stairs, carries a tray, engages in manual tasks while men watch etc
- her efficiency and personal freedom are diminished as she plans her work in order to avoid male co-worker in lift, store room, etc
- illness, nervous depression
- if she complains she is the guilty one — wearing the wrong T-shirt, being over-sensitive, lacking sense of humour, sex-obsessed, sex-hating, vindictive, difficult to work with
- makes women judge one-another from male standpoint: keeps women divided
- women dare not complain because it calls into question their ability to do the job — women often are obliged to take further risks rather than seek help at risk of losing job; fear of 'I told you so' attitude from men
- instead of complaining women often explain S.H. at work by enumerating men's 'problems/excuses', loneliness, sexual frustration, recent divorce, etc
- the fact that men force women to leave jobs because of S.H. reinforces belief and practice that women's work is 'temporary' and not done for reasons of economic necessity, bars women from job promotion and keeps women's wages down — keeps women as source of cheap labour
- if a woman leaves a job in a hurry because it becomes unbearable — likely to get a worse one

Strategy for fighting S.H.
- self-defence classes — assertiveness training
- mutual support between women
- learning ability to show anger at the time
- pooling and sharing of information on particular harassers and overall S.H. as practiced and condoned at workplace
- questioning value of complaining to personnel and management
- confrontation of sexual harassers but not without planning and support
- public humiliation of sexual harassers

- talk with women at work about experience of S.H. whether they define themselves as feminists or not.
- bringing up S.H. at trade union level.
- try to *explode myth that men harass women because they are lonely, sexually uncontrollable* etc. and *replace by knowledge that S.H. is a political act.*

Because a woman at work is defined as inferior to the men with whom she works, she may do boring repetitive tasks and perform service/decorative roles which carry less status and less pay. A woman may be sexually harassed by ANY man — boss, colleagues and men who have inferior status to her at work. Many women are in service jobs in which being pleasant to the men (however insufferable their behaviour) is an essential part of the job. Where women work side by side with men doing the same work, women are defined by men as a threat to the favouritism bestowed on the wives or girlfriends of those men. Women cannot hope to compete with men at work and must only resort to petty infighting among each other to gain male approval.

S.H. at work serves to remind women that they cannot escape male dominance and to keep women divided from each other.

Women at work have 2 'bosses', the boss within the hierarchy of the workplace and the boss with whom she works. Even when a woman works 'for' another woman, she may find that her boss has not only accepted male standards enforced by long service, but uses them to control her subordinate, refusing to delegate responsibility etc.

Male Power is derived from making women powerless
Men enjoy humiliating women
Sexual harassment is regarded as inevitable —
Boys will be Boys

There is no political recognition of the problem of S.H. in this country. It is regarded as an acceptable and normal practice.

Very little information is available about the extent of S.H. in U.K. but trade union surveys done in other countries (e.g. Canada) show that between 70% and 88% of women who go out to work have been victims of S.H. at every job level in every occupation and because trade unions are male dominated this is reflected in the surveys. S.H. covers behaviour which from a male point of view is seen as a 'sexual' advance and does not include the whole range of aggressive male behaviour carried out on the basis of sex difference. All women that I have spoken to have at one time or another been victims of S.H. at work, and many at all times. This is because the insults and injustices practiced at their workplaces are done on the basis of sex differences.

In U.K. there is no legal protection against S.H. Nothing in the Sex Discrimination Act and the E.O.C. has no knowledge of an application made on this issue. The only other option for British women is to take the risk of resigning and sueing for 'constructive dismissal'. Very few cases come up.

Anon

FASHION AS VIOLENCE AGAINST WOMEN

Fashion – so what?
Fashion is not just a trivial, insignificant area of women's lives. If we choose to ignore it, its effects, its reasons do not just disappear. It is a vital element of our oppression, especially effective because the majority of workers in the fashion industry are women therefore it serves to obscure male power by using women as agents.

No, fashion is not trivial – it's survival
A woman's appearance is her income. It governs which stereotype she is placed in at any given moment and that is important in a world ruled by men. I remember reading a newspaper report about a woman being murdered, "She had chipped nail polish and a pencil skirt", there was the implication that the police were not going to take this case very seriously as they thought the woman was a prostitute. Even if a woman is extremely talented or enters a profession, her appearance will determine how men will react to her which will have a large bearing on her promotional chances, etc. Though many women are employed in the fashion

industry it must be remembered that "the emergence of male homosexual sadism from the underground has coincided with the burgeoning of overt sadism against women in all communications" ('Lavender Culture'). Gay men have a lot of power in the fashion industry. The resurgence of the 'feminine woman' can be seen as a backlash to the demands being made by women for greater autonomy and the 'free flowing' styles of the sixties fitted in nicely with men's ideas of 'sexual freedom'. Evidence of this can be seen in the 4" or 5" platform shoes of the mid-seventies and the stilettos and tight skirts of recent years.

You have to suffer to be beautiful

Women are expected to change their appearance as often as once a year, though as we grow older the frequency of this transition decreases. Fashion defines the middle-aged woman as defunct.

Every day women suffer an immense amount of pain through diets (anorexia and compulsive eating), plastic surgery, hair removal (electrolysis, depilatories, waxing), the list is endless. The saddest part of all is the self-hatred that goes with continually trying to live up to an ideal that most of us never reach. Women are being taught to be alienated from their bodies and other women's bodies. What chance does this give us of becoming free if we can't love ourselves?

Fashion is dangerous

It is not an accident that men wear practical clothes while women are incapacitated in tight clothes which restrict movement. Our strength to fight back is undermined.

It is possible to forget your body in loose comfortable clothing. This is not so in tight jeans and a flimsy blouse, for these emphasise our vulnerability. You have to be careful you are not showing too much flesh. These clothes also mark us as a target for attack. "We have no freedom, no language, no behaviour to call our own, all the tight little dresses, single us out as women as effectively as did the yellow stars on the coats of the Jews in Nazi Germany, only today it is done in the name of 'fashion'" (Judith Bat Ada, *Playboy isn't playing**).

*From the collection, 'Take Back the Night', edited by Laura Lederer, Bantam, 1980.

Fashion and Pornography

Pornography is one of the most hateful and violent aspects of misogyny. There is a growing trend towards paedophilia shown in porn. This is reflected in the fashions available for young girls. Previously young girls were dressed in clothes which were distinct from women's, but now they have make-up, tight trousers and even pencil skirts for the under 5's, items which are associated with sexual availability to men. Girls realize from an early age that they receive rewards for offering themselves up as sex objects.

Under male supremacy women's status depends greatly on male approval. If we don't conform we pay heavy penalties. It means that many women mutilate and injure themselves, spending an enormous amount of time, energy and resources in the process. Fashion divides us into angels, whores, dolly-birds and hags. This is important in the maintenance of male power. It prevents us from seeing each other as allies, but sets us up as enemies, always in competition. For many women survival depends on making themselves into sex-objects, this way we can achieve only a superficial identity but "most of us fail as successful sex objects. How better to undermine us than to infiltrate our identity" (Spare Rib 88).

FASHION = CONTROL = VIOLENCE AGAINST WOMEN

Anon

LANGUAGE AS VIOLENCE

This paper occurred to me because:—

(a) I'm interested in the whole idea of how language operates to reinforce our oppression in its many subtle forms which we aren't as aware of as we are the obvious sexist remarks. A lot of this has been looked at by Dale Spender in her book 'Man Made Language'.

(b) ... the way I feel language is used in both its written and spoken form to present a view of women which allows for much of the more specific acts of violence against women that are being discussed in workshops at this conference; it allows these to occur without the reactions of shock, horror, outrage and consequent prevention which one would expect in 'normal circumstances'.

To put it simply and give one example —
Rape — why is rape joked about? Why is it treated lightly as a crime? Why is it sometimes considered to be desired? Why is it not recognised as the direct expression of woman-hatred that it is?

O.K. — so men hold the power, men make the laws, men administer them and men, and only men, rape.

But the 'right-on' man protests he is not a potential rapist and women also joke about rape. I know I used to think women who were raped 'Asked for it'. Yet any woman who has been raped, forced into sex against her will, has any knowledge of rape could not possibly think these things. Or could she? Does she?

At the conference we will be talking about the different acts of violence aginst women. Some will be more immediately obvious than others — e.g. rape as compared to therapy.

I would like to suggest that the way women are talked *about*, talked *to*, helps to support an ideology which has created woman as a possession, a non-human, a sick member of society, irrational, hysterical, emotional, unpractical, a toy, a plaything, something to be used and discarded, and also has created the view of the good woman versus bad woman which divides us off from our sisters and prevents us identifying with all women.

If any of these descriptions of women come as a surprise to you — which they shouldn't! — then have a look at any of the current dictionaries around for a definition of WOMAN.

Pocket Oxford — Adult human female, womanish man
Usage   — 'woman-hater', 'play the woman'

Compare these definitions with that of MAN and you'll easily get the right answer to the question — 'which is the norm?'

This view of WOMAN is perpetrated in novels, in magazines, advertising, films, t.v., in serious and popular journalism, in legal, medical and political discourse, in everyday conversation, and in the many jokes which serve to humiliate and degrade women — the nagging wife, the whore, the mother-in-law, etc.

I'd also like to suggest that the ways women are talked about and written about effectively divide them. A couple of pages of the News of the World convinces us that there are women about who are not like us and that nasty things happen to and we don't want to be like that. In other words the description prevents us from identifying with the victims, although we might be able to see others as the victims.

So just as soldiers learn to label foreigners as wogs, wops and dagos — NOT people or human beings — so no problem about pulling the trigger, dropping the bomb — then women can be positioned through the way they are described and talked about, therefore less need to justify or excuse the atrocities committed against us.

In case you've forgotten:—

'Shall I make you laugh? This feller pays £20 for this whore, right? Only she doesn't fancy him and runs out of the room. He chases her stark naked, down t'street. Cop stops him, says, Where's the fire, lad? Feller says, I've no idea, but if you see a nude bird running down the street, fuck her, it's paid for'. (Comedians — Trevor Griffiths)

Sally

Postscript

The ideas in the paper come from discussions on language and women's position within and to language which have taken place in The Women and Language Group over the past two years. The group, which was initially "open" has been "closed" for the past year during which time we have been trying to put together an article on "Women and Humour".

There are many occasions on which it appears at first sight that women are to blame for things that harm other women. There are many examples of men's power hiding behind women and what women do. When we try to talk about male violence against women or horrible sexual practices which men force on women or when we try to explain to women how it is men who hold power and women who are subservient — women will often argue back by mentioning women who murder women, lesbians who practise sadomasochism, upper-class women who treat other women badly, prostitutes (who 'give all women a bad name'), mothers who, knowing that their husbands are sexually abusing their daughters, do nothing, women who 'of their own free will' act as models in pornographic photos/films, women who campaign against abortion . . . and so on.

Men have developed many ways to use women to enforce their power. This obscures the cause of our oppression — men. And if we blame other women we ourselves are failing to locate, identify and attack the real enemy. A few examples are given below:—

—   We distance ourselves from a particular woman.

This happens when a woman is raped. We do not want to believe that the violence might happen to us — so we find ways of putting the responsibility onto her. Men of course encourage us to do this: then we are less likely to develop a political analysis of rape. (Thus 'she asked for it' etc.)

Similarly, women will focus our anger on prostitutes rather than on the real villains — the pimps and the clients.

—   We disbelieve women, and make excuses for men. This is especially true of women in the 'caring' professions, such as social workers.

A social worker exonerated a father from blame for incest (after refusing to believe the daughter for a year) by saying that he was bringing up a family on his own.

Lots of women in jobs with some power but under the jurisdiction of men 'pass the buck' onto women. This makes it harder for women to be taken seriously. Erin Pizzey is guilty of obscuring the power relations in marriage when she talks about 'cycles of violence' and takes up the cause of 'battered husbands'.

— We make false analyses of women's oppressions or we fail to speak honestly about the sources of our oppression. Academic women have a responsibility to other women not to evade the real issues. Writers owe it to us to make their material available to the WLM and to consult with other women over matters upon which they are not 'experts' (e.g. if writing a history of the WLM).

To locate the source of women's oppression in 'capitalism' or 'society' is to make excuses for wrongs that men do to women.

To present 'individual solutions' is misleading — for instance in novels about women's lives. To suggest that women can and should create a culture and a sexuality outside of 'patriarchy' without tackling men's power over us is misleading and confusing. It can stop women seeing what men are doing to us.

— Women act as the socialisers of other women. It is women who are mothers and teachers, women who are responsible for the early life of girls. It was women who bound the feet of girls in China, who practise clitoridectomy and infibulation and women who pass on the ideology of heterosexuality and marriage. Mothers' concern and anxiety for their daughters make them do terrible things, often to try and make them more 'marriageable'. Mothers also try and protect daughters from abuse by fathers and brothers. But since they are sexually abused and tortured by men themselves women do not always stand up for their daughters in the face of male threat and abuse.

— Women also act as glamour-objects for men's pleasure and present 'acceptable' images of women, showing women being rewarded for conformity (Princess of Wales) and punished for being independent (lesbians). Women are often responsible for propaganda that serves men's interests — women produce thousands of 'romances' and edit/write in 'women's magazines'. We obscure the fact of male control of women by presenting marriage as free choice, by glamour-ising the life and work of models and filmstar women (sex-objects). We persuade each other that we enjoy crippling, deforming and defacing ourselves. But all this happens because men are in control and men want us confined and defined for them.

— Women act as agents for men in their control of women when we as prostitutes procure women for pimps, when we use S & M on each other as 'sexual expression', when we beat one another up or hurt one another, batter our daughters or our mothers ... we express woman-hatred toward one another, which is what men have forced/persuaded us to do.

— And women who fail to challenge what other women are doing when it works in men's interests are also not challenging the ways in which men use us against one another. We have a duty to point out to each other how men hide behind women and get us to do their work for them. We owe it to women to examine what we do and what we say, to say honestly if we know a woman is harming another woman, without blaming her for the root cause, which is men's enslavement of us. Similarly, I believe that we must explain how heterosexuality is central to our oppression and urge women to withdraw from heterosexual relations. And be critical of lesbian sexuality if it copies patterns of hetero (male-defined) sexuality.

- But how far should we hold one another responsible for our actions?
- How far can we make demands of other women?
- How much choice has a woman in her life?
- How can we as feminists work toward our choices such that we will no longer be in positions of aiding men in their hold over women?

If we do not have expectations of one another and do not make demands of each other we are accepting our powerlessness. We may not have a lot of choices but we shall not widen these unless we struggle to do so — that includes exposing how all of us are used by men against one another.

danu

Postscript

This paper was written in 1981. I have several criticisms of it now. There was nothing in it about how women who are able to may use classism and racism against other women.

I think we need a much deeper analysis of the different ways women's behaviour obscures men's power over all of us. Much deeper than is given in this paper. But that's outside the scope of a conference paper, maybe.

And having made an analysis we should not leave it there. Privileged women can work against their privilege. And women with power can use their power in favour of other women, not against them.

danu, 17 March 1983

PORNOGRAPHY — THEORY AND PRACTICE

" . . . The penultimate image of Michelle shows her sprawled between the carved wooden arms of a chair. Across her naked belly, and travelling down the front of her thighs are thick black straps which seem to hold her imprisoned to the seat of the chair — the metaphor of bondage is safely across. Above her breasts her face is partly shrouded by a piece of fabric that seems to fall from her unswept arms. Her one visible eye is closed, her mouth gapes open. Perhaps she has been smothered by the fabric. The centrefold then ensues — Michelle's body is at last completely lifeless. Perhaps she is dead. The picture shows a woman whose body is wrapped in a pale kimono whose torso is unconscious or dead, it has been thrown across a bed. On the far right of the picture we see her head thrown back, eyes closed, mouth open, neck stretched to expose a vulnerable throat, and on the far left of the frame, a similarly exposed and vulnerable vagina, disappearing off the edge of the page" (Pet of the Month — Centrefold).

The above is just one description from a current porn magazine found on, and amongst shop shelves, newsagents' stands and popular book shops. Pornography at the above level, and many would define it as tame, invariably comes

261

down to the same repetitive, inexhaustible celebration of misogyny. The principal content of pornography then is degradation, since the women's bodies involved have no choice or control. It is dehumanised, objectified and reduced to a 'slab' available for any act of humiliation and violence men wish to subject it to. Inevitably the image that 'shines' through the 'glossy' and expensive magazines is the pornographer's hatred of women.

Pornography, then, ranges from page three of the Sun, through to Penthouse, 'Les Girls' and finally terminates in the horror of 'snuff movies'.[1] Each magazine and booklet is full of images of women that are objectified, fetishized, violated, dehumanized and always degraded. An example from a booklet called 'Couleur Sang' (price £5) which is classified as 'hard porn' will perhaps emphasise and reiterate the statements we have so far made.

> "She wasn't enjoying his ways at all but her groanings looked like pleasure mournings. He became furious and held a small sharp chain to whip the woman's sex till blood appeared between the fragile lips ... The huge male organ penetrated her vagina. Her uncle was dominating and raping her. She could do nothing ... The man shrieked with pleasure. The sperm flowed into Caroline's flesh and spoiled her."

The horror of this text is ultimately emphasized with the end sentence which briefly, yet markedly describes Caroline's fate. "Carole was no longer Caroline. Now she could endure everything and no longer hated her uncle". As if not enough — the booklet is also accompanied by sadistic line drawings. The degradation of the above excerpts is obvious, which makes viewing and reading particularly upsetting and disturbing, but for any feminist who wants to understand pornography and hence camapign against it, we have got to force ourselves to view it so as to see what all forms of pornography mean and represent in real terms.

In money terms pornography is an ever expanding industry — over 50 million magazines are sold every year. In the United States the sales returns on the pornography industry are more than the film and recording industry combined. Porn then is not just bought by a few inadequate men stereotyped in raincoats and lurking in Soho doorways

— it is purchased and consumed by the journalist, the headmaster, the policeman, the factory worker, the vicar, our sons, boyfriends or husbands. Where then does porn exist? The ever-increasing sex shops are obvious haunts for such material, but so is the corner shop and modern newsagents. Recently women counted over thirty-eight different publications amongst magazines such as 'Woman's Own' and DIY manuals. It is no longer a product that is kept under the counter — it is on full display in its many varying, but always controlling forms.

How does pornography control and for what purposes? Feminist analysis of pornography is now well established — it shows porn to be a dangerous form of propaganda that deliberately incites men to carry out acts of violence upon women. Pornography gives power to men — it reinforces male supremacy — it advocates women as passive, always willing, and always available. It reduces women to an orifice to be fucked anytime anywhere and in any way. *We* know that it is through patriarchy that women are treated as objects, therefore pornography is surely the most objectionable way of highlighting and glamourizing control of women through sexuality. In short, pornography is about power — the sexual power that men seek to inflict upon women. The sadistic and cruel images of women being tortured, mutilated, raped and killed are rising steadily and along with this increase in such pornography, rape incidents multiply steadily. The statistics available about sex crimes (and these are only the reported cases) show that sex crimes have increased by 124% between 1963 and 1973 (Home Office figures). In that period all pornography has become more freely available. Hard core porn with violent and cruel images of women is proportionally more available, reinforcing all the social attitudes of women as objects, as vehicles, as a way of attaining the glossy sexual experiences thrown at us by every poster in the street, and every article on sex. Exploitation of sex is not to make us all happy and fulfilled. With every poster advertisement and station bookstall displaying us as a lure to buy and own, money is being made and, more importantly, we are being controlled.

To conclude, then, pornography is about male power. This power can be seen in seven subdivisions which are:

1. Men have a metaphysical power — as assertion of self that exists in an absolute form. Men have this self therefore women must lack it.
2. Power is a physical strength.
3. Power is the capacity to terrorize.
4. Men have the power of naming.
5. Men have the power of owning.
6. Money is a male power; and
7. Men have the power of sex.

Pornography exemplifies all the above facts and is central to the social control of women by men and we must take it seriously as a weapon used by men to weaken our resistance and hinder our revolt. Therefore "Sex and desire cannot be separated off from the rest of our lives. Our sexuality exists in relation to the world we live in — which is controlled by men — and men control us into a sexuality that simultaneously empowers them and does us down".[2]

Pornography is a medium that degrades all women everywhere whatever their age or class or race. It frightens some of us into silence, others into angry reaction, some of us laugh nervously, as the reality of the images often forces us to dissociate our minds from our bodies. Therefore we must attack and fight pornography, we must refuse to accept the liberal-mindedness of the sexual revolution, we must refute the arguments put forward describing porn as cathartic (*see note below) and we must struggle not to take part in, or act out sadomasochistic fantasies. Similarly, arguments for the development of a 'female erotica' are diversionary, and inappropriate, restricting and hindering women's ability to name porn as one of the main weapons of our oppression by men. Within a male supremacist system, to believe that erotic images produced by women would not automatically be appropriated for men's use, is not only naive but dangerous. We surely do not need to imitate our oppressor and in so doing weaken our resistance. What use would these images serve anyway, other than to endorse that our sexuality is no threat to men's belief that we fit

---

* The arguments for seeing porn as cathartic rest around the notion that such material will curb men's 'uncontrollable sexual urges'. Such a belief is as naive as it is ludicrous, i.e. do we produce material depicting child abuse in an effort to control and stop child battering?

in conveniently to the norm of male sexuality? We don't — and we will not. If these beliefs are allowed to fluctuate and develop the viciousness of porn will increase alongside the powerlessness of women.

Ruth Grinrod & Maria Katyachild, November 1981

With thanks to members of central London WAVAW and with special thanks to Danu November.

1. Snuff movies are films where women are actually killed as the ultimate climax in the pornographer's 'sick' plot. Cases have been discovered in California.
2. Danu November — unpublished paper, November 1981.

PORNOGRAPHY — STRATEGY

In pornography, the penis=power and woman=object. Pornography feeds and reinforces men's power by portraying women as waiting, willing objects under men's power and control, there to be gaped at, to be fucked, to be manacled with chains.

Pornography operates as male propagandist hatred and contempt of women and like any form of propaganda begins at the level of least resistance — women ourselves. The early days of 'girlie' magazines purporting to be merely expressions of men's admiration of the female form served as a useful tool to introduce the concept of women as objects of hatred without women realising it. Since then, the real message behind porn has become explicit with the slow build up of hard core violent porn. How far can we let them go? They have a £4 million industry now. Our very survival is at stake and that of our daughters.

It is vitally important for us to get in touch with our anger and to develop the courage and confidence to confront porn wherever it exists — pubs, work, newsagents, cinemas, porn shops, bookshops, advertising, the press, galleries, everywhere.

In tackling the issue, whether as individuals demanding the calendar be taken down where we work, or as part of a group picketing the local porn shop, there are potential problems we'll most likely have to deal with, such as,

- men trying to deflect us when we confront them into 'discussion' of why we are offended.
- men refusing to act upon our demand for removal of porn.
- men responding violently when confronted in pubs, the cinema.
- women defending men's need for use of porn.
- feminists differentiating between male porn and 'lesbian erotica'.
- lack of support from other women in confrontation situations.

The problems depend on whom we are talking with ... women in a discussion group, a woman alone or with a man when accepting a leaflet, a feminist or non feminist, co-worker, or on whom we're confronting ... the local newsagent, the porn shop owner, a 'non-sexist' male friend.

And in these situations, there are certain issues that surface to deflect us. One is our stand on censorship. We're brought up believing that censorship is anathema to the idea of freedom of expression. But now we know whose freedom they're talking about. Men's freedom to express their misogyny, men's freedom to continue their enslavement and control of women. To consider censorship as an issue gives credibility to a male concept of freedom, buttresses male power, protects men's interests under the guise of liberalism, permits the continuation of 'an open season' on women and deflects us from the real issue — pornography itself — and divides us in our fight against it. It is a strategy which endangers a clear analysis by making us defensive instead of offensive.

Another concern which undermines us is our possible identification with the Mary Whitehouse - right wing - moral crusaders in the media. But then, men control the media and no matter how clear and convincing our arguments are, it's certainly not in men's interests to present them as such. A good example of its subtlety is Jill Tweedie's reviewing a feminist study of pornography and a book by a self proclaimed female 'masochist' alongside one another. We must not let concern with our image which we cannot control affect our strategies.

A third issue is the existence of 'female erotica'. How is this 'erotica' different from male 'erotica' or porn? The difference is that women control its production. But what is the product? It is 'soft porn'. While it does not contain violence, it is still objectification of women as sexual chattels. This phenomenon 'feminist erotica' is a classic manifestation of women internalising their own oppression. By depicting women as sexually available to other women, we are apeing the male definition of sexuality, acting as agents for men, and providing men with the opportunity to say – See, you want porn too, so what's wrong with ours?

The methods of confrontation are familiar, the ones we've been seeing so far like pickets, sit-ins, leafleting, tabling, lobbying, marches, workshops at schools, women's centres, etc., articles in the press. A few others – taking photographs (or seeming to) of men as they leave the local porn shop or cinema, and group visits to a shop with the twofold aim of exposing ourselves to the incredible range of porn of which we might be unaware, and crowding the space where men are 'browsing' and consuming.

In order to use some of these methods, we must know our legal rights and the possible negative consequences of our actions. We need access to feminist legal advice and a feminist network for arrested women providing both monetary and emotional support.

How do we use these tactics effectively? We see the basic strategy as being a network of local groups. A central group is important for exchange of ideas, contacts, as a base for organising large events and actions, and as an information pool. But, because the display and sale of pornography has spread throughout the country, because it's everywhere, by working in local groups we can keep up to date on what's about in the neighbourhood and act quickly on it. It's a focus for our energy that can be more immediate. We can talk about the porn down the road, then walk down there to do something about it e.g. stand about outside the entrance to the local porn cinema as our male neighbours, friends, sons, etc. turn the corner ready to buy their tickets.

Working locally also makes it easier to develop contacts in the local presses, schools, the council, etc., and to make them accountable to the women's community. We're no longer out there – we're more accessible to a broader range of women, and more visible by concentrating more on local actions. Local commitment is vital if we are to form links with women outside the feminist community. Pornography is in all our neighbourhoods, it's where we fight it most frequently and where we can act most directly against it.

Elis & Linda

THE PRINCIPLES AND PRACTICES OF CONFRONTATION

The choices which society presents to women in response to sexual violence are limited. After we've been assaulted we can either do nothing, go to the police or contact a Rape Crisis Centre (if there is one in our area and we know about it). Confrontation is an alternative which can be used by women who want to take direct action against the men who have sexually harassed, assaulted or raped them. It is a method which has been developed and used *by* women, *for* women. The following is an account of a confrontation which occurred in Vancouver, in 1979:

Twelve year old Melissa was sexually molested by the landlord of the building in which she lived. She told her mother what had happened, and her mother phoned Vancouver Rape Relief to find out information on sexual assault. Melissa, and her mother, decided that they did not want to go to the police, or court, but they did want to do something about the behaviour of their landlord. From the alternatives suggested, Melissa decided to confront the man who had sexually molested her, with the support of other women. A series of discussions were necessary to organize the confrontation. To accompany her, Melissa chose her mother, her best friend, her mother's best friend as well as several other women who had offered her support. Melissa also decided who would speak and approved what they would say to the man who had molested her. The intention of their 'script' was to state their thoughts and feelings to this man without equivocation or interruption from anyone. The group decided it was safest to confront him at his home, when his wife was out. (They also decided that his wife should be told in advance, and suggested to her that she stay at a neighbour's home with two women from the group who would talk to her about what was happening.)

On the day that had been arranged to do the confrontation, two women watched the apartment long enough to be sure the landlord was home. Then they phoned one woman in the telephone tree that had been constructed for the confrontation and continued watching the building until the group arrived. When he opened his door, one woman jammed her foot and shoulder against it to prevent him from closing it. Melissa stood in the centre of the group, protected within a semi-circle of women. She spoke first, facing him directly then each woman with lines followed in turn; the script flowed from one woman to the next as they had already decided who would say what when. The man was not allowed to interrupt; another woman had volunteered to say to him: "Listen — this is not a time for you to speak" as a precaution, necessary in this case, as he kept trying to interject with profuse apologies. When the script finished, a woman gave him feminist pamphlets and articles on rape and sexist behaviour, as well as the telephone number of a men's group prepared to discuss male violence and sexual assault with him. (However, due to the dubious nature of most anti-sexist men's groups, it is worth discussing whether this tactic should be included.) The women then turned and walked away.

Confrontation is not a spontaneous, impulsive act, but a carefully organized and thought-out alternative to the criminal justice system (CJS). A contrast between the principles and practices of confrontation and the institutional legal system follows.

CRIMINAL JUSTICE SYSTEM	CONFRONTATION
1. Rape is defined as a crime against the Crown.	1. Rape/sexual assault is considered a crime against the individual woman and a threat to *all* women.

2. The raped woman is the chief *witness* for the prosecution. Her role is a passive one. She is the receiver of the action and the decisions. Throughout the CJS it is the police, detectives, doctors, attorneys, judge and jury (most of whom are male) who decide whether or not we've been raped. A rapist exercises control over our bodies and choices; the CJS mimics the rapist by maintaining and prolonging the powerless position of the woman who has been assaulted.

2. In confrontation, it is the raped/sexually assaulted woman who is the initiator and decision maker.
She
— decides to confront
— decides when and where the confrontation will occur
— decides how the script will read
— decides who will participate and speak
— speaks first
A confrontation is never done without the woman who has been assaulted. Confrontation counters the myths that she/we do not know what we want, how to make decisions, what is in our best interests and cannot, therefore, be self-determining.

3. In the CJS the burden of proof is upon the woman. The rapist's defense usually hinges upon the issue of consent. The defense attorney attempts to discredit the woman by verbally attacking her until *she* is seen to be the guilty party. Thus, modern day rape trials have the aura of witch trials complete with inquisitors who perform the cross-examination, clothed in ritual, costume and procedure.

3. In a confrontation, we believe the woman who states that she has been sexually assaulted. The man is not allowed to plead innocence or employ a highly paid professional to construct a case in his defense. It is not a dialogue between him and ourselves. It is clearly our turn to speak and his role is to listen. We agree ahead of time not to talk with him but to deliver the words and the feelings and to leave despite any attempt on his part to speak.

4. The CJS is a patriarchal institution created by men, for men. Sexist myths are formalised in the laws. For example: in all cases of sexual interference, the judge must warn the jury that it is dangerous to convict on the uncorroborated evidence of the witness. As the *overwhelming* majority of sexual offenses are committed by men, the 'witness' (whose evidence alone is not to be believed) is most likely to be a woman. *In no other area of the law is this warning applied.*

Note: Witchcraft was also made a "crimen exceptum" (a crime

4. Confrontation was developed by women, for women. We are not relying on male authority figures to validate our experience or 'protect' us. We are organizing ourselves to confront male violence. It is important for us to stand together, strong with our belief in ourselves and our power to create change. Confrontations are not just an action; they are changing the way we as women feel and think by teaching us how to use our anger and speak for ourselves. In a sexist society women are isolated from one another; we are encouraged to believe that it is *our personal*

distinct from all others, outside ordinary judicial rules) to legitimate the torture of witches [women].

problem if we are sexually assaulted; *we* should change our locks, our clothes, our lifestyle. *There are no private solutions to sexual assault.* VAW is such a general social relation that we all know how it feels to be harassed to some degree. Through confrontation we assert that it is the behaviour and attitudes of men that have to change — they are the problem.

5. During the trial, the man remains anonymous. His identity is protected from public knowledge; he is referred to as Mr. X. The rapist is thereby protected from community pressure.

5. Confrontation is a form of co community pressure and disapproval. The rapist/attacker does not remain anonymous. Many people know that he has attacked a woman, and say that they know. He is not protected by silence. Rape/sexual assault is made a speakable crime rather than a private matter of shame. Sexual assault has been/is used to control women through intimidation, fear and guilt. Confrontation is an attempt to overcome this oppression.

6. If the rapist is convicted and sentenced, he is usually poor and from a racial or cultural minority. Nothing will be done in prison to change his attitudes and behaviour towards women. Relationships of power are *reinforced* by the penal system. Many (most?) rapists get out of jail and rape again.

6. No class or racial exceptions are made in confrontations. We believe that sexist behaviour is socially conditioned and supported by patriarchy; it can be unlearned and replaced with non-sexist attitudes and behaviour. In a confrontation we demand that a man change his attitudes and behaviour towards women. We leave feminist literature and if possible the contact address of a men's group *attempting* to become aware of the sexist attitudes they have that maintain male supremacy.

7. The date of the trial is unconfirmed. The woman who has been assaulted must live in a state of suspense for months and sometimes years, uncertain of when she will be expected to appear in court. In the meantime, she must keep alive the memory of the assault as she must relive the scene in morbid detail when she testifies. This contributes to the emotional

7. The confrontation is a chance for the woman to express what she feels and thinks to her attacker. Therefore, the woman who has been assaulted does not confront until she is ready. Usually the confrontation will happen long before the time it would take for a court decision to be made. Confrontations must be nonviolent; it must not be a mimic of

trauma of an assault. The re-enactment in court is a further assault and provides a voyeuristic experience for men so inclined to exploit the opportunity. Throughout, the CJS is focused upon what is proper and procedural rather than upon the woman's suffering.

the assault — taking power by violence or violent threats. Treating people violently to teach them non-violence doesn't work. As much force as is necessary will be used to defend ourselves if need be, but it is not our intent to provoke such a situation.

Confrontations are not always the right action and are chosen and planned carefully depending upon, among other realities, the risks of violent retaliations from the man being confronted, during and after the confrontation.

Steps can be taken to make it safer for the woman and her friends involved in the confrontation. There should be good locks on the doors and windows of their homes. All exits should be clear of obstructions which would delay escape. A telephone tree can be set up with friends and neighbours so that help can arrive immediately. There should be at least seven or eight people (mainly women) confronting to reduce the risk of violence on his part.

In many instances confrontation has not provoked a violent response — but no firm generalizations can be made. Consequently, it is up to the individual women to decide whether or not they have the desire, anger and support necessary to confront their attacker.

ACTION AGAINST MALE VIOLENCE
(This paper was written after the Conference)

Confrontation

Confrontation is a way of dealing with known, individual men who have been violent.

The tactic of Confrontation allows a woman who has previously been powerless in a situation of male violence against her, to have the support of other women and to have complete control over the situation. The Confrontation should be set up by her, and discussed before hand with the other women who will help.

The Confrontation may only last a few minutes, on

average anything between four to eight minutes in which the woman physically confronts the man who has been violent or threatens violence to her. She has the opportunity to impress upon the man that she does not welcome his attention, that he must stop whatever it is that has hurt her. This will differ depending on the example of male violence, whether it is sexual harassment at work, battering within the relationship or rape. A man who has already been violent or has threatened violence may, of course, respond to a Confrontation with more violence, but our experience and the experience of feminists using Confrontation in Canada is that if several women accompany the woman (Canadian women recommend as few as four other women, but we suggest eight), the effect is to shock and intimidate the men.

Do not allow the man to speak, but instead make him listen to the woman confronting him. We simply told the man to shut up, and this worked. Several other women added things to back up what the woman was saying. This had all been rehearsed before the actual Confrontation. We had talked through the possibility of his being violent, and how we should respond. In the event, it was not necessary to restrain him, because he was intimidated by our numbers and our determination. After the Confrontation, which took about six minutes, we went somewhere else to talk about it so that we could release our tensions.

We think that Confrontation is an excellent tactic in many situations where the man is known; it can be done by women in their neighbourhoods and at work. We recommend it in cases of:

1. Sexual Harassment at work
2. Rape
3. Battered women (but not all cases)
4. Flashers.

Pros

The advantage for all the above cases is that it does have an effect on men, and evidence from Canada and the USA suggest that men are so shocked by the Confrontation that most do not return to violent acts against women. The woman herself feels strong, she receives support from other women and has the opportunity to express her anger.

Since we are not looking for male protection, Confrontation is an ideal way of taking control of our own lives. However, we are not suggesting that women do not resort to police aid if Confrontation does not work; we merely feel that Confrontation is more useful to us than police action for the reasons described above and below.

Cons

There is a fear that a Confrontation may provoke a violent man to more violence, but our experience shows that this is not so. We suggest that if a man is violent afterwards, he was likely to have been anyway, and although Confrontation did not stop him, at least it allowed the woman a chance to have her say.

OTHER FORMS OF ACTION AGAINST MALE VIOLENCE

Pickets: Of sex shops, video shops, Drag shows, Strip shows, sexually violent films, courts and trials.

Needed:
1. Placards focusing clearly and simply on the protest.
2. A leaflet explaining to women on the street why you are protesting.
3. Press Release, a signed statement from a member of your group, with a telephone number to go out to local and national newspapers and radio stations explaining why you are protesting, giving details of the protests; where when and why. We have found that the press are more likely to come if a contact telephone number and name is there.

Pitfalls: Obstructing highways; avoid it by keeping moving! If the police do come, do as they ask, but you do not need or have to give them your names or the name of the 'woman in charge'.

Self-Defence

It is important to overcome our reluctance at defending ourselves. Feminist Self-Defence Teachers Networks now exist throughout the country.

Pitfalls: 1. Carrying a weapon in self-defence is still illegal in this country.
2. A self-defence course does not 'protect' women from male violence, but it helps us respond individually to it in a more positive way.

Questionnaires/Exhibitions

Door to door surveys or high street surveys to find out the extent of male violence. The questions, if direct, like, 'Have you ever experienced male violence?' may result in negative replies. Ask instead, less direct questions because what may be violent for you might not be seen as violent by another woman. Women should be encouraged to express what they feel, so a good opener is 'Do you ever feel afraid to go out alone at night?'. From that, women may then talk about their experiences, which they may never have mentioned before. A public exhibition of posters, photographs, etc. is a very good way of getting women to talk about it. But the pictures there should not depict violence (a problem?)

Civil Disobedience

A tactic used much in other campaigns particularly Desegregation in America. This method could be used more widely in Britain against male violence, particularly when most women are in agreement in opposing it. Civil Disobedience means breaking the law, doing something which will mean the police will arrest you, like sitting-in at a sex shop, or video shop which is selling sexually violent material, and refusing to leave when asked. This has to be done en masse, otherwise there will be a few heroic martyrs. Even when arrested (a likely consequence), we refuse to be bound over to keep the peace, and are likely to be gaoled. Sentence, currently seven days. But if sufficient numbers of women were prepared to do it, it would definitely have an effect, if only in publicizing the cause.

Pitfalls: Women in sensitive jobs, or women with children can rarely risk arrest. So it should be only those who can afford to go to prison, but that still leaves enough of us all the same.

Reclaim the Night Marches

A feminist response to a particular attack on women, best if done in the locality where a woman out at night has been attacked. Recently, there have been problems, like an RTN organized in a Red Light Area. We think it is best to talk with the women in the area first, so that prostitute women join/support the march as in the first RTNs in Soho, rather than seeing the march as against them. Likewise, a recent march in London, in which the organizing group also called for more police on the streets, ran into trouble because they had not considered either the implications of their call or the fact that it was through a mainly Black area. Again prior consultation and consciousness-raising should proceed any action.

Pitfalls: Possible arrests, in London particularly, the police have deliberately provoked violence at the beginning or the end of marches. It is best therefore to have a hall, if possible for the beginning and the end of the march, and for *all* women to know the route. Also publicize available solicitor members.

Sit-ins

Like Civil Disobedience, except that one does not have to be arrested. An action to take against an institution, like a newspaper or college that is encouraging male violence against women. Having made your protest, go when, and if, the police arrive.

Talks, Radio, Television Programmes and Press

We have found that some of our most productive and effective work has been simply explaining our objections to male violence. Either by giving talks in schools, women's groups or at conferences. We rarely do mixed talks although some of us are prepared to, because we might otherwise not have the opportunity to put our case to the women, but it is restricting.

Willingness to use the male dominated media has meant that many more women have been made aware that they are not alone in suffering male violence. By talking about male violence on the radio or on television, thousands of women can hear feminist arguments that they otherwise might not hear. Doing interviews with women's magazines has the same effect. Counter propaganda is an effective way of fighting back, and increasing our numbers.

Pitfalls: Possible risk of being misquoted, or saying completely the wrong thing if under pressure. We advise media training within WAVAW groups in order to overcome this, since it spreads skills and experience.

Press Releases

Writing a statement to be sent to the Press and particular institutions in response to news which effects women, but where no other action is taken, e.g. the recent case of three British footballers raping a Swedish woman. A press release showing solidarity with the woman may catch the attention of the Press. Other occasions where a press release is a suitable form of action are those when an institution or organization has made suggestions and/or proposals which encourage male violence e.g. the Hunt Committee Report on Cable Television.

Pitfalls: Too many, and the Press will soon stop listening.

Petitions

Where a specific demand or request can be made, which if sufficient women sign, is likely to be met e.g. safe public transport for women; the right to self-defence: that a woman who kills a man in self-defence should go free. Even if the petition does not bring pressure upon the authorities (although we know that they sometimes work), they give those who sign the petition a good introduction to the issue of male violence against women.

Pitfalls: None, but petitions do take quite a lot of effort.

Posters and Stickers

Printed posters and stickers are an effective way of protesting against particular advertisements, record covers, paintings, etc. which depict violence against women. One recent example of such a sticker is one which reads, "You call it Art, we call it violence against women."

Lobbying of Parliament and Local Government

Similar to petitions. Best if a specific demand is being made e.g. a minimum sentence for rapists (although we have no idea as to what the latter should be). A demand made of local government might be that it refuses to grant licences to sex shops in its area. Lobbies are useful in that they enable women to question their M.P.'s and/or councillors.

Pitfalls: Maybe a waste of words, time and effort, but at least the M.P. or councillors know that violence against women is an issue which has been taken up by those whom it concerns. If the Press pick it up it definitely has more impact; they often want local television and radio interviews, interviews which reach women, even if the councillor was unimpressed.

Writing to Advertisers

Advertisers are using increasing levels of real/simulated male violence against women in order to sell their products. Writing to the Advertising Standards Authority is something which can be done on an individual level by any woman. The Authority claims to take protests and objections seriously, so it is worth writing.

Pitfalls: What men find objectionable and what women do is somewhat different!

These are some of the ways that we have used to fight back against male violence. There are, we are sure, more. New ones will be evolved to deal with new situations; old ones changed as we all gain in experience. We hope meanwhile that these will be of help. Good luck!

Central London Women Against Violence Against Women
October 1982

USEFUL ADDRESSES

WIRES PO Box 20, Oxford. Tel: 0865-240 991
WIRES stands for The Women's Information, Referral and Enquiry Service. Write to WIRES if you want to find your nearest local women's group, women's centre etc.

But if you live in London contact:

A Woman's Place (AWP) Hungerford House, Victoria Embankment, London WC2. Tel: 01-836 6081.
AWP is a central London women's centre who can give you local London addresses and contacts for more specialised groups.

Women's Aid Federation
London Women's Aid
Women's Reproductive Rights Campaign
Rights of Women
Lesbian Line
all at: Tindlemanor, 52/54 Featherstone St., London EC1. General enquiries: 01-251 9276.
London Lesbian Line can also give you information for other parts of the country.

National Abortion Campaign 75 Kingsway, London WC2.

Women Against Violence Against Women c/o WIRES

Incest Survivors Campaign c/o AWP

Sisters Against Disablement c/o AWP

London Rape Crisis Centre PO Box 69, London WC1. Emergency 24-hour telephone: 01-837 1600. They (or WIRES) can give you local contacts.

Women and Medikill Practice c/o The Women's Centre, 32a Shakespeare Street, Nottingham.
(Women and Medikill Practice newsletter 50p from above address)

Asian Women's Resource Centre 134 Minet Ave, London NW10.

Black Women's Centre 41a Stockwell Green, London SW9.

Please enclose a stamped addressed envelope with all letters.

280